Criticism and Modernity

This book is for Bridie and Hamish,
and for all my other teachers

Criticism and Modernity

AESTHETICS, LITERATURE, AND NATIONS IN EUROPE AND ITS ACADEMIES

THOMAS DOCHERTY

OXFORD
UNIVERSITY PRESS

OXFORD
UNIVERSITY PRESS

Great Clarendon Street, Oxford ox2 6DP

Oxford University Press is a department of the University of Oxford.
It furthers the University's objective of excellence in research, scholarship,
and education by publishing worldwide in

Oxford New York

Athens Auckland Bangkok Bogotá Buenos Aires Calcutta
Cape Town Chennai Dar es Salaam Delhi Florence Hong Kong Istanbul
Karachi Kuala Lumpur Madrid Melbourne Mexico City Mumbai
Nairobi Paris São Paulo Singapore Taipei Tokyo Toronto Warsaw

with associated companies in Berlin Ibadan

Oxford is a registered trade mark of Oxford University Press
in the UK and in certain other countries

Published in the United States
by Oxford University Press Inc., New York

British Library Cataloguing in Publication Data

Data available

Library of Congress Cataloging in Publication Data

Docherty, Thomas.
Criticism and modernity: aesthetics, literature, and nations in
Europe and its academies/Thomas Docherty.
Includes bibliographical references and index.
1. Criticism—Europe—History. 2. Criticism—Political aspects—
Europe. 3. Aesthetics, European. I. Title.
PN99.E9D63 1999 801'.95'094—dc21 98-49303
ISBN 0-19-818501-4

1 3 5 7 9 10 8 6 4 2

Typeset in Sabon
by Cambrian Typesetters, Frimley, Surrey
Printed in Great Britain
on acid-free paper by
Bookcraft Ltd., Midsomer Norton, Somerset

PN
99
.E9
D63
1999

Preface

The idea for this book has been with me for some time. I began to promise myself that I would write about criticism and modernity while I was in my first tenured academic position, in University College Dublin, about a decade ago. There, I received warm encouragement from my colleagues and the most generous support from Seamus Deane, the acuity of whose thinking made me realize that the project was more extensive and more complex than I had imagined. Quietly, and with a generosity of spirit for which I will be ever grateful, he allowed me to see that questions concerning the relation of aesthetics to politics have a life inside and outside of the academy. When I took the Chair of English in Trinity College Dublin, I entered the world of wall-to-wall administration which is part and parcel of being a Head of Department in today's Irish or British university system. Smaller-scale projects then occupied my time; but the students of my seminars in theory, film, and post-modernism taught me by allowing me to work with them through some of the ideas that would eventually surface here. I am grateful also for the support or work of Ian Campbell Ross, Aileen Douglas, Penny Fielding, and Stuart Murray. Buried in a footnote in this book, the reader will find a hint of why I made my next move, to Kent, where I was enabled to make progress with this book. My thanks go to my colleagues and students in Kent, most especially to Lyn Innes whose brave struggles with the timetable made it possible for me to have some structured time away from the travails of organizing the research of the department.

Parts of the work have appeared or been tried out on audiences before. Chapter 1 was published in a different form in *Textual Practice*; and I was encouraged in the work at that time by Alan Sinfield. Part of Chapter 7 was given as my inaugural lecture in Kent, where the response of colleagues enabled me to sharpen up and clarify some issues. Some of Chapter 2 figured in a keynote lecture given at the 'Re-examination of Character' conference held in honour of Baruch Hochman at the Hebrew University of Jerusalem. I thank my hosts, Ephraim Gerber, Shlomith Rimmon-Kenan, and Baruch

Hochman, and the audience. The British Council helped to fund my visit. Frances Ferguson and Walter Michaels gave me a hard time in trying to make me justify some of my moves, the effect of which has been to sharpen my focus and clarify my claims; for which, many thanks. I presented some of Chapters 3 and 5 in Edinburgh University, where Penny Fielding, Cairns Craig, and others forced me to reconsider some issues. Chapter 4 had its first outing in the 'Criticism of the Future' conference, organized by Brian Dillon in the University of Kent. He and others among my graduates - Robert Duggan, John McMahon, Paula Quigley in particular - have been supportive and enabling in their work with me. I thank all of the above for making the time and for having the gracious generosity of spirit to listen to my work and to enable me to improve on it. Others have heard and commented on aspects of this work in progress: I thank David Ayers, Andrew Benjamin, Steve Connor, Valentine Cunningham, Andrew Gibson, Caroline Rooney, David Trotter. I alone am accountable for any errors in which I persist.

At a crucial turn in the making of this book, Bridie Sullivan sat me down and forced me to make the argument of the whole. It was at this point that I realized for the first time that I had a project with a discernible shape; and Bridie made it possible for me not only to see it but to see how it might be done. Hamish Docherty put up with listening to the work of Adorno by way of a bed-time story - until he discovered the joys of his own books; but now we can argue about philosophy, and he teaches me always.

In Oxford University Press, Jason Freeman and Kim Scott Walwyn commissioned this book, and encouraged me in my early efforts with it. Sophie Goldsworthy has seen it through with the same degree of commitment. I thank them here for their support; and I now beg your indulgence.

Contents

Introduction

This book examines the relation of criticism to modernity. In doing so, it investigates the ways in which the formulations of aesthetic theory that occur within philosophy and literature impinge upon the political formations of the modern European nation-states. Hence, the book offers a study of the relations of aesthetics to politics in the emergence of what we now think of as a specific kind of 'democratic' society; but within this, questions regarding the relation of taste to democracy must also be addressed. The premises on which I build my argument are threefold: first, modern aesthetics develops in an explicitly nationalist arena; second, the issues surrounding the emergence of nation-states within Europe are involved with philosophical questions pertaining to the time of the aesthetic and with social questions pertaining to the formulation of the autonomous human subject, freely determining her or his own relation to others and to objects; and, third, these issues are regulated by something that we have learnt to describe as the academy. That is to say, questions of major national concern find their mediation in the teaching of humanities disciplines in the university, and most especially within that discipline that we recognize, in all its variant guises, as 'English'.

The aims of this book are simple, if multiple. I explore the relation of aesthetics to politics in the formation of the modern autonomous human subject in the period of the emergence of a 'democratic' Europe and its academic institutions. The claim is that the engagement with, and the teaching of, English (in particular; but of many humanities disciplines in general) has been marked by a nationalist politics that has been inimical to the development of democracy, to the establishment of an autonomy marked by freedom in the human subject, and even to the very possibility of aesthetic experience—and its attendant intellectual work, criticism—itself. I argue this by tracing the development of an aesthetic philosophy through a series of primarily literary and philosophical confrontations from about 1660 to about 1830 in Europe, showing thereby how Europe formulates itself ethnically, how it characterizes itself as 'democratic', and how the legacy of such aesthetic philosophy impinges upon the academy, most specifically in the twentieth century's formations and deformations of 'English'.

That this subject is important may not be immediately self-evident. For many—especially for many in government today—the question posed to the university and most pointedly to its human-ities disciplines is simple and crude: how can you justify your exis-tence and your privileges? The answer required by governments is equally simple and crude: we are to justify our existence in terms applicable not to the academy, but in terms applicable rather to industry and business, that is, economically and instrumentally. 'English', for example, is to be justified not by its contributions to the cultural formation, freedom, and betterment of autonomous and critical human subjects, but rather by how efficiently it oper-ates in the production of individuals who will—as a more or less direct consequence of their engagement with literature—contribute directly to the economic profile and profit of themselves and, yet more importantly, of the nation. It is partly as a consequence of the rage that any intellectual must feel at the grossly inadequate over-simplification of such a view (and at the inadequacy of the acade-my's response to it) that a book such as this demands to be written. I have written it partly, therefore, in an attempt to show that the questions of 'English' as an academic discipline are already com-plex, and that their prehistory requires some elucidation if we are to address the legitimacy of academic work in the humanities and elsewhere sufficiently.

It should be made clear from the outset, however, that this book is not another re-run of the by now rather tedious arguments about the ideological formation of English in the nineteenth century, with its later development, shifting, and eventual overcoming by a pro-ject called 'theory' in the late twentieth. There have broadly been two ways of addressing the history of criticism within English stud-ies. The first of these would be best exemplified by those works in the late 1970s and early 1980s which traced 'The Rise of English Studies', as Eagleton called it in the opening chapter of *Literary Theory*, a story told in variously inflected ways by Eagleton (and behind him Williams), by Chris Baldick, by Tony Davies, and taken up by British 'theory' in the writings of Terence Hawkes, Antony Easthope, and others. The reader will look in vain here for that

particular understanding of the Arnold–Eliot–Leavis-'cultural studies' trajectory, however. It is not here for the simple reason that,
interesting narrative though it might once have been, it is limited
by its excessively narrow scope and ambit and by an unwarranted
optimistic belief that we have 'progressed' towards a happy state of
affairs in which we can reflect meaningfully and self-consciously on
our critical activities, unlike our forebears, who simply went ahead
in their ideological corruption or blindness. In this project, instead,
I have set out to widen the scope of our understanding, taking
account of the national confrontations and conflicts shaping aesthetic philosophy within the European Enlightenment.

The second way in which the prehistory of our present predicament has been charted is best thought of in terms of an 'aesthetic
history', in which the construction of our contemporary theory and
criticism has been traced back to foundations lying in Germanic
philosophy. The trajectory here is most insistently that mapped by
Kant–Hegel–Nietzsche, as in the splendid study by Luc Ferry of
Homo Aestheticus. That map, with all the various digressions and
counter-mappings (Schiller, Schopenhauer, Marx; later, Adorno
and the Frankfurt School, Heidegger) has suited arguments within
philosophy; but again effectively isolates the Germanic tradition
from the pressures exerted upon it historically by, for examples,
late Renaissance Italian thought, or a Franco-Scottish enlightenment, or Irish or Indian philosophies.[1]

In place of these understandings of the emergence of modern
criticism, I discover a number of more specific and less consistently centred conflicts. These include, for example, England against
France (in the figures of Dryden and Corneille) at the time of the
Second Dutch War, when the core of the conflict is to be found in

---

[1] It should be stressed that Luc Ferry in *Homo Aestheticus* (Grasset, Paris,
1990) does frequently locate the three Germanic thinkers of his central trajectory in
relation to French philosophy (and at one key moment, also to Hume); but the centrality of Germanic thinking to aesthetic philosophy, and its isolating prioritization,
remain unquestioned. Terry Eagleton's *Ideology of the Aesthetic* (Basil Blackwell,
Oxford, 1990), remains firmly (if, perhaps, with a disturbingly light scholarship)
committed to this lineage; but, as my arguments later in this book will show, it is
marred by its fundamental alignment to what is the 'gentlemanly' style that it sets
out to critique. A more useful example in anglophone writing is Andrew Bowie's
Aesthetics and Subjectivity (Manchester University Press, Manchester, 1990), which,
though it widens the philosophical scope to include Fichte, Hölderlin, Schelling and
others, thereby effectively re-centres contemporary theory in relation to a specific
(and, in literary terms, quite narrow) version of Romanticism.

Africa and attempted colonizations; Scottish anglophilia (and the resistance thereto) in the wake of 1707 set against Genevan ideas of democracy and the individual agent (in Hume and Rousseau); arguments over benevolence, love, hypocrisy in the formulation of Enlightenment philosophy in England (Shaftesbury), Ireland and Scotland (Hutcheson), and France (Molière); questions concerning the centrality of the State in the regulation of the health and happiness of its subjects in an emergent Germany (Schiller, but also Hegel and Schopenhauer); variant models of the university and its inaugurations of critical possibilities for the student (Vico in Naples, Blair in Scotland, Humboldt in Berlin, Newman in Ireland, Jaspers in Germany, Leavis in England); and so on.

This diversity allows for a widening of the usual terms of the argument, such that I am able to complicate notions of autonomy, modernity, and the stakes of aesthetic criticism itself. In the opening chapters, I argue that aesthetic judgements are fundamentally linked to a *theatricality* on the part of the critic, and that such theatricality is to be found in both philosophy and cultural criticism. Following this, I trace the importance of *tragedy* for giving a set of guiding principles to the act of criticism. The key here is that neo-Aristotelian notions of tragic *fear* are acted out in terms of a fear, within emergent nation-states, of alterity and foreignness; and the theatre of Corneille and Dryden, together with their comprehensions of the nature of tragedy, become the cover for an only slightly veiled debate about national supremacy between France and England as proto-colonial powers. There is, however, another side to neo-Aristotelian tragic theory, and that is *pity*, here reconsidered in terms of the placing of love as the primary subject for a *comic* theatre, such as we see it in Molière. Molière's explorations of love become explicit philosophical examinations of the question of how and on what basis matters of aesthetic preference ('liking' this rather than that) devolve immediately into matters of ethical import, and thus, of how and on what basis we can construct the rational society that requires the possibility of human interactivity.

While these arguments are being laid out in theatrical performance, Shaftesbury is also constructing an entire philosophy based upon a version of love or pity that he calls benevolence. But when his student, Hutcheson, takes this on, he finds that the question now emerging is that which we recognize as the founding question of modernity itself: legitimation. Further, Hutcheson's particular historical and cultural situation ensures that his understanding of legitimation in acts of critical judgement (both aesthetic and ethical) is not a simply formal philosophical affair, but is instead a matter marked by the problematic politics of 1707's Act of Union between Scotland and England and its legacies. The matter of the subject's autonomy is now firmly intertwined with the location of the subject in relation to a nation-state which may or may not exist as a fact. It is here that we see the explicit linkage of aesthetics to politics; but here also that we see attempts to think those politics not just at the level of national self-determination but also at the level of what we begin to call democracy. The full complexity of this is elaborated in the confrontation of Hume with Rousseau. I argue that the determination of the subject's autonomy as a matter whose legitimation depends upon spatial (national) self-identifications occludes what the philosophers and writers know to be central to aesthetic judgement: the temporal 'becoming' (as opposed to the spatial 'being') of the subject. This subject-in-formation is a subject whose business, among other things, is the education of the senses or, better, the regulation of experience by the operations of reason. Such a regulation is demanded on behalf of the social; and it is thus confronted with the counter-demand for the regulation of the operations of reason by the pleasures and pains of experience. This dialectic of the regulated autonomy of the modern and democratic subject requires an attention to the *time* of aesthetics, to the historical mutability of judgement and of the self; and there is thus a tension between two versions of democracy: one version thinks democracy is a matter for regulation by a State within a nation; the other requires that democracy attend to the absolute primacy of the singularity of the subject and her or his experience, temporal development, *formation* or *Bildung*.

It is in the light of this 'archaeology' of aesthetics that we can then situate the more familiar Germanic materials; but that situating demonstrates the necessity of elevating Schiller to a more central position than he has traditionally been accorded, given that he usually exists in a Kantian shadow. This allows me to chart aesthetics in its primary relation to pedagogy or *Bildung*. Given that aesthetics in my delineation of it is marked by a politics and an ethics, education becomes central to the ways in which philosophers account for the importance of aesthetic activity: to criticize is also to be engaged in a process of self-construction, self-autonomization, with or without a nation-state to sustain and legitimize specific critical judgements. Aesthetic education becomes central to the formulation of the autonomous subject, and hence also to the articulation of democracy—however much that term is semantically debated—itself.

Such education, of course, has the effect of relocating criticism within the academic institution; and it is here, in a final chapter, that I can outline the nature of the problem that we have been dealt by the prehistory of criticism. Fundamentally, I am able to argue that in the expression of an aesthetic that has been fundamentally tied to place or nation, there has been a crucial elision of what is a basic element of aesthetics itself: the historical and temporal experience of the subject who confronts art and is moved, changed, forced to take a stand by it. The argument of the book is one in which I want to enable the possibility of criticism by rehabilitating the category of experience, not as that which will legitimize our judgements, but rather as that which will ground them and make them possible in the first place. Consequently, I argue for aesthetics as an *event*, and not as an action whose validity is guaranteed by its location. It is only when we return the possibility of the event to criticism that we can begin to be modern, can begin to achieve an autonomy, can begin to establish anything that might resemble a democracy that is lived as much as argued about.

SECTION I

CRITICISM AND NATIONAL THEATRICALITY

I

Tragedy and the Nationalist
Condition of Criticism

I

Criticism, as we know it in modernity, depends upon an attitude which is, tacitly at least, nationalist in fact and in origin: within modernity, there is a specific relation between aesthetic criticism and the formulation of the emergent nation-state, especially within what is becoming known as Europe. The political nationalism in question here is profoundly allied to that aesthetic or cultural theory whose determinant formation is that of tragedy, and specifically that aspect of tragedy usually identified in the neo-Aristotelian concept of *terror*.[1] The consequence in modernity for criticism and theory, ignoring its own topographical locatedness and its own debts to a tragic consciousness, is the occlusion of the object of criticism in the interests of the production of what is fundamentally (if silently) a nationalist identity for the subject, the critic herself or himself.

Criticism has been most concerned to make a place for the critic which will offer the solace and assurance of the *heimlich* even when it seems to be most uncanny; and such solace—the 'solace of good form' as Lyotard has it—can only be mediated in terms of the

---

[1] In what follows in this present chapter, it will be clear that the Aristotle in question is the Aristotle of the *Poetics*. In later chapters, the Aristotle of the *Nicomachean Ethics* and of the *Politics* will assume a greater importance. In this first case, Aristotle is mediated primarily through the conflicting readings of Corneille, Dryden, and, behind them, Castelvetro; in the latter case—that of the ethical Aristotle—the primary mediations will be seen to involve Aristotle with Augustine. See esp. Ch. 6 below. In both cases, the centrality of Aristotle proposes as a consequence a specific mapping of Europe, whose centrality in a Graeco-Roman axis, is not devoid of politics.

comforting *legitimation* of the critic's practice in terms of its theoretical rather than topographical foundation, for any acknowledgement of the kind of locatedness of which I write—of a 'location of the cultural'—not only relativises the criticism but, more importantly and problematically, demands a justification of its otherwise tacit nationalist (some might say 'racist')—even terrorizing—attitude.[2]

It should be made clear at the outset here that I am not making the banal and mistaken claim for any *equation* of modernity (or Enlightenment) with terror (the Holocaust and associated results of nationalist Fascism).[3] My argument in this opening chapter is proposed as a different and more complex one. Starting from a consideration of the Cartesian and *theatrical* roots of cultural modernity, I examine the late Renaissance production of subjectivity as the foundation of a specific type of critical consciousness persisting from

[2] For 'the solace of good form', see Jean-François Lyotard, *The Postmodern Condition* (trans. Geoff Bennington and Brian Massumi; Manchester University Press, Manchester, 1984), 81. Although my phrase, the 'location of the cultural', is meant to allude to the work of Homi Bhabha, especially his *The Location of Culture* (Routledge, 1994), the allusion is not intended to signal my identification with that work. Bhabha's concerns, in the essays that make up that study, are differently focused, differently prioritized, from my own concerns here. In this present part of the study, I am addressing the rather simpler question of how we legitimize judgements that are properly subjective, in that they are given partly by the subject's ideological locatedness or historical and cultural singularity: how do we move from such singularity to the normativity of issues of value. I deal with this in a more pointedly philosophical fashion in Chapters 4 and 5 below.

[3] Zygmunt Bauman, in *Modernity and the Holocaust* (Polity Press, Cambridge, 1989) argues most precisely the relation between the Enlightenment and the Nazi terror. He points out that, structurally, the techniques used by the Nazis in the death-camps (for example, the exercising of fear as a tool to ensure that victims would—*entirely reasonably*—inform upon each other and thus collude 'efficiently' with their torturers) were the obverse side of the otherwise positive uses of an instrumental reason whose method had been most clearly described by the general tendency of Enlightened modern thought. That is to say, there is no simple equation between Enlightenment and Holocaust, or between reason and terror; rather, it is the case that within Enlightenment reason there lurks an evil which, though repressed, can threaten to return in such a way as to overturn all the positive values of Enlightenment thinking—and modernity—itself. The argument over a so-called post-modernism, often caricatured, journalistically, in the equation of reason and terror is, in fact, much more complex than this, involving, for examples, the work of Theodor Adorno and Max Horkheimer on *The Dialectic of Enlightenment* (1944; trans. John Cumming; Verso, 1979); or of Walter Benjamin in his famous seventh thesis on the philosophy of history (in *Illuminations*, (ed. Hannah Arendt; trans Harry Zohn; Fontana, 1973), 258); not to mention Freud on the return of the repressed.

Descartes up to a kind of liminal point in the fascination with the threatening power of the object that one finds in Baudrillard. The theoretical result of this is my claim that modern criticism conspires to elide alterity—the Other as such—and to erase, with this elision, the very object of criticism (most usually the text) from history.[4] In the second part of this chapter's argument, I shall attend to a detailed examination of one aspect of cultural relations between England and France in the late seventeenth century (more specifically still, in the period 1664–8); and I shall consider Dryden's response to the Second Dutch War and to Corneille. Here, we shall see the emergence of a new discourse in which the aesthetic and the political are fused—even confused—in a particular fashion which is specific to the emergence of modernity and its attendant criticism or self-theorization. Such self-theorization—the theory that is constitutive of modernity itself—establishes itself through the elision of a specific historical Other: Africa. Finally, I will bring together the conflicts over the neo-classical theory of tragedy and the emergence of this new discourse in an argument which shows that, even within the terror shaping modern—nationalist—criticism, there is the possibility of a different order of things, marked by tragedy's counterpart of terror: pity, or, in the terms used here (and by Dryden, Corneille, and their contemporaries), love. It is this love, embarrassing to a criticism which pretends to be scientific, abstract, counter-metaphysical, which has been the more general casualty of the nationalism constitutive of modern theory.[5]

---

   [4] I want to stress here that by 'the text' I mean to reinscribe the very precise Barthesian sense given to this term in his formerly well-known essay 'From Work to Text', in Roland Barthes, *Image–Music–Text* (ed. and trans. Stephen Heath; Fontana, 1977). Criticism now speaks largely unthinkingly of 'texts'—just as unthinkingly as, prior to that essay by Barthes, it spoke unthinkingly of 'works' or 'art' (in the sense of 'craft'). Hence, the 'object' that I claim is elided here is, in fact, not just some static or monumental 'work', not 'poems', but rather the very processes and practices of textual criticism or reading.

   [5] This shadowy presence of love is explored more fully in the chapters that follow; but it should be noted immediately that by 'love' I do not intend to evoke contemporary notions of 'desire', for this latter is, I suggest, itself a term which covers the embarrassment the critic feels whenever her or his subjectivity is under threat. The love of which I write is marked precisely by such a threat, in the face of which the scientism of a non-metaphysical discourse provides no solace. In later parts of this book, I shall be writing of the experience of love and of the relation of that experience to the aesthetico-political domain germane to modernity. For immediate purposes here, see the socio-cultural account given by Ulrich Beck and Elisabeth Beck-Gernsheim, *The Normal Chaos of Love* (trans. Mark Ritter and Jane Wiebel; Polity Press, Cambridge, 1995).

II

Modernity understands criticism primarily in terms of *difference*. For the modern, the possibility that a pronouncement about an aesthetic event or act will discriminate or distinguish—will 'make a difference'—is a precondition for describing that pronouncement a *critical* statement.[6] It is not enough to 'appreciate' a text or artifact and to evaluate it in neo-Arnoldian positivist terms by 'seeing it steadily and seeing it whole' or by 'seeing it as in itself it really is' (for it is argued, certainly after Kant if not already before, that this is not in any case strictly possible); rather, the critic, insofar as she or he is critical at all, must strive to see the text in a neo-Wildean mode of negativity, 'as in itself it really is *not*'.[7] Hence, perhaps, the frequent vilification of much modern (twentieth-century, post-Wildean, paradoxical) criticism on the grounds of its ascribed innate *aestheticism*.[8] At the most basic level, the modern critical

---

[6] On the centrality of discrimination such as this to criticism—and on its excessive sociological effects and consequences—see Pierre Bourdieu, *Distinction* (trans. Richard Nice; Routledge, 1984). For a more specific instance of this, one which demonstrates the work of such a critical consciousness in institutions (and one which will be of increasingly central importance in the rest of this book), see G. E. Davie, *The Democratic Intellect* (Edinburgh University Press, Edinburgh, 1961) and *The Crisis of the Democratic Intellect* (Polygon Press, Edinburgh, 1986), in both of which a critical intelligence, produced from a 'generalist' education (actually the Scottish university system, but practically any 'liberal' as opposed to 'vocationalist' or 'instrumentalist' pedagogy) is seen to be central to the functioning of democracy itself. For a further examination of this in terms of Scottish culture, see also Craig Beveridge and Ronald Turnbull, *The Eclipse of Scottish Culture* (Polygon Press, Edinburgh, 1989) and *Scotland After Enlightenment* (Polygon Press, Edinburgh, 1997); and see also Chs. 3 and 4 below. The kind of criticism in question here is that usually associated with Kantian philosophy and with the Frankfurt School.

[7] Most recently, the paradigmatic literary example of this attitude would be most typically seen in the writings of Alain Robbe-Grillet, where the fixed and steady gaze upon an object (attempting to see it as in itself it really is, at least in relation to its perceiving subject) always transforms the object itself, such that 'what it is' becomes identified with 'what it is not'; and the most celebrated example of this is the perfect/imperfect tomato described in *Les Gommes* (Minuit, Paris, 1953), 145–6.

[8] The attack on much contemporary criticism for its supposed neo-formalist aestheticization of politics is, of course, most heavily indebted to particularly weak readings of Benjamin's essay on 'The Work of Art in the Age of Mechanical Reproduction', in *Illuminations*, 243. The debate in our time has unfortunately degenerated into the banalization of politics in which 'political correctness' has been set in contest with an equally vacuous banalization of culture called variously 'the defence of the canon' or 'the defence of western/traditional/family values'. Few have

attitude or mood reveals as its foundation an intrinsic *hermeneutic* determination: modern criticism involves the insistent revelation of what had been covert, in an act of demystification whose purpose is to reveal the different within the same.[9]

For most, the specifically 'modern' project of criticism begins in the Enlightenment, whose objective is the gradual emancipation of the human subject from her or his enchantment by and enslavement to myth and superstition through the progressive operations of a critical reason. The goal of the project—and what characterizes it as one aspect of modernization—is the production of the human as an *autonomous subject*, an agent of history rather than history's victim.[10] The autonomy in question is to be apparent in the subject's capacity for making choices regarding her or his course of action; and such choices are seen to be free precisely because, or to the extent that, they originate in the subject and are *critical*, that they make the specific *difference* in history which reveals—or, indeed, produces—the identity of the agent as an individual, individuated from the determinations of the social, leaving the traces of her or his actual presence, and determining the course of her or his own history, even if, as Marx pointed out, not entirely under conditions of her or his own choosing.[11]

It is thus that criticism, in modernity, is aligned with freedom; and it is also thus that criticism is established as the fundamental

---

commented upon the forms of political correctness that were already in place and implicit in the forms of legitimization adopted by criticism prior to the eruption of this pseudo-debate. The political situatedness of aesthetic practices is much more complex—and much more important—than the pseudo-debates that surround it in 'theoreticist' arguments would suggest.

[9] See, e.g., Paul Ricoeur, *De l'interprétation* (Seuil, Paris, 1965), 35–6. See also Ch. 3 below for the roots of this in Francis Hutcheson.

[10] According to Jürgen Habermas, it is the importance of this emergence of autonomy for the validation of modernity that a postmodern thinker such as Lyotard 'has never understood'; and it is this which basically drives the wedge of a difference between Habermas and Lyotard (conversation with the present writer, Dublin, 14 Apr. 1994).

[11] Karl Marx, *The Eighteenth Brumaire of Louis Bonaparte* (Foreign Languages Press, Peking, 1978), 9. On the intimate, if initially merely etymological, relation between criticism and difference, see Barbara Johnson, *The Critical Difference* (Johns Hopkins University Press, Baltimore, 1980). It should be noted in passing here that freedom, in the kind of argument outlined above, has been reduced in the discourses and practices of contemporary 'democratic' politics to the extraordinarily circumscribed limitations of consumer choice, and that it has little to do with the autonomy it is supposed to exemplify.

link between epistemology and ontology, between theory and practice, between pure and practical reasonings. For modern criticism, to know is to be in a position to do: *savoir* is the precondition of legitimate *pouvoir*; and the legitimacy of such power is guaranteed through the critic's making of a reasonable, responsible (or, more pointedly here, *answerable*—'accountable') choice of the course of action to be followed or endorsed. In this, it is reason itself to which the critic is responsible or accountable, a reason which, because it is theoretically grounded or foundational, *legitimizes* the critical act; but answerability is also *measured* through the *distance* or difference established between the state of affairs prevailing before the critical intervention and that resulting from it. According to Peter Gay, Enlightenment, governed thus by reason, 'can be summed up in two words; criticism and power';[12] and the purpose of such criticism and power is the establishment and prioritization of difference.

Yet this kind of thinking does not originate in the eighteenth century. One can trace a genealogy of such a critical attitude at least as far back as Descartes. It is Descartes who initiates—and modernizes—philosophy in terms of a series of formulations designed to overcome a hypothetical illusion (governed, at the extreme, by an 'evil demon', the *malin génie* who eventually returns in French thought in Baudrillard's 'evil demon of images') in the face of which there is a requirement for the self-evident, for 'clear and distinct ideas', whose very clarity will guarantee the validity of actions or thoughts grounded upon or accountable to such ideas. Cartesian philosophy is to empower through a criticism differentiating the (illusory—imaged or figural) given from the (logically— linguistic or discursive) self-evident or self-evidencing; and thus Descartes initiates that tendency in which the ostensible is seen as somehow intrinsically differing from itself, such differing being in fact constitutive of the very identity of the given object of contemplation as such. The modern is the site of this contest between the relative priorities of the sensually or empirically visual (the sensible, the 'evidence') and of the discursively rational (which is considered to be occluded by the visual, but yielding to an abstract mathematical logic that is effectively autonomous and independent

12 See Peter Gay, *The Enlightenment* (Oxford University Press, Oxford, 1966), *passim*.

of any specific sensible experience); and what we call 'representation' (the fundamental issue of modernity) is nothing more or less than this tension between the ostensible priority of the *visual* as fact and the preferred priority of the *linguistic* as the ground of truth.[13]

I do not wish to linger here on the claims for the pre-eminently visual priority that has been given to philosophy and to modernity, for that has been more than adequately treated by Irigaray and (with a rather different agenda) more recently by Martin Jay.[14] Yet I will stress at the outset one important corollary of these and similar observations. Modernity is intrinsically linked to acts of demystification whose predominant aspect is visual; but what is this if it is not a specific kind of *theatricality* in critical philosophy? Such theatricality can be easily described: it involves the display of identity in the form of a visual difference (the *larvatus prodeo* on which much of the work of the early Barthes was based); or, in a word, it is 'spectacular' as well as being specular and speculative.[15] The object of the critic's contemplation finds its identity constituted through its specific mode of self-differing, through its

---

[13] Such thinking initiates a tradition in French philosophy which culminates in Jean-François Lyotard's *Discours, figure* (Klincksieck, Paris, 1971); but it is a problem worked through in German philosophy—and subsequently in most Continental philosophy—in Kantian terms as a distinction between the demands of the sensible and those of the rational impulses. In Chs. 3–5, I shall be arguing the case for a specifically 'located' version of this in the thought of Hutcheson and then Hume. Relevant to the kinds of argument at stake here, among contemporaries, is for example the work of the Chicago Laocoon group, perhaps most specifically that of W. J. T. Mitchell, in *Iconology* (University of Chicago Press, Chicago, 1986) and *Picture Theory* (University of Chicago Press, Chicago, 1994). A literary origin for the question in English literature is quite possibly properly to be located in Shakespeare's *Othello*, a play which explicitly asks its audience and viewer to set the quite clear and visible difference between Othello and the rest of the players in contest with the linguistic powers heard in Othello's own rehearsal of the rhetorical power of narrative (which enabled him to win Desdemona) and Iago's rhetorical manipulation of Othello in a gulling plot: it asks where we locate 'truth' in this play between what it sets up as the visibly obvious and the linguistically persuasive and logically verifiable. In short, it plays a contest between eye and ear.

[14] See Luce Irigaray, *Speculum* (Minuit, Paris, 1974), and *Ce Sexe qui n'en est pas un* (Minuit, Paris, 1977) for the initial influential work in this area; and cf. Martin Jay, *Downcast Eyes* (University of California Press, Berkeley and Los Angeles, 1995).

[15] Some new historicist work, including that of Jonathan Goldberg and Louis Montrose, has picked up and developed this notion theoretically; for a clear and explicit example of this, see Leonard Tennenhouse, *Power on Display* (Methuen, 1986).

self-representation, in a word; and it is the task of the critic not only to see it as it appears, but also to see it as and for what it represents. The critic bears witness to a profound constitutive difference in her or his object of contemplation, seeing its 'presence' while also acknowledging what cannot be presented in unmediated form, its unpresentable absence or ground, and seeing both these things at once. As this book will make clear, the aesthetic object is seen both as a particular and as the example (or representation) of an abstract (unrepresentable) type at once. Such 'spectacular' (or speculative, inventive, 'economical') philosophy is also, as Derrida has recently noted, 'spectral'. It is a kind of 'seeing things', a 'hearing of voices' in the manner of Hartman in criticism, Joyce in his texts. It is, in short, a criticism indebted to a specific theatrical source with which modernity has been insistently obsessed: *Hamlet*, whose most famous soliloquy enacts the Cartesian realization that being is inescapable for one who thinks and who speaks her or his thoughts.[16]

Modernity thus knows criticism primarily as *representation*; and the representation in question is always governed by the critic's attitude to her or his object. That object is always identified through difference; and what is this representation if it is not the production of an identity constituted in difference? For modernity, criticism is inescapably 'spectacular' (or speculative), dramatic, *theatrical*.

Descartes knows this when he dramatizes his own project in the proto-*Bildungsroman* form of the *Discours de la méthode* and the *Méditations*. In these texts, it is by now a truism to say that Descartes proposes his philosophy in a remarkably literary form, telling a story in which he presents himself as the hero of knowledge, risking the existence not only of the external world that seems to support his body, but also risking his very own existence.[17] The story is intended to be terrifying, and Descartes is at some pains to stress that his stratagem is not suitable for everyone:

---

[16] See Jacques Derrida, *Spectres de Marx* (Galilée, Paris, 1993); and cf Geoffrey Hartman, *Criticism in the Wilderness* (Yale University Press, New Haven, 1980), 55–6. On Hamlet as a first 'modern', see Franco Moretti, *The Way of the World* (trans. Albert Sbraggia; Verso, 1987), and see my own comments on the ghostly or spectral relation between hearing and seeing things in Thomas Docherty, *Alterities* (Oxford University Press, 1996).

[17] On the 'literariness' of Descartes, see Hugh Kenner, *Samuel Beckett* (John Calder, 1962), 81; on Descartes as himself the 'hero' of the *Discours de la méthode*,

If my work has given me a certain satisfaction, so that I here present to you a draft of it, I do not do so because I wish to advise anybody to imitate it … I fear much that this particular [design] … will seem too venturesome for many. The simple resolve to strip oneself of all opinions and beliefs formerly received is not to be regarded as an example that each man should follow … But like one who walks alone and in the twilight I resolved to go slowly …[18]

The method leads Descartes to assume that the world—the given— is ideological, in that it is misleading illusion or the determinant of a false consciousness: 'I shall then suppose … [that] some evil genius not less powerful than deceitful, has employed his whole energies in deceiving me'.[19] Further than this, having doubted the existence of all exteriority, Descartes takes the story in the terrifying direction of self-annihilation: 'I shall consider myself as having no hands, no eyes, no flesh, no blood, nor any senses, yet falsely believing myself to possess all these things'.[20] It is this presentation of the philosophy as a kind of horror-tract that makes it exciting and, despite Descartes's proclamations to the contrary, *exemplary*. The terror arising from the story, however, is merely a tactical terror (as in the best exemplary horror-tales or theatrical tragedies). The Cartesian strategy is one in which the world's *meaning*, if not necessarily its very *being*, is finally to be referred back to a self-present subject of consciousness, Descartes himself (even if, in a further twist of the tale, the veracity of this subject's logic is to be grounded in a transcendent God).

Descartes founds his philosophy basically upon a voice, an act of utterance, that paradoxically unspoken *loquor* (a verb hovering uncertainly between speaking and being spoken) governing the possibility of uttering—and 'inhabiting'—the famous *Cogito*. In this, the text of the *Méditations* silently reduces the ontological to the linguistic. Geometer that he is, Descartes operates at the level of the linguistic—mathematical—abstraction: his proofs are guaranteed by a *formal* truth of linguistic self-coherence, not by any *experiential* truth guaranteed by correspondence to an empirical

see Jacques Barzun, *Classic, Romantic and Modern* (Secker & Warburg, 1962). See also Jean-François Lyotard, *The Postmodern Condition*, 31 ff. on the difference between the intellectual as hero of knowledge and as hero of emancipation.

[18] Descartes, *Philosophical Works*, rendered into English by Elizabeth S. Haldane and G.R.T. Ross (Cambridge University Press, Cambridge, 1969), i. 90–1
[19] Ibid. 148.　　　　　　　　　　　　　　　　　　[20] Ibid.

and non-linguistic state of affairs. One might lay the same complaint here as Derrida does when faced (in 'Force et signification') with Rousset's structuralism, that force is being reduced to form through a spatializing philosophy whose effect is to circumscribe the material historicity of the object of contemplation which, in the Cartesian case, is the object-world itself in all its secular complexity. For Descartes, truth is a function of propositions (the articulation of clear and distinct ideas); and, in this, he offers a model for the much later de Man, another philosopher who preferred to work at the level of the linguistic rather than at that of the factual.[21] Having laid the linguistic foundation for his philosophy, Descartes can reconstruct exteriority, guaranteeing it as essentially a *linguistic* phenomenon (that is, as representation or as a 'sign' of the real) dependent upon a speaking subject of consciousness whose very extreme asceticism is testimony to the truth of its propositions.[22]

This terror at the death of the author, then, is merely a proto-de Manic exercise in *katharsis* (which, in de Man's case, might take the form of self-exculpations, 'excuses' or evaded 'confessions'), instrumental in the production and conditioning of a subject purged of ideological (imagistic/figural) blindness, and gifted with (linguistic) insight whose stringency derives precisely from its extremist, terroristic origins. This extremist terror has its literary

---

[21] See Paul de Man, *The Rhetoric of Romanticism* (Columbia University Press, New York, 1984), p. viii: 'I have myself taken refuge in more theoretical inquiries into the problems of figural language.' This statement, made in passing, could be applied to almost every intervention made by de Man in his work through deconstruction; cf. the further explicit articulation of this in *The Resistance to Theory* (Manchester University Press, Manchester, 1986), especially the title essay. On the notion of the *loquor* as the founding condition of the *cogito* in Descartes, see Thomas Docherty, *Reading (Absent) Character* (Oxford University Press, 1983), ch. 3. Beckett remains, in one dominant critical view, the greatest modern literary inheritor of the Cartesian example in which the deconstruction of exteriority is explicitly dependent upon a voice, not necessarily one's own, which speaks the subject in neo-Heideggerian fashion as much as it speaks the text: 'A voice comes to one in the dark. Imagine' (Samuel Beckett, *Company* (John Calder, 1979), 7). On the geometrization of structuralism and its consequent evasion of ontological force (with which, in one sense, the whole of this present study is concerned) see Jacques Derrida, 'Force et signification' in *L'Écriture et la différence* (Seuil, Paris, 1967).

22 Against my claims here, Hans Blumenberg, *The Legitimacy of the Modern Age* (trans. Robert M. Wallace; MIT Press, Cambridge, Mass., 1983), 404, argues that it is in the eighteenth century that the absolutism of truth is measured for the first time by its austerity. His argument should also be set alongside that of Page DuBois, *Torture and Truth* (Routledge, 1991).

counterpart in Shakespeare's *King Lear*, in which the visual blind-
ing of Gloucester vies for priority with the question regarding
Lear's rational capacities, capacities measured in part by his language: 'What! Art mad? A man may see how this world goes with
no eyes. Look with thine ears' (IV. vi).

Such a tragic terror forms the basis for an essentially *autobiographical* criticism which predominates from Descartes to the present day and which is, predictably, most often described in terms of
the neo-romanticism shaping and informing much twentieth-
century theory.[23] In short, one might propose (in an admittedly
very general form) an explanation of the history of modern criticism through reference to an anxiety about exteriority, construed
variously in different historical moments as, say, the world in
Descartes, 'nature' or the *Ding-an-sich* for romanticism, 'history'
for the post-romantic theory of the twentieth century, and so on all
the way down to 'otherness' for postmodernism. (Where I wish to
evade the generalities involved in this proposition is in my claim,
gradually emerging through this study, that the specific anxiety in
question has always some reference to the nation-state.)

The modern critic is she or he who begins from the anxiety
about her or his supposed object, be it a text or other aesthetic
product whose source is ostensibly independent of the critic herself
or himself. The modern critic's response to such a fear of otherness,
or to this fear of the object-as-such, is the production of a specific
kind of subject: a linguistic subject of consciousness characterized
first by a presumed capacity for understanding of, and for the consequent appropriation of, objects; and subsequently by mastery or
control over its recalcitrant Others.

This tendency, however, has more recently been stalled in its
otherwise stately and unquestioned progress. In the contemporary
moment Baudrillard rewrites Descartes, this time from the point of
view of Descartes's feared *malin génie*, the evil demon of images
and illusions. In the earliest stages of his work, Baudrillard
addresses the object and exteriority in a fairly conventional fashion. The contemporary world deals with its fear of the object

---

[23] On autobiography, see Philippe Lejeune, *Le Pacte autobiographique* (Seuil,
Paris, 1975). For a recent series of engagements with the question of biography, see
David Ellis (ed.), *Imitating Art* (Pluto Press, 1993). For a more recent exploration
of autobiography, see Robert Smith, *Derrida and Autobiography* (Cambridge
University Press, Cambridge, 1995).

through the practices of consumerism, commodity fetishism, and archivism; and Baudrillard's formative work is the analysis of a culture dominated by the forms of consumerism. The analysis is simple but forceful and consequential: in an exercise of its seductive power, the object controls the subject precisely at the moment when the subject believes itself to be in control of the world through the mercantile appropriation and semiotic comprehension of objects.

Further, however, Baudrillard incorporates into his thinking Debord's realization that the most important commodity in our times is the image itself; consequently, it follows that it is images—representations—that give, control, condition, organize, and regulate subjectivity as such. Representation—indeed theatricality (parody, fakes, simulacra)—must occupy a central and guiding position in any subsequent socio-cultural analysis. What we witness in Baudrillard, fundamentally, is the mirror-imaging (a 'fatal' evil re-presenting) of Descartes. For the earlier philosopher, it is vital to establish the priority of the 'I' as a linguistic subject over the world of exteriority; in a postmodern moment, however, Baudrillard argues that this is a strategy always condemned to failure.[24] For the contemporary, the problems and issues regarding the relation to exteriority remain the same; but Baudrillard has simply taken the threat of the evil demon of images more seriously, with the consequence that a fundamental priority is given, in his 'fatal strategies', to the object over the subject of consciousness, and with the consequence of a problematization of the very autonomy upon which modernity founds itself. Hence the quite necessary condemnation of Baudrillard by a leftist criticism which requires the maintenance of a notion of autonomous agency if there is to be any belief in the efficacy of a critical consciousness to change the world, to emancipate the subject from oppressions. Let me say here simply that such condemnation is not (and has not yet been) entirely satisfactory; and one must—and probably this is true *especially* if one is of the left—face and engage with the problematization of autonomy consequent upon the implications of even Baudrillard's most extreme forms of postmodernism.

---

[24] If not condemned to failure, the strategy is condemned at least to a form of hypocrisy. The priority of the 'I' is a fiction sustained at the cost of various repressions, or (and perhaps worse) oppressions. In the matters most pertinent to this study, it will be seen that the oppression in question is that of the victims of an emergent colonialism; the repression that of the nationalist impetus implicit in modern critical consciousness.

The persistent problem with which these philosophers attempt to deal, and which Baudrillard's work lays bare, can be characterized as a prevailing terror of alterity. The fear governing modern criticism is that the subject—indeed, even consciousness itself—might not be entirely autonomous, that it might in some way be fundamentally dependent, contingent upon its others or, worse, upon objects. (That is to say, of course, that the fear is that Baudrillard might be correct; just as the fears of Descartes and of Milton were that Satan might be not only seductive, but fundamentally right and therefore an exemplary model to be imitated.) Further, the subject (in whatever guise) might not therefore be—contra Marx—the agent of history at all, and may even be incapable of understanding an exterior, empirical, material world. The dangerous alterity figured in the object as such must therefore be tamed, most commonly in post-Cartesian (i.e. modern) terms through the reduction of the empirical to the linguistic.

It is from this desire to rein in the object that we can trace the 'imperialism of consciousness' foreseen in Hegel's master–slave dialectic, a dialectic in which the relation between the subject and object is displaced on to a more interpersonal relation between subject and subject, each vying for power and control of its others, fundamentally through the control of rhetoric or discourse. Here we have the beginnings of that power–knowledge nexus which begins, in class terms, by proposing the validity of a specific class-consciousness and a class-based agenda as normative and neutral, and which culminates in more explicit forms of colonialism, as Todorov has recently demonstrated with reference to de Tocqueville and others.[25]

Modern criticism is (among many other things, of course) that which deliberately attempts to absent the empirical other—alterity—from history in an effort to legitimize the critic as an autonomous subject of language or discourse; modern criticism is thus profoundly *semiotic* and inherently aestheticising in its determinations to find a form under which the force that is a recalcitrant alterity might be assimilated in the product of autobiography or subject-legitimation. A more direct way of absenting this other—this Derridean 'force'—from history is, of course, through the

[25] See Tzvetan Todorov, *On Human Diversity* (trans. Catherine Porter; Harvard University Press, Cambridge, Mass., 1993), esp. 91–207.

political actions which culminate in war; and my contention is that it is in a war mentality that we see the condition of modern criticism emerging, most specifically in the late seventeenth century, to which I now turn directly.[26]

III

In the late seventeenth century, a specific aesthetic battle was beginning to engage Europe, commonly known as that battle of the books contesting the relative merits and values of the ancient authors and the moderns. This is a historical instance of the emergence of a self-conscious modernity, in which writers distinguish themselves from their immediate precursors in the interests both of cultural progress and political modernisation. This aesthetic contest is partly formed by more pressing battles, in those military conflicts which shape a modern Europe into its emergent nation-states, governed broadly by the primacy of mercantilism and the ascendancy of the bourgeois classes, in a period going from the English Restoration through to the French Revolution, the latter of which articulates the modern nation-state itself understood as a 'space of legitimation'.[27] I will focus here on one particular military conflict in order to trace its intimate relation to the aesthetic itself in this emergence of an incipient modernism or cultural modernity.

Dryden published *Annus Mirabilis* in 1667, and his *Essay of Dramatic Poesy* in 1668, though both were written during 1666 when Dryden was living in Charlton where he could escape the effects of the London plague. In both texts, he attends to the 'recent conflict'—the Second Dutch war—fought between 1665 and 1667. That war, ostensibly initiated by Charles (even if its origin is in fact more complex), was a disaster for England; and, at least until the scapegoating impeachment of Clarendon in 1667, Charles faced a mercantile population which required some form of appeasement. The first question one must ask is why a poet, and one who has since been described—not entirely unfairly—as 'the age's most

---

[26] For a different theoretical explanation of the importance of a war mentality to criticism, indebted heavily to the thinking of Paul Virilio, see Docherty, *Alterities*.

[27] Todorov, *On Human Diversity*, 175.

enduring sycophant'[28] and who was an ardent supporter of Charles, would wish to linger over this war, even if in an attempt to justify or support Charles.

The occasion of these two texts has been variously described. For some time (since George Williamson's 1946 article in fact) it has been taken as a commonplace that the *Essay* was a product of a 'notable exchange of opinion', fundamentally that between Samuel de Sorbière, whose mocking *Relation d'un voyage en Angleterre* produced Thomas Sprat's defence of England and of the honour of the Royal Society in his response, the *Observations on M. de Sorbier's Voyage*.[29] Sorbière's text is an often satirical attack on the English as a nation of *fainéants* and tribal xenophobes. His narrative includes attacks on religion and governmental politics, as well as on the incidents of daily life such as the discourtesies suffered on being called 'French dog' by urchins in the port of Dover and such like. The section of the text which would have been of most interest to Dryden as a critic would have been that dealing with theatre, in which Sorbière claims that the English plays would not pass muster in France:

Mais les Comédies n'auroient pas en France toute l'approbation qu'elles ont en Angleterre. Les Poëtes se mocquent de l'vniformité du lieu, & de la règle des vingt-quatre heurs. Ils font des comédies de cingt-cing [*sic*] ans, & après avoir représenté au premier acte le mariage d'vn Prince, ils représentent tout d'vne suite les belles actions de son fils, & luy font voir bien du pays.[30]

In his response to this—and to Sorbière's more general complaints—Sprat argues that he will not attack the French *nation*, but will instead limit himself to a personal attack on the credibility of Sorbière himself; indeed, it is Sorbière's error, claims Sprat, to generalize about a nation from, for example, the particularity of schoolboys behaving rudely to foreigners arriving in Dover (though he himself, in trivializing Sorbière's complaint, generalizes about the rude behaviour of schoolboys everywhere).

---

[28]   Ronald Hutton, *The Restoration* (Clarendon Press, Oxford, 1988), 128.

[29]   George Williamson, 'The Occasion of *An Essay of Dramatic Poesy*', *Modern Philology*, 44 (August, 1946), 1–9; Samuel de Sorbière, *Relation d'un voyage en Angleterre* (Paris, 1664); Thomas Sprat, *Observations on Monsieur de Sorbier's Voyage into England* (1665).

[30]   Sorbière, *Voyage*, 167–8; long 's' modified in transcription.

Sprat's specific replies on the question of theatre amount to a claim that Sorbière is simply out of date, and that what he mocks as English irregularity may have been the case under Elizabeth, but that now, 'for these last *Fifty* years, our Stage has been as Regular in those Circumstances, as the best in *Europe*'.[31] The terms of Sprat's response show a desire to defend not just cultural practices but also political entities and identities. Though lacking the easy availability of the concept of the modern nation, Sprat argues in a vocabulary constitutive of a nationalist case. For instance, he claims against the French that 'as long as we exceed all the World, in the *Fabricks of Strength*, and *Empire*, we may easily allow him to object to us our want of those of *Pleasure*'.[32] More pointedly still, he compares Sorbière unfavourably as a traveller and observer with English travellers:

The *English* have describ'd, and illustrated, all parts of the Earth by their Writings: Many they have discover'd; they have visited all. And I dare assure him, that they have been always most tender of the Reputations of *forein States*, which they have gone to visit, as they have been most merciful in sparing the *Natives* blood, in those Countries which they have discover'd.[33]

Despite Sprat's claims to the contrary, the terms of the debate are inescapably those of the nation-state. What is being compared is not just a stereotypical 'national character', but that much more important thing, national identity as formulated in the congruence of aesthetics and politics, art and public policy.[34]

Sprat and Sorbière are at odds over the relative centrality or place in the world of their two countries; and Sprat is more aware of this than Sorbière, for whom the travel-book is primarily a kind of satire, an aesthetic or literary exercise (written at the request of the pleasure of the Marquis of Vaubrun-Nogent) rather than a singularly political gesture. Yet though the tone of both texts may differ, the governing ideology supporting both is profoundly patriotic; and Sprat's response is undeniably and unmistakably political in intent:

[31] Sprat, *Observations*, 245; long 's' modified in this and all subsequent transcriptions.
[32] Ibid. 46.
[33] Ibid. 60–1.
[34] For a useful historical survey of the ways in which cultural policy affects and effects the civic subject, see Toby Miller, *The Well-Tempered Self* (Johns Hopkins University Press, Baltimore, 1993).

'Tis true that *England* is not the seat of the Empire of the world: But it may be of that which confines the world it self, the Ocean. ... The time wherein we live is upon the recovery of an Universal peace; a peace establish'd on the two surest foundations of Fear, and Love.[35]

The incidental comparisons between national theatres is a part of a 'war of letters'. The stakes of this war are neither merely aesthetic nor merely political; rather, the argument finds itself constantly arguing the one case in terms of the other, fusing the two lexicons in what becomes the beginnings of a new discourse, the discourse of 'national character', itself a precursor of a more fully articulated discourse of nationalism such as we will see in, for instance, Burke.[36]

If the occasion of *Annus Mirabilis* is political, then so too is that of the *Essay*. Cedric Reverand sees in the *Essay* a parallel being drawn between the English military victory off Lowestoft at the start of the Second Dutch War and the English aesthetic victory over French theatre seen, he claims, in the joy of a group of French people celebrating their 'liberation' from French dogma and rules at the end of the piece:

the parallel between these two sets of events ... argues that what these poet-critics decide out in the boat may be just as relevant to England's greatness, just as significant in defining England, as what the English navy achieves with its guns.[37]

Once more, this analysis shows that it is an issue of patriotism or of an emergent nationalist consciousness that is at stake. In what follows, I will theorize this more fully, and will argue for what might be the surprising turn in which we will see the specifically *African* roots of a modern European critical consciousness, a criticism firmly tied, through its autobiographical impetus, to questions of national literature and the morality of citizenship, and a criticism based in an anxiety about what we can identify as a specific *geographical* exteriority.

---

[35] Sprat, *Observations*, 286–7. These two foundations, note, are exactly akin to Aristotle's key concepts of fear and pity in his definition of the functioning of tragedy. Sprat's universal peace is, at best, a tragic peace, and perhaps tragic because universal.

[36] On Burke, the French Revolution and national character, see Seamus Deane, *The French Revolution and Enlightenment in England* 1789–1832 (Harvard University Press, Cambridge, Mass., 1988).

[37] Cedric D. Reverand II, 'Dryden's "Essay of Dramatic Poesy": The Poet and the World of Affairs', *Studies in English Literature*, 22 (1982), 381.

In order to theorize this, however, one must first have in mind some more historical information (for which I am largely indebted in the following three paragraphs to the work of Bliss and of Hutton). The year 1651 saw the passing of the first Navigation Act in England, and, as Robert Bliss has pointed out, the effect of this Act exceeded its actual propositional context or intent, for it ' "nationalized" England's trade, not in the sense of state ownership but because it was blanket legislation which on its face applied to all trades and equally to all Englishmen'.[38] The space of the nation is thus formed, if only implicitly; and, almost incidentally, the proto-citizen is produced. If this is an example of nationalism in an emergent condition, it is what Todorov characterizes as 'internal' nationalism: that is, it is not in the first instance concerned to establish the primacy of one nation-state over others, but rather to homogenize the internal relations of citizen to citizen such that all are equal before the law; and the state—rather than the king or any divine orders—becomes the space of legitimation or court of appeal for the citizen.[39]

Such an act of 'nationalization' reveals the absolute centrality of trading to the concept that 'England' has of itself at this time, a concept firmly and explicitly made apparent in Sprat's rejoinder to Sorbière. 'England' is defined as that which is successfully mercantile; yet the Dutch at this time are, paradoxically, more English than the English in these terms, being even more successful in their trading, and the resulting anxiety among the English about their national identity is an anxiety over the occlusion of what the Cartesian would see as the clarity and distinctness of the idea of Englishness. More importantly, it follows that any war about trade at this time is, at least implicitly, a war about the quality of 'Englishness'.[40] The trade in question for both countries depended upon colonies, with the Dutch in control of the East Indies and also of the vital strategic port of New Amsterdam in the very midst of England's American colonies, a port through which tobacco was

---

[38] Robert M. Bliss, *Revolution and Empire* (Manchester University Press, Manchester, 1990), 59.

[39] Todorov, *On Human Diversity*, 175. This position for the State is seen at a later historical moment, and in another emerging modern nation, the Germany in which Schiller made his *Letters on the Aesthetic Education of Man*. For more detailed argument on this, see Ch. 6 below.

[40] For the Dutch side of this story, and for an examination of self-invention by the Dutch, see Simon Schama, *The Embarrassment of Riches* (Collins, 1987).

smuggled to deny the English the due taxation incomes, thus putting the international relations between the two countries under stress.

It was when the English, with governmental backing, claimed New Amsterdam in 1664, renaming it New York, that the Second Dutch War became inevitable; but although it may appear thus as the act that instigates the war, this action itself was the result of earlier engagements off the coast of Africa. Aware of the growing Dutch presence on the coast of Guinea in the early 1660s, the impecunious Charles invested 6,000 pounds in the Royal Company of Adventurers Trading into Africa (later renamed the Royal African Company). In 1661, this Company stakes a claim on exclusive trading rights along virtually the entire West African coastline; and, predictably, increasingly violent skirmishes broke out between English and Dutch ships in this area. The taking of New Amsterdam was a tactic meant to force a peace settlement to bring these naval conflicts to a close; but, when the Dutch recaptured all their previous holdings in a series of battles between October 1664 and February 1665, the Royal African Company turned to Charles, as a major investor, for official—that is, political and national—support. The pressure to declare war became irresistible, and formal hostilities between these two major imperial powers, fighting over trade routes, began in March 1665. Essentially, then, the Second Dutch War—a war which, it is my central claim, has an aesthetic and cultural as well as a military determination—has its origins in the West Coast of Africa in a conflict over the imperial control of trade routes and over colonial mastery in the Gulf of Guinea.

As is now well known, the war began propitiously for the English, with their famous victory, alluded to by Dryden, off Lowestoft on 3 June 1665; but things rapidly degenerated as Charles pressed the very merchant ships on whose behalf the war was supposedly being fought into military service, while plague (ironically imported into Europe via a Dutch ship bringing goods from Smyrna) focused the attention of the people on a more immediate and dangerous threat to life.

In commemorating this war, Dryden makes, in both *Annus Mirabilis* and in the *Essay of Dramatic Poesy*, an interesting swerve away from the surface conflict. In the poem, the war is seen—and justified—by Dryden in terms which might seem more apposite to an imperial war. Importantly, however, this war was not for Dryden a conflict between the English and the Dutch at all, but rather a war between the English and the French (who, though entering the war as an ally of the Dutch, actually made little military contribution to it). Dryden writes:

> Behold two nations [England, Netherlands] then, engaged so far
>   That each seven years the fit must shake each land;
> Where France will side to weaken us by war,
>   Who only can his vast designs withstand.
>
> See how he feeds the Iberian with delays,
>   To render us his timely friendship vain;
> And while his secret soul on Flanders preys,
>   He rocks the cradle of the babe of Spain.
>
> Such deep designs of empire does he lay
>   O'er them whose cause he seems to take in hand ...

And, argues Dryden, 'This saw our king' (lines 25-37), making the case for Charles as a perspicacious strategist forced into war by the presence of France in the background of the Anglo-Dutch conflict. Louis is the real—if ghostly or spectral, theatrical—villain of *Annus Mirabilis,* just as the ghost of Cardinal Richelieu will become apparent as the implicit villain in the Essay. This rather astute, if politically serendipitious, piece of analysis by Dryden forges the link between his own aesthetic activities as a writer and the political activities of the emergent imperial—or at least nationalist—powers, England and France. McKeon offers a yet more precise reading of Dryden's message, which, he argues

is international, and not strictly imperial. He imagines a world economically one, a universal collective resembling a city like London but comprehending the entire earth. ... The international scope of this Utopian vision is only an extension of the collectivizing tendency of a zealous nationalism which recognizes the general necessity of mercantile operations.[41]

In the poem, Dryden reveals, necessarily indirectly, the stakes of the *Essay:* the link between aesthetics and politics forged through the construction of the nation-state or, perhaps more pertinently, via the strategies of colonializing war and the experiences of a terror located in the place of the geographical (and now geo-political)

---

[41] Michael McKeon, *Politics and Poetry in Restoration England* (Harvard University Press, Cambridge, MA, 1975), 71.

exterior, in this instance Africa, as a site for potential exploitation or financial speculation (and I intend 'speculation' here to refer not only to economic matters but also to that theatricality for which I make my claim as a founding condition of modern criticism and philosophy above).

The stakes can only be revealed indirectly for two reasons. First, the very concept of the modern nation-state is unclear at this time, still awaiting full and proper delineation, with its attendant discourse or lexicon. Todorov (in common with thinkers as diverse as Gellner, Hobsbawm, Said, Bhabha and others) has pointed out that the term of the 'nation' comprises notions of cultural as well as political (in the first instance, 'civic') nationalism; cultural nationalism being that which 'is a path that leads towards universalism—by deepening the specificity of the particular within which one dwells', while civic nationalism 'is a preferential choice in favour of one's own country over the others',[42] and thus anti-universalizing. Additionally, within political nationalism, there is a further conflict between what Todorov calls 'internal' and 'external' nationalisms, the former being characterized as a space of 'the equality of all citizens' determined internally, the latter being, once again, the setting of one nation in opposition to others. For Todorov,

It is precisely the encounter between these two meanings, internal and external, cultural and political, that has given rise to the specifically *modern* entities of nation and nationalism.[43]

Dryden finds himself precisely at the moment of the emergence of this conflict, with the result that the only real terms available for the expression of his case are those of patriotism in which there is a *fusion* of the cultural with the political notions of nationalism.

In the second place, Dryden is indirect because he sees that the real conflict in question in this newly emerging discourse of nationalism involves him not with the Dutch at all, but rather with the French; and it is thus upon the latter that Dryden turns his literary and aesthetic guns. Consequently, the emergence of modern criticism, tied firmly to the place-logic of the nation-state, is fought out in the *Essay* between Dryden and Corneille in what is essentially a rather recondite argument over the aesthetics of tragedy. It remains clear, however, that the historical source of this modern critical

---

[42] Todorov, *On Human Diversity*, 172.   [43] Ibid. 176.

consciousness lies elsewhere, in an imperial and colonial contest in and over Africa, without which modern criticism could not fully articulate itself.

It is in this indirect revelation of the stakes of Dryden's argument that we can see what I claim to be at the root of modern criticism as such. The swerve made by Dryden, in shifting attention away from the Dutch to the French, serves more than a direct political purpose in terms of presenting a favourable image of the king. It directs attention away from Africa, and allows for the formulation of an argument whose constituents are all immediately recognizable as European. Africa is thus and at once constructed as the Other of a modern Europe and is simultaneously elided from a history now constituted by Europe in its own image. In Lyotardian terms, a differend is avoided and a tort committed. Dryden displaces the issues regarding the political materiality of Empire on to an argument about culture. In so doing, he maintains the emerging discourse of nationalism but elides Africa from the concerns of European culture (now presented simply *as* culture *tout court*). Africa remains simply as an object to be appropriated, its historical subjectivity or agency removed from historical concerns. Yet this modern critical consciousness, with all its emergent nationalist baggage, is dependent precisely on the very African alterity which remains 'forgotten', reappearing only as oddity or exoticism until the next major rehearsal of these same political issues in the Berlin conference of 1884.

IV

The cultural contest between England and France had been enjoined before Sorbière so irritated Sprat with his *Relation d'un Voyage*. In 1660, Corneille had published his plays in the three-volume edition, each volume of which was prefaced by one of the *Discours* outlining the terms and conditions proper to tragedy. The text of Corneille shares with the debate between Sorbière and Sprat one interesting intersection, for one particular attack made by Sorbière was not properly answered in an otherwise thorough riposte by Sprat. Sorbière complains that the English are difficult to understand because of the way they speak; and Sprat in fact concedes this claim: 'the obscurity of our Speech being not only his complaint, but of many other Foreiners, I will not stand long in its justification'; but he argues that it is a trivial point: 'I will not regard this small objection, wherein there may be others, that agree with him'.[44] Corneille, a provincial, was also aware of his verbal peculiarities. In his *avertissement au lecteur* in the 1663 and subsequent editions, Corneille advises the reader of certain innovations he has made in orthography in order to facilitate proper pronunciation of the French; and, perhaps most pertinently to a Dryden aware of the Sorbière–Sprat controversy and aware also of the contest with the Dutch, Corneille indicates that he is following the Dutch example in this:

L'usage de notre langue est à présent si épandu par toute l'Europe, principalement vers le Nord, qu'on y voit peu d'Etats où elle ne soit connue; c'est ce qui m'a fait croire qu'il ne serait pas mal à propos d'en faciliter la prononciation aux étrangers, qui s'y trouvent souvent embarrassés par les divers sons qu'elle donne quelquefois aux mêmes lettres. Les Hollondais m'ont frayé le chemin.[45]

It is order and regulation such as this that characterizes the content of the three *Discours*; and it is the argument *over* such regularity that structures and determines much of Dryden's *Essay*, written largely in response to the increasingly apparent international preeminence of Corneille.

Corneille, by 1660 the foremost playwright and cultural authority in France, takes issue with Aristotle, arguing that the shortcomings in his great theoretical precursor are due to the simple fact that Aristotle has not seen the triumphs of French theatre (effectively, the plays of Corneille himself, explications and critiques of which substantiate, in practical terms, the theoretical arguments—which we may now call 'subject-legitimizing' or autobiographical—made in the discourses). Incidentally, though perhaps more importantly, Corneille also takes issue with the stringent orders of Richelieu who, before his death in 1642, had demanded a strict maintenance of and adherence to the neo-Aristotelian 'rules' regarding tragedy. For Richelieu—and also for Corneille—tragedy was not just a formal

---

44 Sprat, *Observations*, 219. For the attacks to which this weak response is made, see Sorbière, *Relation d'un Voyage*, 94 (on the incomprehensible Latin spoken by the English); 167 (on pronunciation in the theatre); 169 (on the laziness of the English whose lips hardly move when they speak: a 'stiff upper lip' to set against Irigaray's lips which speak together, perhaps).

45 Pierre Corneille, *Œuvres complètes* (Seuil, Paris, 1963), 820.

aesthetic exercise: it was also a practice that had a political determinant as a manifestation of a national culture, and consequently it
demanded rigorous policing. Corneille agreed with the necessity for
regulation, but argued that the rules should themselves be subject to
modification in the light of practice (thus offering further legitimacy to his own theatrical practices).

Corneille sees that Aristotle's elements of pity and terror, as
aspects of tragedy, are so important that he must reserve a dominant place for them in his discussions. He begins from the proposition that tragedy is that kind of theatre which, through pity and
terror, leads to the purgation of similar passions. The theoretical
terms of his argument are extremely instructive, for they offer an
instance of precisely the kind of relation to exteriority which is
intrinsic to a specifically modern critical consciousness.

According to Corneille, Aristotelian theory does not require the
presence of both pity and terror; and thus, in suggesting that one
of these is sufficient for tragedy, Corneille claims that he is not at
odds with Aristotle:

il est aisé de nous accomoder avec Aristote. Nous n'avons qu'à dire que
par cette façon de s'énoncer il n'a pas entendu que ces deux moyens y
servissent toujours ensemble, et qu'il suffit selon lui de l'un des deux pour
faire cette purgation, avec cette différence toutefois que la pitié n'y peut
arriver sans la crainte, et que la crainte peut y parvenir sans la pitié.[46]

Further than this, Corneille understands the terms in a fashion
extremely germane to the terms of my present argument. Pity, he
says, is that which is aroused when we *identify ourselves* with the
sufferer, seeing her or him effectively as our *representative* on stage.
The pity in the face of an evil into which we see someone like ourselves fall brings about the fear that the same might happen to us.

In short, this aesthetic terror is aligned with a process of identification in which an Other is seen as the representation of a subject:
terror is brought about through a philosophy of identity in which
difference—the Other—is seen as but an aspect of the same, a
deferred version of the same, 'I'. Now, literary terror such as this, as
my argument above has shown, is but one instance of a more general—political—condition of terror: terror arises when we fail to see
the Other as singular, or whenever we reduce a radical alterity to a

mere surface difference.[47] In the terms recently advanced by Marc Guillaume in his discussions with Baudrillard, terror arises when we reduce *l'autre* to *autrui*:

dans toute autre, il y a autrui—ce qui n'est pas moi, ce qui est différent de moi, mais que je peux comprendre, voire assimiler—et il y a aussi une altérité radicale, inassimilable, incompréhensible et même impensable. Et la pensée occidentale ne cesse de prendre l'autre pour autrui, de réduire l'autre à autrui.[48]

In the case of the contest between Dryden and Corneille, between English and French theatres, the radical Other—that which is absented from history even as it is the founding moment of modern critical consciousness—is, as we have seen, Africa, the battles over whose geography and topography lie at the source of these critical conflicts between emerging national cultures. Yet perhaps it would be true to say that Africa, around whose coastline we saw the battle for the imperialist control of trade routes, is but one example of a more general anxiety about a geo-cultural alterity, manifested in an incipient general 'exoticism'.

Todorov points out that exoticism is a system in which 'otherness is systematically preferred to likeness';[49] and that geographical remoteness forms an intrinsic aspect of exoticism: 'it would not occur to anyone to idealize well-known neighbors'.[50] Hence, I claim, the peculiarity of a mutual anxiety shared by the English and the French, both of whom are engaged in acts informed by an exoticism in order to formulate the terms of their own national characters. The 'locatedness' I ascribe to criticism is perhaps also apparent in the plays of Corneille and Dryden themselves. Corneille's great success in adapting from Spanish sources, especially in *Le Cid* (1637), stimulates a thematic interest in geo-political otherness continued in plays such as *Rodogune, princesse des Parthes* (c.1645), *Héraclius, empereur d'Orient* (1647), not to mention the almost incidental exoticism (a temporal as well as spatial exoticism) of

[47] For a fuller exploration of this, argued from what is basically a Kierkegaardian philosophy, see Sylviane Agacinski, *Critique de l'égocentrisme* (Galilée, Paris, 1996), esp. ch. 5, in which she argues that one fundamental aspect of a 'racism' is the failure to singularize the other, or the tendency to see the other homogeneously.

[48] Marc Guillaume et Jean Baudrillard, *Figures de l'altérité* (Descartes & Cie, Paris, 1994), 10.   [49] Todorov. *On Human Diversity*, 264.

[50] Ibid. 265.

those of his plays set in the ancient world; Dryden, at the same time as engaging with the arguments advanced in Corneille's discourses, is making plays such as *The Indian Queen* (1663-4), *The Indian Emperour* (1665), and *The Conquest of Granada* (1668).

My final refinement of this argument, following on from the foregoing evidences, is that modern criticism is itself conditioned by a specific tragedy germane to the formulation of a nation-state. For Dryden, one question shaping the *Essay* is how to justify English theatre against the pre-eminence of Corneille who, by this time, has effectively become a 'national poet', thus giving credence to a specifically cultural idea of the nation-state itself and, almost incidentally, thereby demanding a concept of 'English theatre' with its corresponding 'national poet'. Along with others, but primarily with William Davenant, Dryden attempted to construct an earlier national poet than Corneille, producing—and adapting—Shakespeare for the purpose, as Dobson has convincingly argued.[51] My claim here is that Dryden saw that the question of a national theatre effectively superseded the capacity of any individual to embody it: nationalism—though he did not use the word in its present sense—was a matter for a more generalized patriotism, and was best expressed in a terminology fusing the aesthetic with the political.

The *Essay* makes a number of explicit comparisons between the theatre and the nation, imbricating cultural with political questions. The fortunes of national theatres are themselves aligned with the fortunes of nations in these 'wars of the theatre'; Ben Jonson is described as one who 'invades authors like a monarch' in the 'empire of wit'; new languages of poetry are produced from imperial battles; and, of course, the occasion of the fiction of the essay itself is 3 June 1665, 'that memorable day in the first summer of the late war when our navy engaged the Dutch'.[52]

Dryden is at pains to validate modern English theatre against both the persistence of a slavish repetition of the ancients and the threats to supremacy proposed by the French. In this, he sets up

---

[51] See Michael Dobson, *The Making of the National Poet* (Clarendon Press, Oxford, 1992).

[52] John Dryden, *An Essay of Dramatic Poesy*, in *John Dryden*, ed. Keith Walker (Oxford University Press, 1987); for the allusion to the link between nations and their theatres see 93–4; for the passages quoted, see, in order, 80, 111–12, 116, 74.

Shakespeare as a writer who is advanced as being 'natural' against the regulatory and formulaic Corneille and other French writers:

To begin then with Shakespeare. He was the man who, of all modern and perhaps ancient poets, had the largest and most comprehensive soul. All the images of nature were still present to him, and he drew them not laboriously, but luckily. . . . Those who accuse him to have wanted learning give him the greater commendation. He was naturally learned. He needed not the spectacles of books to read nature. He looked inwards, and found her there.[53]

As Dobson has pointed out, this presentation of the 'naturalness' of Shakespeare was a common tactic of the period; but importantly, Shakespeare has to be 'adapted'. He is adapted—that is, rewritten—by Dryden, Davenant and others to suit the necessities of the Restoration period, in which the norms of Elizabethan–Jacobean tragedy no longer have the same currency as they had, and when themes and issues of a seemingly more domestic interest, such as love, make a strong claim not (as they had heretofore) on comic, but rather on tragic theatre. Such 'love', associated with the emergence of a strongly felt feminine presence in theatre and culture more generally, retains its stereotypical associations with the threats posed to masculine order by sexual irregularity and promiscuity;[54] and, of course, the matters of aesthetic regulation of sexuality are thoroughly informed by matters concerning the political regulation of the monarch's voracious sexual appetites, as evidenced by Rochester or by the comic playwrights of the moment, such as Congreve or Wycherley. The *Essay* provides many instances in which the specific irregularities of Shakespearean form are held

---

53 Ibid. 110.
54 It is important to note that this 'feminization of culture' was not as straightforward as some contemporaries, such as Rapin, would have had their readers believe. More recently, critics such as Elaine Hobby and Moira Ferguson have rendered a greater complexity to these issues. See, for relevant examples, Moira Ferguson, *Subject to Others* (Routledge, 1992) and Elaine Hobby, *Virtue of Necessity* (Virago, 1988). Gerald MacLean, in 'Literature, Culture and Society in Restoration England', in id. (ed.), *Culture and Society in the Stuart Restoration* (Cambridge University Press, Cambridge, 1995), 4, points neatly to one aspect of this complexity when he writes that 'Women, though granted certain novel freedoms like that of professional acting, often found themselves subjected to gender codes that they had been busily undoing during the revolutionary decades'. It is typically in the theatre of the male writers (Dryden, Congreve, Wycherley, Vanbrugh, Farquhar, and others) that the stereotypical identification of woman with mobility is made.

to be superior to the rule-governed theatre of contemporary France (still misrepresented here as the France of Richelieu's *académie*). Once again, it would be an over-simplification at this point to oppose simply the feminine and the masculine, the former to be associated with disorder while the latter is characterized as 'regular'; rather, it is the case that the theatre—and more importantly, the *theory*—of the period formulates the questions of national culture in terms which are not, in the first instance, directly of a state–political nature. The result of these confrontations is that the age sees, in England especially, a supervention of comedy, especially domestic comedy, in which the French, it is claimed (and despite the obvious example of Molière), have neither expertise nor any national characterological predilection.[55] Here we have Dryden's fundamental proto-national insight advanced in theoretical terms. He claims in his examen of Jonson's *Silent Woman* that humour (and the term itself is undergoing an important semantic shift) is that which attends precisely to *singularity*; it is thus the perfect riposte to a tragic orientation in culture and criticism in which the potential singularity of *l'autre* is reduced to the *comparability* explicit in *autrui*, a comparability which marks the availability of otherness for taxonomical theorization: 'humour is the ridiculous extravagance of conversation, wherein one man differs from all others'.[56] In a strict sense, therefore, such humour is simply inimical to representation at all, and thus tends to evade the problems of the 'specular' in modern criticism.

Semantically, 'humour' is moving away from its intimate relations to an elementary somatics and is approximating here to a sense captured in 'mood', 'attitude' or 'inclination'. The humour in question is one seen in Aphra Behn's *Love-Letters to a Gentleman* (itself modelled on the *Lettres d'une religieuse portugaise*, written, aptly enough, not by a Portuguese nun but almost certainly, if anonymously, by the French diplomat, Guilleragues). Such an attitude is conditioned principally by the vaunted singularity and incomparability of a desired object.

In its attention to such singularity, this humour is thus also akin to an emerging construction of 'love', seen as the 'piteous' counterpart of Cornelian terror. Both Corneille and Dryden make the case for the importance of love as an aspect of theatre, even of

55   Dryden, *Essay*, 194–5.   56   Ibid. 113.

tragedy; but it is here that we see the understirrings of the prioritization in Dryden of pity over terror, the reiteration of the importance of love as that which thus denies the possibility of theoretical
regulation.

The argument can now return to the theoretical relation obtain-
ing between tragic theatricality and the nation-state, a relation
worked out through the mediation of cultural criticism. According
to Clément Rosset, tragedy is properly to be thought of as factored
and conditioned by change. There is no such thing as a tragic situation or state of affairs; rather, tragedy is that which describes the
change between states of affairs. Rosset gives the example of the
stonemason who tumbles to his death before our eyes. What makes
this specifically *tragic* is the fact that there is an identification
between differences, an identification between the living and the
dead:

> Je suis le seul à avoir saisi le tragique de la mort, non parce que le maçon
> s'est écrasé à mes pieds, mais parce que je l'ai vu, en l'espace d'une sec-
> onde, vivant, mourant, puis mort. ... Le tragique, ce n'est pas ce cadavre
> que l'on emporte, c'est l'idée que ce tas de chairs sanguinolentes est le
> même que celui qui est tombé il y a un instant, qui vient de faire un faux
> pas.[57]

For Rosset, 'le tragique est et sera toujours *le surprenant par
essence*'.[58] In my description of the stakes of modern criticism, the
pertinence of this is clear: the modern critic is she or he who is sur-
prised by the essence of her or his text, always discovering that the
essence of what is given as an object in a site of alterity is actually a
covert form of the subject herself or himself (*autrui* and not *autre*;
Europe and not Africa, say). The prime explicit example of this is, of
course, Stanley Fish who, at the time when he advocated a form of
reader-response criticism, finally identified his ideal 'reader' as not
just any non-specific reader, but none other than the nameable
Stanley Fish[59]. Modern criticism, in order to accommodate its fear
of alterity, to 'contain' its object-as-such (be it a text, a nation-state,
another individual) which threatens the autonomy of the subject,

---

57   Clément Rosset, *La Philosophie tragique* (1960; repr. Quadrige/PUF, Paris,
1991), 9.
   58   Ibid. 18.
   59   See Stanley Fish, *Is There a Text in This Class?* (Harvard University Press,
Cambridge, Mass., 1980), 49.

works to reduce that part of the object constituted by a radical alterity (*l'autre*) to a mere otherness (*autrui*), in which the self can always
be recognized. The critic finds, in the object which is ostensibly proposed as the site of difference, an underlying site of the same.

The result is that the modern is founded upon the production of
a subject of consciousness characterized first by an assumption that
the object-world is available primarily for the subject's understanding and appropriation, and subsequently by a mastery over this subject's ostensibly recalcitrant others who turn out not to be fundamentally Other at all. These others, in Rosset's terminology, will 'surprise' the subject by their 'essence', an essence which will always be
discovered to be not different, not 'themselves', but rather the same,
'me' (and, from one angle, it can be claimed that it is such thinking
that excuses, silently, the barbaric acts of colonial appropriation carried out in its name). Thus we have in criticism precisely the *anag-
norisis* constitutive of tragic terror: a recognition of the self in the
Other, such that the Cornelian identification and representation will
take place. The structure of such criticism is (like its politics) tragic.

'English' literature, 'French' theory, 'American' criticism, and so
on all depend upon this tragic structure in which the others of
'England', 'France', 'America', are constructed precisely in order to
be elided or absented from history. The theoretical ground of modern—we might as well say 'tragic'—criticism depends upon a specific historical instance in which the national Other (exotic
colonies) is itself elided from history in the interests of the protection of the English national identity at the close of the seventeenth
century. The paradoxical consequence of this is that, in a specific
sense, criticism has not even yet begun to happen for the simple
reason that the object of criticism is being structurally circumvented in the production of a subject whose truth is guaranteed by
autobiographical self-coherence (or subject-legitimation) rather
than by historical engagement.

Yet this contest, at the root of modernity, between England and
France over the primacy of a national aesthetics of theatre and
specifically of tragedy, is not the whole story. In the second part of
this opening section, I turn to the counterpart of terror in aesthetics: love, friendship, pity; and I trace the importance of a comic aesthetic for the emergence of a link not just between the aesthetic and
the political, but also between the aesthetic and the moral.

2

Love as the European Humour

I

In 1665, while Dryden was writing his *Essay* and pondering Anglo-French cultural antagonisms, Molière found himself enjoying the favour of Louis XIV, even through the scandals and socio-cultural troubles caused by his controversial *Tartuffe*, with its satirical attack on moralistic hypocrisy, in 1664. He had begun to receive a pension from Louis in 1663 of some one thousand francs; but this was multiplied sixfold when, in the August of 1665, Molière's company received the official patronage of the king. Within a month of that date, and while the Second Dutch War was going on, Molière proposed an entertainment for Louis at Versailles with his ostensibly light-hearted *divertissement* called *L'Amour médecin*. This play is very typical of Molière's comic output at this period, containing many of the staple characteristic elements of comedy so deftly deployed in his mature theatre: a satire on medicine and its inefficacy, a uselessness consequent upon medicine's extremely 'theoreticist' abstraction from the material realities of patients; a father who acts as an obstacle to the fulfilment of a daughter's erotic desires; a tricky servant of the kind Molière lifted from the Italian *commedia dell'arte*; a plot whose dénouement depends upon a particularly ironic deception. However, to regard these formal features as an adequate summation of the stakes of this play is to miss entirely the most salient points in its cultural and historical significance. These formal features and the dexterity demonstrated by Molière in his handling of them tell us a great deal about Molière as a craftsman, as an 'artisanal' playwright; but the play is more important in cultural history than this would suggest.[1] At its core, *L'Amour médecin* is a play about the very power of aesthetics to shape and control life: it is about the power of theatre or of art to shape history; and consequently, it is better viewed as every bit as much a symptom of the cultural antagonisms which plagued Dryden as were that English writer's tortuous justifications of his neo-Shakespearean 'English' national theatre and of Charles's military strategies and of his equally tortuous attempts to unite his aesthetic concerns with political realities.

L'Amour médecin opens with Sganarelle, the father in the case, agreeing with the proposition that 'qui terre a guerre a', a proposition being acted out clearly in the proto-colonial wars going on around the theatre, concerning the relations I discussed above among the French, the English and the Dutch. Sganarelle sees the principle as a description of the everyday as well as of the national–political. Having just lost his wife with whom, when she was alive, he constantly argued, he now faces the problem that his daughter, Lucinde, is in a dark melancholy. The reason for the melancholic humour has nothing to do with the death of a mother—no echoes of the tragic Hamlet here—but rather with her desire for a husband. Sganarelle calls in the doctors to diagnose her trouble; and this opens the way for Molière's satire on contemporary medicine in this play. The doctors speak the usual jargon of the 'humours' in a discourse which serves to reduce the possible diagnoses and treatments effectively to two possibilities: either Lucinde needs to be bled, or she needs to be given an emetic:

M. *Tomes*: Monsieur, nous avons raisonné sur la maladie de votre fille, et mon avis, à moi, est que cela procède d'une grande chaleur de sang; ainsi je conclus à la saigner le plutôt que vous pourrez.

M *des Fonandres*: Et moi, je dis que sa maladie est une pourriture d'humeurs causée par une trop grande réplétion: ainsi je conclus à lui donner de l'émétique.

M. *Tomes*: Je soutiens que l'émétique la tuera.

M. *des Fonandres*: Et moi, que la saignée la fera mourir.

. . . .

---

[1] This notion of the artist as 'craftsperson' is, as Barthes has shown, a development of rather recent date; and yet it is a guiding principle for criticism that has been read back into a historical period for which it was actually much less important. See Roland Barthes, *Le Degré zéro de l'écriture* (1953) repr. in *Le Degré Zéro de l'écriture suivi de nouveaux essais critiques* (Seuil, Paris, 1972).

M. Tomes: Si vous ne faites saigner tout à l'heure votre fille, c'est une personne morte. (*Il sort*)

des Fonandres: Si vous la faites saigner, elle ne sera pas en vie dans un quart d'heure. (*Il sort*)[2]

The medical 'discussion' of the case among the doctors actually manages to circumvent any examination or physical consideration of Lucinde or her ailments; and instead, the doctors prefer to discuss the questions of 'form', decency and decorum in medical matters and in their practices. After all, 'un homme mort n'est qu'un homme mort, et ne fait point de conséquence; mais une formalité négligée porte un notable préjudice à tout le corps des médecins';[3] and 'Il vaut mieux mourir selon les règles que de réchapper contre les règles'.[4] These doctors are, as it were, 'theorists' who prefer to legitimize their practice according to the governing theories which underpin it; they are unprepared for the particular case which would generate a new theory or disturb their self-legitimizations. These doctors prefer to observe the proprieties of their calling while ignoring entirely the material content of the reality of their actions. Like the 'subject-legitimising' theorist whom I introduced in the opening chapter above, these doctors apprehend the *form* of their object—medicine—but ignore its *content*—actual, material patients or specific illnesses. The consequence is that Sganarelle finds himself in a predicament uncannily prefigurative of a Lyotardian differend: he has to judge what to do in the case; he has two mutually disjunctive propositions or prescriptions; he lacks any overarching 'metamedical' discourse, some discourse beyond the 'humours' and their determining authority which would allow for an adjudication between the competing diagnoses. He is left then having to judge, but, in Lyotard's neo-Aristotelian phrase, to 'judge without criteria'.[5]

For Molière, this is a disabling consequence of the subscription to a particular 'science', the science of a medicine based on a baffling but ostensibly extremely methodical (and thus plausible) understanding of the human body as a play of forces or of physical 'humours'. What is under satirical attack here is the institutionalization of the *force* that

[2] Molière, *Œuvres complètes* (Seuil, Paris, 1962), 317.
[3] Ibid. 316.   [4] Ibid. 317.
[5] See Jean-François Lyotard et Jean-Loup Thébaud, *Au Juste* (Christian Bourgois, Paris, 1979), *passim*.

is the humours into a discourse which can turn that force into a self-legitimizing, self-sustaining, and autonomous *form* whose primary function becomes the legitimation of the form itself, in blind or wilful ignorance of the forces which required the necessity of form in the first place. In this, Molière prefigures Derrida's great 'Force et signification' essay; and what is under attack in both the seventeenth-century theatrical production and the late twentieth-century theoretical production is precisely a philosophy of self-legitimation, a self-legitimation which articulates itself through a wilful ignoring of its object or of alterity (construed as unpredictable force) as such, a philosophy which I outlined in Chapter 1 as the condition of tragedy.[6]

In *L'Amour médecin*, Molière proposes what might be construed as an 'alternative medicine', a 'complementary' medicine which turns out to be nothing more nor less than theatre itself: it is theatre that will efficaciously address the imbalance of the humours. Clitandre, in love with Lucinde, plays a role and disguises himself as a doctor with the aid of the servant Lisette. He describes this new therapy thus:

Monsieur, mes remèdes sont différents de ceux des autres. Ils ont l'émétique, les saignées, les médecines et les lavements; mais moi, je guéris par des paroles, par des sons, par des lettres, par des talismans, et par des anneaux constellés.[7]

This medicine, a form of 'talking cure' involving music, literature, and magical seduction, distinguishes itself from that of the alchemy of the humours by working on the spirit before attending to the physical body: 'ma coutume est de courir à guérir les esprits avant que de venir au corps.'[8]

---

[6] See Jacques Derrida, 'Force et signification' in his *L'Écriture et la différence* (Seuil, Paris, 1967).

[7] Molière, *Œuvres complètes*, 319.

[8] Ibid. 320. In this set of propositions, Clitandre is actually opening a significant pedagogical controversy, whose relevance for this book will become more apparent in Chs. 6 and 7. His medicine, based upon the arts, is one which calls into question the efficacy of an instrumental form of knowledge which pretends to be able to ignore the human spirit and aspiration in favour of a supposedly more real, more 'immediate' (that is, less mediated), more 'applied' set of practices more usually associated with the 'applied' sciences, with commercial business or mercantile relations in the social realm. This, of course, has much affected twentieth-century pedagogical policy in Europe, in the form of debates over the relative values of science or arts education. A clear starting-point for a discussion of this would be the 'two cultures' controversy between F. R. Leavis and C. P. Snow; but it reaches a much fuller articulation in the so-called 'postmodern' condition, as initially

In the dénouement of the plot, Clitandre gets to marry Lucinde by the effective working of a self-deconstructing disguise: he reveals explicitly to Sganarelle exactly what he is doing in 'faking' a marriage to Lucinde, thereby gaining Sganarelle's complicity in the action. By 'pretending' to be what he is, by making his theatrical self-representation match his being, Clitandre gets his way: theatre—representation or acting—shapes the real. This not only prefigures some of the terms of the Searle–Derrida debate over the functioning of Austinian 'speech-acts', but also uncannily foreshadows the arguments between Lacan and Derrida over the function of revealing and concealing letters in Poe's tale of 'The Purloined Letter', in which concealment can be achieved precisely by revelation.[9]

Of more immediate significance is the fact that Molière is here calling into question the notion of truth-telling. As in many of his plays, hypocrisy is here a key concern; but hypocrisy is a word whose etymology suggests an extremely intimate link with 'acting' itself, and Molière demonstrates here, as he will do again later and at greater length in *Le Misanthrope* that there is more to telling the truth than just enunciating true propositions. Hypocrisy turns out here to be the very condition of the possibility of truth itself, insofar as 'the true' is associated with or identified with 'the good' or with a match between desire and reality. Molière writes as if aware of the power of fakes and simulation so recently described by Eco or Baudrillard when Sganarelle, not believing that the simulations around him constitute the real, goes along with the 'humorous'

---

discussed by Lyotard, in terms of the pragmatics of knowledge in narrative and the legitimation crisis in scientific forms of validation for knowledge. See C. P. Snow, *The Two Cultures*, introduced by Stefan Collini (Canto edn.; Cambridge University Press, Cambridge, 1993); and, alongside Collini's introduction, see also Ian MacKillop, *F. R. Leavis* (Allen Lane, 1995), 314–25. For a more recent engagement of the relations of science to the humanities with respect to knowledge, see also Jean-François Lyotard, *The Postmodern Condition* (trans. Geoff Bennington and Brian Massumi; Manchester University Press, Manchester, 1984); Bill Readings, *The University in Ruins* (Harvard University Press, Cambridge, Mass., 1996; repr. 1997); and cf. Chs. 6 and 7 below.

9 For the key positions in the Searle–Derrida debate, see John Searle, *Speech Acts* (Cambridge University Press, Cambridge, 1970), and Jacques Derrida, *Limited Inc. a b c* (Johns Hopkins University Press, Baltimore, 1974). For the Lacan–Derrida debate, see Barbara Johnson *The Critical Difference* (Johns Hopkins University Press, Baltimore, 1980; repr. 1985), ch. 7, 'The Frame of Reference: Poe, Lacan, Derrida'.

joke and finds that his situation—the truth of his reality—has changed irrevocably.

In the plot, we have a major and central opposition between, on one hand, a belief in 'the humours' with all their 'objective' or material 'physicalism' (or 'physick') and, on the other, a belief in 'humour' or in the power of aesthetics, of art and of artifice, especially in the theatrical form of comedy. The new medicine of aesthetics counters an older medicine in which the human body was to be understood in the ostensibly materialist (but actually merely 'instrumental') terms of the play of counterbalancing forces. On one hand, then, we have the human being dissociated such that the 'physick' has no intimate relation with the spiritual; on the other, the human body affected by affairs of the spirit. When T. S. Eliot considered the English literature of this same period, he famously found a 'dissociation of sensibility' at work. This is what he must have meant.[10]

II

Molière's doctors are, fundamentally, rhetoricians; and their links to the literary precedents of the *rhétoriqueuers* should not be underestimated.[11] Their language is one which is, as it were, relatively autonomous: its self-referential and formal integrity, its answerability to a governing discourse called 'medicine' which determines it, is more important than its referential function. These doctors speak, and immediately the world-as-object is well lost; but in inverse proportion to that loss of the world, their own position in the world, or in the system of communications that forms the social, is correspondingly assured and further legitimized. They enact a specific logic of deconstruction articulated by de Man when he considers Baudelaire's essay on comedy, 'De l'essence du rire', according to which their 'predicament' (to borrow de Man's term) is that their language drives them further and further from practice

---

[10] See T. S. Eliot, 'The Metaphysical Poets' (1921) repr. in *Selected Essays* (3rd edn.; Faber and Faber, 1951; repr. 1980), 287–8.

[11] The rhétoriqueurs are not much remembered in literary history, but their work did lead to the better-known poetry of Colin Muset, Clément Marot, Hélinand and others; and it is useful to set this poetry alongside Molière here for the purposes of comparison.

the more theoretically reasonable and truth-driven it becomes;[12] for what guarantees truth in this case is the institution that legitimizes their linguistic practice and the community of interpreters who sustain it as an institutional and authoritative form in the first place.

While Molière is making theatrical comedy out of this in France, Milton is deploying a broadly similar practice in his epic attempt to 'justify the ways of God to men'. In 1665, Milton's position is very different from that of Molière, of course: his political desires for a Commonwealth based on a parliamentary democracy had taken their major setback in the Restoration. *Paradise Lost* might usefully be regarded as a text in which Milton's 'left-handed' prose—those writings whose referents are immediately visible—finally cedes place to a writing which regards itself as (necessarily) a relatively 'autonomous' work whose political and historical referents—visible though they may be to those who, even if blind, are capable of the required insight—may be occluded precisely by the rhetorical manoeuvres where 'cloud instead, and ever-during dark | Surrounds me, from the cheerful ways of men | Cut off'.[13] The text is, in some ways, as much a 'fantasy' as the medicine of Molière's doctors, as Milton wants to 'see and tell | Of things invisible to mortal sight'.[14]

It is this kind of fantasy—this rhetoric of the linguistically autonomous—that produces the self-legitimation of Satan, of course, who is able to ask, in one of Milton's most daring rhetorical manoeuvres, that 'Evil, be thou my good'.[15] The kind of self-legitimation at work here leads precisely to that state of affairs

---

[12]   The de Manian logic to which I refer here is that governing the argumentation of 'The Rhetoric of Temporality', in which de Man establishes a difference, in the 'philosophical' person (*par excellence*, the critic) between a 'linguistic' self (which can know itself) and an 'empirical' self (caught up in the world's travails, but fundamentally untouchable, unreachable, by the linguistic self). De Man drives a wedge between our modes of knowing the world (which can be guaranteed by reference to the language in which we know it), and our ability to shape it as agents (which has no direct link to our epistemological certitudes). This 'predicament' is examined more closely in my study *After Theory* (expanded 2nd edn.; Edinburgh University Press, Edinburgh, 1996), 119–26. It is of course significant for my present purposes that de Man makes this argument in a consideration of an essay on *comedy*.

[13]   John Milton, *Paradise Lost*, ed. Christopher Ricks (Penguin, 1968), 58–9; Bk. 3, lines 45–7.

[14]   Ibid. 59; Bk. 3, lines 54–5.   [15]   Ibid. 81; Bk. 4, line 110.

called the 'dissociation of sensibility' as characterized by Eliot: a linguistic legitimation is prioritized in the face of empirical evidences which would de-legitimize the self.[16] Satan's language enables him to ignore the physical or empirical facts of his case, just as much as Milton ignores his physical blindness to gain his rhetorical and suasive insights. There is, in such circumstances, a kind of struggle being waged between the demands of empiricism and the capacities of linguistic authority or rhetoric, a conflict of the faculties between the factually true and the linguistically correct. This conflict is enacted as a war within the subject, waged here at the cost of the object or the real world.

The philosopher of this war is Hobbes. In 1640, Hobbes's *Elements of Law* began to circulate in manuscript form, some ten years before its unauthorized publication in its two constituent parts, *Human Nature* and *De corpore politico*. When these texts appeared in England, Hobbes was already working on *Leviathan* in Paris, having fled there for his own safety after the manuscript circulation of the *Elements* had begun to arouse some controversy and unwelcome kinds of interest in England. Hobbes tries, in his political philosophy, to avoid precisely the possibility of a differend—such as that faced by Sganarelle in Molière's theatre—ever arising; and he does so by an appeal to the 'sovereign'. The sovereign in Hobbes is a concept functioning as a court of last appeal to which we must all subscribe if we are to have a social being—by which he means a life—at all.

Hobbes's philosophy begins from a peculiar amalgam of Montaigne and Descartes. From Montaigne, he inherits the view that 'Le monde n'est qu'une branloire perenne. Toutes choses y branlent sans cesse. ... Je ne puis asseurer mon object.'[17] Hobbes conceives of the world as primarily and fundamentally a play of forces in motion; and this allows him to extend the Cartesian anxiety about the existence of objects of perception. In Hobbes's view, there is nothing 'in' the object of perception to be perceived: rather,

---

[16] Although I am identifying this version of the 'dissociation of sensibility' with Eliot here, it is important to note that Eliot is not the only—and certainly not the first—critic to be concerned with what is fundamentally a dissociation of the consciousness from empirical reality. See esp. Ch. 6, in which I trace a similar concern in Schiller.

[17] Michel de Montaigne, *Essais* in 3 vols. (Garnier-Flammarion, Paris, 1969), iii. 2 'Du repentir', 20.

there is a play of forces which constitutes the world in terms of the constantly mobile, ever-shifting establishments of relations between momentary 'subjects' and equally fleeting 'objects'; and, if we are located as subjects within such a play of forces, these relations constitute what we call 'experience'.[18] Thus, for instance, he writes that the 'apparition of light without, is really nothing but motion within', and that 'image and colour is but an apparition unto us of that motion, agitation, or alteration, which the object worketh in the brain, or spirits, or some internal substance in the head'. Such thinking leads to the more general principle that:

whatsoever accidents or qualities our senses make us think there be in the world, they are not there, but are seemings and apparitions only. The things that really are in the world without us, are those motions by which these seemings are caused.[19]

Force is thus constitutive of cognition, and is also thereby constitutive of our perception of the self or of the subjectivity in relation to which we make a sense for experience and for the world. Force allows us, accordingly, to narrate ourselves (and thus to legitimize our actions); and, by the same token, force disallows the object from such a possibility of self-narration (and thus gives it no autonomy, no authority, no possibility of 'legitimate' action, for its very being becomes dependent upon the arrangement or *agencement* that brings it into its temporary existing).[20] It is perhaps needless to say that people can be objects in this state of affairs; and the positive and progressive aspect of Hobbes—the attempts to curb random violence and anarchy and thus institute a necessity of ethics in a situation inimical to altruism—are driven by the demand to deal with the emerging dialectic of subjectivity for the human agent in this ostensibly dire political situation. That, of course, is a situation which persists in philosophy and which is commonly considered under the terms of Kantian ethics, the Hegelian master–slave dialectic, Sartrean existentialism: it is the problem concerning autonomy and the pursuit of freedom in a situation in which the

---

[18]   This, as I shall show in Ch. 6, prefigures Schopenhauer, and also foreshadows more recent philosophies of the 'event' such as we see it in Lyotard, Deleuze, Badiou.

[19]   Hobbes, *Elements of Law* ed. J. C. A. Gaskin (Oxford University Press, Oxford, 1994), 24, 24–5, 26.

[20]   The term *agencement* is taken from Deleuze.

limits of human freedom and autonomy must condition the pursuit of such freedom *as an absolute* in the first place.

The specific force which becomes of most interest in this situation is precisely that force which would seem to be intrinsically ethical or driven by forms of attention to Otherness, alterity: that is to say, the force of something that Hobbes calls 'love'. Forces which help the 'vital motion' or the continuance of life are called pleasant or delightful by those experiencing them; and such forces are the occasion of love which, in the materialist terms of Hobbes, is nothing but a movement or inclination of a subject towards what it takes as an object.[21] While, for Molière, love is a therapeutic which is productive of happiness and of comic laughter, in Hobbes there is a disjunction between love and laughter. For, as is well known, laughter in Hobbes is occasioned precisely by forms of ridicule and by an at least implicit (though more usually explicit) mockery of the Other. Laughter, according to the *Elements*, is 'nothing else but a sudden glory arising from the sudden conception of some eminency in ourselves, by comparison with the infirmities of others, or with our own formerly'.[22] Laughing at the infirmity of others might be a description of the attitude of the doctors in Molière (but for the fact that, in Molière's practice, they are precisely the object of laughter or ridicule); but it is hardly an adequate description of the laughter associated with the fulfilment of an erotic desire between, say, Clitandre and Lucinde. When Hobbes reiterates and extends this view of laughter in *Leviathan*, he proposes laughter as a marker of social standing and of value:

Sudden glory is the passion which maketh those *grimaces* called LAUGHTER, and is caused either by some sudden act of their own that pleaseth them, or by the apprehension of some deformed thing in another, by comparison whereof they suddenly applaud themselves. And it is incident to them that are conscious of the fewest abilities in themselves, who are forced to keep themselves in their own favour by observing the imperfections of other men. And therefore much laughter at the defects of others is a sign of pusillanimity. For of great minds one of the proper works is to help and free others from scorn, and compare themselves only with the most able.[23]

Here, we get the beginnings of a theory of comedy and of its social function. It is important to note, at this point, that a comedy based

---

[21]   See Hobbes, *Elements*, 43–4.   [22]   Ibid. 54–5.
[23]   Hobbes, *Leviathan* , ed. Edwin Curley (Hackett, Indianapolis, 1994), 32.

on Jonsonian notions of the 'humours' is, courtesy of Hobbesian thinking, no longer easily tenable; for Hobbes's materialist view of the world as a play of shifting forces which constantly changes and challenges our subjectivity is one which effectively damages the idea that each individual subject is easily identified according to her or his presiding (and thus more or less stable) 'humour': those humours, even within the human body, are themselves constantly involved in the Montaignesque 'branloire perenne' and thus never result in any fixed or stable individual identity. The humours now demand *regulation*.

That Hobbesian theory of comedy, then, is one which is clearly associable with the tragic orientation in critical consciousness I outlined in Chapter 1. Its laughter is dependent upon the assertion of a superiority over the Other against which the laughing subject defines itself, thereby effectively absenting the Other from history through the tactic of ridicule. Yet what is being ridiculed is precisely, as Dryden was becoming aware, the *singularity* of the Other. The laughter against the Other is thus, at least covertly, a mechanism which allows a subject to assert superiority in the face of the possibility that the Other might actually resist comprehension, that, in its singularity, it might not be easily assimilable (and thus that it might be threatening to the putative stability of the subject). As Hobbes shows, the judgement of the Other made by the laughing subject is one designed to allow that subject to reflect upon itself and to strengthen its assurance of its own righteousness and legitimacy.[24]

By 1758, when Hutcheson was to write his *Reflections on Laughter*, such a Hobbesian version of the form and function of comedy could be explicitly attacked. Those *Reflections* are a direct response to the perceived limitations of Hobbes and of Mandeville; and Hutcheson is able to argue that laughter is conditioned by an ethical demand based on the very counterpart of the tragic terror so intrinsic to late seventeenth-century critical consciousness: pity.

---

[24] Pierre Bourdieu, *Distinction* (trans. Richard Nice; Routledge & Kegan Paul, 1984), advances a similar kind of argument with respect to the social functioning of taste, arguing the case that judgements of works of art are made not solely with the works of art in mind, but rather with a heavy sense that the judgement in question says more about the social standing of the critic/judge than it does about the work ostensibly being judged or evaluated.

For Hutcheson, laughter in the confrontation with something perceived as amiss in the Other arises from a basic love for the Other, and from the consequent ethical demand for gentle, if satirical, correction. I shall discuss this more fully in the next chapter; but for present purposes, I shall be asking what it is that happens, culturally, between 1650 and 1758 to make the Hobbes/Mandeville 'terrifying' (tragic) thesis untenable and to replace it with the more benevolent, pitying, love-centred thesis of Hutcheson (and behind him, Shaftesbury) more readily available. The name for what happens is, fundamentally, Molière; and, in the rest of the present chapter, I shall be attending in particular to two key texts: *Le Misanthrope* of 1666, and *Le Bourgeois Gentilhomme* of 1670.

III

If Molière had tried to represent Hobbes in the theatre, he would have done well to call his character Alceste, for if this misanthropist is not the theatricalization of Hobbes, then he is at least the dramatization of a Hobbesian ethos or disposition: a rather curmudgeonly extremist who pushes his rhetorical argumentation to the point where it gets him into untenable positions, and who nonetheless sticks to the consequences of what he has to say, regardless of how complicated those consequences of his rhetoric might be for the maintenance of logic or for the sustenance of the real, lived and political life he faces. Molière satirizes here the figure of the man who lives his philosophy for real,[25] a man who sees

---

[25] To this extent, Alceste can be seen as what we might now call a 'strong thinker', by which I mean to distinguish the character of Alceste from both that of the Rortean pragmatist and from the philosopher of Vattimo's *pensiero debole*. For Rorty, the intellectual has no special social responsibilities: she philosophizes, certainly, and she lives her social and political life, equally certainly; but there need be no programmatic determination of the latter from the former. Similarly (but with important differences), Gianni Vattimo and Pier Aldo Rovatti recently formulated a notion of 'weak thinking'—*pensiero debole*—according to which it was possible to be only loosely committed to the social or political philosophies sustained by one's intellectual engagements. Sartre would have seen all this as the merest *mauvaise foi*, and much Marxism would concur with this judgement—or, equally, with that of Alceste, for whom such sophistries would be seen as a hypocrisy founded in insincerity or 'theatricality'. For Rorty's argument, see Richard Rorty, 'Postmodernist Bourgeois Liberalism' in his *Objectivity, Relativism, Truth: Philosophical Papers* 1 (Cambridge University Press, 1991), repr. in Thomas Docherty, ed., *Postmodernism:*

any discrepancy between, on one hand, one's intellectual or abstract commitments and beliefs and, on the other, material life, as hypocrisy, 'theatricalization' and insincerity: Alceste ostensibly does not know the dissociation of sensibility.

Le Misanthrope opens with a rather Hobbesian set of presuppositions being advanced by Alceste. Philinte, Alceste's friend, warmly embraces someone; but then reveals that he cannot recall the name of this anonymous character. Angered by this show of benevolent emotion towards someone who obviously means so very little to Philinte, Alceste complains that 'Votre chaleur pour lui tombe en vous séparant'.[26] Behind that statement is the same philosophy that allows Hobbes to describe perception as force, and imagination or memory as nothing more than 'decaying sense' or a force which is dissipating because the object of perception is no longer forcing itself upon our brain.

The play then sets up a presiding opposition between Alceste, who claims to favour truth and sincerity over social ritual and nicety on the one hand, and, on the other, Philinte, who acknowledges that there is a specific play of quasi-economic forces at work in the very constitution of our being in a social sphere, and that such forces require adherence, if not yet commitment, if the social is to be regulated (and thus to persist) at all. Alceste thus comes to represent the force of self-justificatory rhetoric, while Philinte represents the necessity for the observation of empirical realities as they affect the human subject; Alceste wants the world to conform to his consciousness, while Philinte accepts that the empirical realm affects the language in which we come to self-presence as subjects. Lacking a comic sense of humour, Alceste is nonetheless driven by a specific 'humour' or mood, clearly given at the start of the play in his *contretemps* with Philinte: 'Je veux qu'on soit sincère, et qu'en homme d'honneur | On ne lâche aucun mot qui ne parte du cœur.'[27] Against this, Philinte proposes a mode of sociality, a decorum based upon economics or upon

A Reader (Harvester-Wheatsheaf; Columbia University Press, Hemel Hempstead and New York, 1993); for Vattimo, see Gianni Vattimo e Pier Aldo Rovatti (eds.), *Il pensiero debole* (Feltrinelli, Milan, 1983), and cf. the more recent work of Gianni Vattimo, *Credere di credere* (Garzanti, Milan, 1996), in which this philosophy allows for a *rapprochement* between nihilism and a Catholic theology.

[26] Molière, *Œuvres complètes*, 324 (line 23).
[27] Ibid. 324 (lines 35–6).

what is fundamentally a logic of representation as evidenced in the effecting of social exchanges:

> Lorsqu'un homme vous vient embrasser avec joie,
> Il faut bien le payer de la même monnaie,
> Répondre comme on peut à ses empressements,
> Et rendre offre pour offre, et serments pour serments.[28]

For Alceste, the problem with such economic balance ('offre pour offre', 'serments pour serments') is precisely that the social decorum produced by it is based upon a logic of *representation* (my 'offre' is re-presented—and, indeed, adequately if not perfectly represented—in yours), against which he favours the immediacy of the sincere heart, or the *presence* of the subject in her or his social being (and not a mere social appearing or representation of the being): 'Je veux que ... Le fond de notre coeur dans nos discours se montre.'[29] Consequently, a social exchange in which each subject or participant matches the other in that perfectly balanced economy—the representation—that constitutes Philinte's decorum does not allow for the possibility of Hobbesian distinctions or the social superiority that distinguishes one as a particular, singular, individual: 'Je veux qu'on me distingue', as Alceste puts it in this same conversation. Alceste sees that what is at stake in this is the very fabric of the social, yet he argues vehemently against what he sees as a social formation that is ostensibly based upon the equality of all participants but which through that pretence of equality thereby serves only to elide distinctions and to disregard the quiddity of the individuals who make up the society. That is to say, he argues that Philinte's position is that which governs a false or premature Utopia of a form of 'democracy' which understands democracy as an argument for the essential equality (and thus indistinctness) of all participants. For Alceste, this false democracy observes the *forms* of democracy only by ignoring social reality—and it is this that makes it prematurely Utopian:

> Non, je ne puis souffrir cette lâche méthode
> Qu'affectent la plupart de vos gens à la mode;
> Et je ne hais rien tant que les contorsions
> De tous ces grands faiseurs de protestations,
> Ces affables donneurs d'embrassades frivoles,

---

[28] Molière, *Œuvres complètes*, 324 (lines 37–40).
[29] Ibid. 324 (lines 69–70).

Ces obligeants diseurs d'inutiles paroles,
Qui de civilités avec tous font combat,
Et traitent du même air l'honnête homme et le fat.
.   .   .   .
Et c'est n'estimer rien qu'estimer tout le monde.[30]

This is not to suggest, of course, that Alceste is a democrat or egalitarian (except insofar as he treats *all* others pretty equally in terms of the extent of the contempt in which he holds them). He is concerned throughout to establish his identity and standing as one who is superior to those around him.

Alceste allows the rhetoric of reason to force him into unreasonable extremities; but Philinte knows that the supremacy of reason needs to be tempered, its force regulated, if it is to be reasonable at all. Accordingly, he proposes a reason moderated by mood, sense, or by the emotional pull of 'sobriety'. While accepting that Alceste's argument is unanswerable in rhetorical terms (that is to say, the language in which it is made is formally correct, and its mode of reasoning observes the rules of linguistic reasoning), Philinte nonetheless asks for a little less rigour and for a bit of sympathy for our human failings:

A force de sagesse, on peut être blâmable;
La parfaite raison fuit toute extrémité,
Et veut que l'on soit sage avec sobriété.[31]

Most importantly in the context of my present argument, it is precisely this 'tempered reason', this impure form of reasoning (or this *pensiero debole*), that allows Philinte to see the objects of his perception—human beings—as in themselves they really are:

Je prends tout doucement les hommes comme ils sont,
J'accoutûme mon âme à souffrir ce qu'ils font;
Et je crois qu'à la cour, de même qu'à la ville,
Mon flegme est philosophe autant que votre bile.[32]

Phlegmatic humour contests truth with bilious humour, in these terms.

Alceste's extremist subscription to the form of reason, and to its rhetorical extremes, is displayed fully in the development of the

---

[30] Ibid. 324 (lines 41–58).   [31] Ibid. 325 (lines 150–2).
[32] Ibid. 325 (lines 163–6).

play's action. The real concern of this play is a rather self-reflexive one, for its plot turns crucially on an issue of aesthetic judgement: how do we know what constitutes the good work of art (how do we evaluate a poem); and how do we love another human subject (on what grounds can we legitimize—and thus validate or prove—moral approbation and love)? In a word, what is beauty?

The play brings together two modes of judgement: the aesthetic and the litigious. When it opens, we quickly see revealed one possible reason for Alceste's choleric misanthropy, in that he alleges that he has been betrayed, robbed, and slandered by someone whom he trusted. Alceste and his unnamed adversary in this case are now at law. Alceste proposes to rest his case entirely on reason itself, refusing to play the system of influence and corruption that runs the legal system. That is to say, having identified his rhetoric as 'sovereign' in the Hobbesian sense, he expects all other possible modes of acting to be answerable to that rhetoric as the final arbiter of the true. His rhetorical self legitimation pushes him to an extremist position: 'J'ai tort, ou j'ai raison';[33] and he asserts that he will not intervene, preferring instead to rest his case on the supposed self-evidencing of the legitimacy of his case before the eyes of the world and thus also before the eyes of the law. When Philinte points out that he will surely lose his case, Alceste's response leads him into utter paralogy:

> J'aurai le plaisir de perdre mon procès.
>
> .   .   .   .
>
> Je verrai dans cette plaiderie
> Si les hommes auront assez d'effronterie,
> Seront assez méchants, scélérats, et pervers,
> Pour me faire injustice aux yeux de l'univers.
>
> .   .   .   .
>
> Je voudrais, m'en coutât-il grand-chose,
> Pour la beauté du fait, avoir perdu ma cause.[34]

Here, the (aesthetic or formal) beauty of seeing his humour legitimized—that is, the beauty of seeing his subject-position corroborated and validated—prevails over his supposed desire for empirical truth on which Alceste claims to be basing his entire practice.

33 Molière, *Œuvres complètes*, 326 (line 192).
34 Ibid. 326 (lines 196–202).

Explicitly, Alceste will now be shown to be in the right precisely to the extent that he is shown by the judgement of his legal case to be in the wrong: he cannot lose, therefore, because to lose his case is precisely what will make him win his argument. Alceste's paralogical characterology is one which establishes a particular condition which will reappear in later aesthetics (especially in that of Rousseau):[35] the desire for truth is pushed to the extreme in which a truth conditioned by empirical validation cedes primacy to a 'truth-to-the-self', or what we have learned to call 'authenticity' or 'sincerity', according to which the legitimation and authority of the self is more important than the veracity of factual propositions about the world.

In *Le Misanthrope*, further, this juridical case which precedes the play and thus conditions it is immediately linked to another judgement, that aesthetic judgement in which Alceste judges Oronte's sonnet. Given the establishment of Alceste's character, it is clear that the extremely negative judgement made is, in fact, preconditioned: it is a judgement that is inevitable given the establishment of Alceste's paralogical character, and its basis is to be found not in Alceste's empirical engagement with the poem but rather in Alceste's engagement with his own desire for 'sincerity', a sincerity that can only be demonstrated by a conformity of the actual judgement with a given character of misanthropy. Once more, we have a state of affairs in which the critic—Alceste—makes a judgement whose function is to consolidate a subject-position, a judgement which therefore neglects its supposed object (the sonnet): the function of criticism here is to provide solace for a subject which is itself the foundation of the critical act, and self-legitimation triumphs over the critical engagement with an aesthetic object.

Both these judgements converge in a third, in which, even for Alceste, extremist and paralogical reason does not regulate love: 'la raison n'est pas ce qui règle l'amour';[36] and it is Célimène, object of Alceste's 'humour' (or affection) who sees the (almost necessary) self-contradictoriness of the 'sincere' character:

> L'honneur de contredire a pour lui tant de charmes,
> Qu'il prend contre lui-même assez souvent les armes;

35 For the full exploration of this, see Ch. 5.
36 Molière, *Œuvres complètes*, 326 (line 248).

Et ses vrais sentiments sont combattus par lui,
Aussitôt qu'il les voit dans la bouche d'autrui.[37]

This mode of criticism, then, in which 'sincerity' (or the authentic validation of a character for the subject which can then act as a foundational ground for all judgement) triumphs over a respect for alterity (or for the possibility that an empirical fact might threaten the foundation on which a subject's judgement is being made) leads to a peculiar state of affairs. The subject can legislate *only* for itself: when its judgement is corroborated by others, then, *ipso facto*, the authenticity of the self—and its identifiable singularity—is threatened. If someone else agrees, then the subject must axiomatically disagree with their agreement, and thus lapse into self-contradiction.

That paradoxical state of affairs is known to us more immediately as a paradox associated with a liberal humanist criticism which shies away from 'solidarities'; we see it expressed, for instance, in Edward Said, who argues:

Were I to use one word consistently along with *criticism* (not as a modification but as an emphatic) it would be *oppositional*. If criticism is reducible neither to a doctrine nor to a political position on a particular question, and if it is to be in the world and self-aware simultaneously, then its identity is its difference from other cultural activities and from systems of thought or method.[38]

Crudely put, to agree with this is to oppose it, and *vice-versa*. The position is one which cannot legislate a generally applicable norm from the singular fact of a specific aesthetic judgement made by one subject; and if one says that this position does not in fact wish to make such a normative legislation, then one is opening the door to a form of liberal individualism that is actually close to anarchy. If all judgements are made in the interests of the corroboration *merely* of the factual response of the individual critic, then we have a state of affairs in which criticism is about the production of an *autonomy* in which every subject is its own law, but no community of interpreters can ever exist, for no general norms of judgement (aesthetic *or* juridical) can be established.

---

[37] Molière, *Œuvres complètes*, 326 (lines 677–80).
[38] Edward Said, *The World, the Text, the Critic* (1983; repr. Faber and Faber, 1984), 29. For a fuller exploration of the paradox involved in this position, see my *After Theory* (2nd edn.; Edinburgh University Press, Edinburgh, 1996), 249–50.

The paradox of 'distinction' follows from this: if everyone is singular, an individual, then the only way to be an individual is by not being an individual. To put this in terms more directly germane to the present argument, if 'I' am identified as my rhetoric, then I must axiomatically disagree with anyone who agrees with me or who 'quotes' me (that is to say, reiterates my rhetorical judgement) and thereby confuses the singularity of my identity with that of another subject. Clearly, an ethical problem is visible here, in that a mode of criticism which proposes itself as sincere appears to be at odds with the establishment of a community whose norms for judgement could be based on such a sincerity.

Molière, however, is exploring that in terms of the contradictoriness of a love expressed by Alceste in necessarily (because grounded in a given character) misanthropic (misogynist) terms. The condition of love, in this play, makes explicit what is more or less tacit in the theatrical treatment of the amorous theme in European writing at this time: love is contradiction, and is hence unamenable to those forms of thinking or of reason which are seen increasingly to depend upon their normativising powers, those forms of quantifiable reason emerging in the dominant form of mathematics practised by Newton and Leibniz. Love in the writing of this time is an inexplicable condition which is unavailable for the regulations of an emerging powerful reason; and, by its very nature, it is incalculable. It is in *Le Misanthrope* that such non-measurability, such unquantifiability, such ineffability is made apparent. In English theatre of this time, apparently unable or unwilling to cope with such an alternative to formal or mathematical reason, love is reduced in Hobbesian terms to lust, explained in terms of a materialist and transitory desire for gratification of physical impulses; but it is Molière who sees that this inexplicability of love—its very sincerity—is also a question of the legitimation of the self, and, by extension, a significant ethical problem regarding the establishment of social or communitarian norms.

Alceste, the great reasoner and the character who will rest his very juridical status on the self-evidencing of reason, cannot 'explain' his love for Célimène. He does not love her for any specific quality in her; and, were this an English Restoration play, such a state of affairs would be translated in the comprehensible, if unsettling, terms of material lust or appetite. In Molière, however, the question that arises is that regarding the proper relation between reason and love or, to write this large, between objectivist philosophy itself and the subjectivity of the experiencing of love. This once more opens an issue that we have seen before: what is the status of the object for the critical subject, and how 'available' is that object for the operations of the reason—or now also the love—of that subject?

The basic terms of the argument in philosophical terms are relatively easily put. Suppose I am able to quantify or measure love in terms of the love of specific qualities perceived in the object of my affection (a position that English culture might have known as the 'King Lear hypothesis'); and now hypothesize that someone else appears, displaying the same qualities. Is the love which I had applied to one object (call it 'S') universally applicable? Can I at least establish a communal normative response to the loved object, even if I cannot yet found community as such? The philosophical terms are thus put by Roger Lamb:

You love S. Furthermore, you love S in virtue of the fact that S manifestly has properties $F(1), \ldots F(n)$. Now as it happens there is someone else who also manifests properties $F(1), \ldots F(n)$. Call this other person 'J'. *J now appears on your scene.* The question for us to consider is not whether you do (for at this point you do not)—nor, indeed, whether you ever will—love J. You may, but you may not. Rather the question to consider … is whether, all other things remaining equal, you are under any rational constraint to love J (as well as S). And thus, the question is whether, under such circumstances, you must, as a rational being, love J.[39]

If I am rationally constrained to love J, then I lose the very singularity that I had prized in S, a singularity which is single precisely because it cannot be represented either as an enumerated set of qualities $(F(1), \ldots F(n))$ or characteristics alleged to constitute the object, or represented as or in the objective figure of another person (J).

A form of reason that bases itself upon such an understanding of the object—that is, on an understanding that objects can be represented, and that in Hobbesian fashion their very being depends upon the force of their representation as a felt experience within the subject—is clearly antipathetic to a system of love which respects singularity or uniqueness. Love, thus, emerges now as a

³⁹ Roger E. Lamb, 'Love and Rationality' in id. (ed.), *Love Analyzed* (Westview Press, Oxford, 1997), 25–6.

problem for a Hobbesian philosophy based, as it necessarily is, upon the logic of theatricality or of representation. Hobbes, perhaps paradoxically, requires a subscription to some version of 'the humours', not as objects that can be perceived in the Other, but as effects perceived in ourselves as representations of the Other. Molière, on the other hand, is looking for a philosophy that is not thus incommoded; and so, for him, 'humour' (not 'the humours') takes that Drydenesque turn in which it relates to comedy and singularity, rather than to physical representability. Recall Dryden here: 'humour is the ridiculous extravagance of conversation, wherein one man differs from all others'—a phrase that might equally well describe the condition of love as it is explored in Molière: a fixation on the singularity of the loved object.

There is a politics to this. In the first instance, we have again the issue of a national culture and a national politics (here with a very different inflection from that given in Chapter 1, because here concerned with the question of the very foundation of community as such); and, in the second place, we have the stirrings of a new kind of political thinking in the emergence of a philosophy governing 'democracy', the need for which is urgent in the face of the threat of an anarchy masquerading as autonomy. To make a proper way into this, I turn to my other key text, Molière's *Le Bourgeois gentilhomme*.

IV

In November 1669, an envoy of the Sultan Mahomet IV was received at the court of Louis XIV. He amused Louis by appearing to be very unimpressed by the extremely showy and extravagant reception laid on for him; and it may well have been the case that Louis requested from Molière some elements of 'turquerie' in his next play, *Le Bourgeois gentilhomme*. There was, alongside this, an emerging aesthetic interest in the 'exoticisms' of Turkey, from Guys de Scudéry's successful 1641 novel, *Ibrahim ou l'illustre Bassa*, through Lully's musical work of 1669, the *Récit turquesque*; and the interest and topicality of the exotic subject-matter persists into 1672, when Racine puts on *Bajazet*. The question of Turkey, and of an emerging 'Europe' or European identity defining itself against an exotic Turkish otherness, ghosts Molière's 1670 text, and explicitly continues the investigation of the relation of love to philosophy and to democracy.

Le Bourgeois gentilhomme is a play about class, certainly; but it is about class marked and identified through aesthetic taste, class-distinctions being apparent through the liking or disliking of objects of aesthetic perception.[40] Jourdain enters the scene, reminiscent of a Shakespearean Malvolio, ridiculously dressed: 'je me fais habiller aujourd'hui comme les gens de qualité.'[41] As in *L'Amour médecin*, the therapeutic power of art itself—the political practicalities of aesthetics—is a dominant issue, as Jourdain tries to appreciate music, to learn how to dance and to engage in the rituals of the martial arts: 'Sans la musique, l'état ne peut subsister', and 'Sans la danse, un homme ne saurait rien faire'.[42] His very body becomes the site of taste as he learns how to fence:

Allons, monsieur, la révérence. Votre corps droit. Un peu penché sur la cuisse gauche. Les jambes point tant écartées. Vos pieds sur une même ligne. Votre poignet à l'opposite de votre hanche. La pointe de votre épée vis-à-vis de votre épaule. Le bras pas tout à fait si étendu. La main gauche a l'hauteur de l'œil. L'épaule gauche plus quartée. La tête droite. Le regard assuré. Avancez. Le corps ferme ...[43]

On one hand, this text demonstrates every bit as clearly as does *Le Misanthrope* the validity of Bourdieu's work on taste, in which he argues from the point of view of the sociological evidence that aesthetic judgements have less to do with judgements about works of art than with the establishing of distinctions between classes of people, between those endowed with taste and those scarred by bad taste. In such judgements, the ostensible object of judgement is ignored as we try to legitimize ourselves over against other subjects vying for greater social legitimacy and power. For Bourdieu, the question of taste directly impinges on economics, for what is at stake here is the amassing of 'cultural capital'; and it is this paradoxical situation regarding taste—or aesthetics, justice and politics—that is explored in Molière's satire. For Jourdain, taste is a physical matter, something that tortures his very body; and thus, in

---

[40] The classic analysis of this confusion between aesthetics and class or social status (though not with direct relevance to Molière) is, of course, Pierre Bourdieu's *Distinction* (trans. Richard Nice; Routledge & Kegan Paul, 1984).

[41] Molière, *Œuvres complètes*, 508.

[42] Ibid. 509.

[43] Ibid. 511.

this torture, Jourdain's taste is lived, vital, experienced as a physical reality or necessity.

When Giorgio Agamben considers the origins of modern aesthetics, he turns to this example of Jourdain, 'un *homme de mauvais goût* qui veut devenir *homme de goût'*.[44] Jourdain, with his desire to become a man of taste, is not treated as an object of scorn, but rather one of sympathy, argues Agamben, acknowledging in this that he is rehearsing exactly what Rousseau had said about the play in his *Lettre sur les spectacles*. In that piece, Rousseau asked: 'Quel est le plus blâmable d'un bourgeois sans esprit et vain qui fait sottement le gentilhomme, ou du gentilhomme fripon qui le dupe?'[45] Agamben picks this up and develops it in an argument in which he claims that:

Le paradoxe de Monsieur Jourdain est qu'il est non seulement plus honnête que ses maîtres, mais en quelque sorte plus sensible aussi et plus ouvert face à l'œuvre d'art que ceux qui devraient lui apprendre à juger: cet homme fruste est tourmenté par la beauté, cet illettré qui ne sait ce qu'est la *prose* a tant d'amour pour les belles-lettres que la seule idée que ce qu'il dit puisse être de la prose est capable de le transfigurer.[46]

That is to say, Jourdain retains the ability to experience art empirically, sensibly, while his masters are actually rather distanced from their art and their practices. Their attention is to the form or formalities, but not to the content, of their art; Jourdain, having no mastery of form or no abstract conception of the art, is lost in content, drowned in experience. Jourdain's 'teachers' are, as it were, his bad doctors, 'theorists' lifted straight from the pages of *L'Amour médecin*, and transferred from the discourse of medicine into the discourses of the various aesthetic practices of music, dance, philosophy, martial arts, and so on. What makes Jourdain's masters 'modern', in Agamben's view, is precisely this distancing of themselves from experience, precisely what I am calling the triumph of their abstract or intellectual 'theory' over the empirical engagement with the content of their practices.

The turn in the plot depends upon disguise, in which Cléonte—who has admitted that he is not a 'gentilhomme' (in a speech that

44 Giorgio Agamben, *L'Homme sans contenu* (trans. from the Italian by Carole Walter; Circe, Paris, 1996), 33.
45 Rousseau, *Lettre à M. d'Alembert sur les spectacles*, introduction de L. Brunel (5th rev. edn.; Hachette, Paris,1910), 55.
46 Agamben, *L'Homme sans contentu*, 33-4.

shows, ironically, that he has all the qualities of the gentil-homme)—appears as the 'son of the Great Turk', in which guise he has the social status required to persuade Jourdain that his daughter, Lucile, can marry him. The trick depends upon that very philosophy of love called into question by *Le Misanthrope* some three years prior to this play, as the scheming trickster Covielle points out here:

> *M.Jourdain*: Tout ce qui m'embarrasse ici, c'est que ma fille est une opiniâtre qui s'est allée mettre dans la tête un certain Cléonte, et elle jure de n'épouser que celui-là.
>
> *Covielle*: Elle changera de sentiment quand elle verra le fils du Grand Turc; et puis il se rencontre ici une aventure merveilleuse, c'est que le fils du Grand Turc ressemble à ce Cléonte, à peu de chose près. Je viens de le voir, on me l'a montré; et l'amour qu'elle a pour l'un passera aisement à l'autre...[47]

That is to say, if love is understood to be quantifiable in terms of the love *for* specific qualities in Cléonte, then, when another appears bearing the same qualities, in this case the 'son of the Great Turk' (actually Cléonte in disguise), then Lucile will be rationally constrained to love this new person. The trick in the text is that the two putative objects of Lucile's affection share the same qualities because they are the same person.[48] Where Jourdain's aesthetic is one subscribing to a neo-Hobbesian position inimical to love as such, Cléonte and Lucile offer a new attitude to love, one in which love is a gesture towards the singularity of alterity.

There is a politics to this love, *une politique de l'amitié* as Derrida might have it, here. Derrida begins his study of the politics of friendship from a meditation on a phrase from Aristotle, as cited in Montaigne's *Essais*, specifically in the essay 'De l'amitie';[49] 'O

---

[47] Molière, *Œuvres complètes*, 532.

[48] Later, we will see that this issue assumes a central importance in German aesthetics, specifically in the work of Schiller, who makes a distinction between what he calls 'Person' and 'Condition' to try to deal with the post-Humean anxieties over the persistence of personal identity in the face of obvious historical change. One can be the same Person, but appear under different Conditions. For the full exploration of this, see Ch. 6 below. In the present chapter, what is of importance is that an ostensibly temporal condition—that of change and development within the individual—is mediated in this trick as a 'spatial' condition—Cleonte is here and not here simultaneously.

[49] Jacques Derrida, *Politiques de l'amitié* (Galilée, Paris, 1994); Michel de Montaigne, *Essais* (Garnier–Flammarion, Paris, 1969), i. 231–42.

mes amis, il n'y a nul amy.' The *Essais* were, of course, hugely influential in the shaping of Renaissance and early modern European literature, the Florio English translation appearing in 1613, and Ginammi's Italian version in 1633. In 1635, a new French edition, edited by Melle de Gournay, had appeared, reprinting continually through the seventeenth century, until 1669, when Montaigne became the object of intense political and religious scrutiny; and the *Essais* were placed on the index in 1674—not before they had had a massive influence on Descartes, Pascal, and most importantly for present purposes, Molière.

With respect to Molière, there is, in the essay 'De l'amitié', a better place to begin than that from which Derrida weaves his speculations. The first reference to Aristotle in this essay is one in which Aristotle makes explicit the link of friendship (and love) to politics: 'Et dit Aristote que les bons legislateurs ont eu plus de soing de l'amitié que de la justice.'[50] This is taken to corroborate Montaigne's view that nature leads us inexorably to the formation of society, to a being sociable or to a human essence of sociability and relatedness. Within that sociability, however, there are various kinds and modes of relation to be distinguished; and when Montaigne thinks of the familial affections and their bonding obligations, he comes to an important hypothesis linking love to the assertion of freedom and autonomy:

Le père et le fils peuvent estre de complexion entièrement eslongnée, et les frères aussi. C'est mon fils, c'est mon parent, mais c'est un homme farouche, un meschant ou un sot. Et puis, à mesure que ce sont amitiez que la loy et l'obligation naturelle nous commande, il y a autant moins de nostre chois et liberté volontaire. Et nostre liberté volontaire n'a point de production qui soit plus proprement sienne que celle de l'affection et de l'amitié.[51]

---

[50] Montaigne, *Essais*, i. 232. Cf. Aristotle, *Ethics: The Nicomachean Ethics* (trans. J. A. K. Thomson, revised by Hugh Tredennick, introduced by Jonathan Barnes; Penguin, Harmondsworth, 1976), Bk. viii, p. 258. Aristotle, in fact, goes slightly further than Montaigne: 'Friendship also seems to be the bond that holds communities together, and lawgivers seem to attach more importance to it than to justice', he writes; but as he glosses that statement, he goes on to say that 'Between friends there is no need for justice' (ibid. 259).

[51] Montaigne, *Essais*, i. 233. This differs in orientation from Aristotle, for whom perfect friendship is marked by durability, a durability itself grounded in the essential 'goodness' or ethics that constitutes the perfection of friendship in the first place. See Aristotle, *Ethics*, 263.

Love, friendship, is the arena in which we assert our autonomy most vigorously, according to this. For Montaigne, this is for the simple reason that love is precisely a matter of singularity, and consequently of non-quantifiability. As he puts it, if we ask him why he loves someone, 'je sens que cela ne se peut exprimer, qu'en respondant: "Par ce que c'estoit luy; par ce que c'estoit moy".'[52] It is this singularity—of both the subject and the object (or, as one should say, of the other subject)—of affection to which Molière bears witness when he has Jourdain duped by a disguise in which Cléonte, paradoxically, reveals himself *not* as the son of the Great Turk, but precisely as himself. The love in question is not a matter for rational constraint, but primarily a matter of singularity and of an 'event' in which love is constituted as the identity of a relation between two free and autonomous subjectivities (in this case, those of Cléonte and Lucile).

Although I begin from a different part of Montaigne's essay than does Derrida, I nonetheless want to build on Derrida's observations, in order to expand my argument now to include the question of the constitution of 'Europe'. Derrida establishes that there is a fundamental difference between the lover and the loved: one can be loved without knowing that fact, but by contrast one cannot actively love and remain unaware of *amitié*. *L'amitié* is, above all and in the first place, a matter for the lover and not for the loved. As Derrida puts this:

On peut *penser et vivre* l'amitié, le propre ou l'essentiel de l'amitié, sans la moindre référence à l'être-*aimé*, plus généralement à l'*aimable*. En tout cas sans avoir à en partir, comme d'un principe. Si nous nous fiions ici aux catégories de sujet et d'objet, nous dirions dans cette logique que l'amitié (*philia*) est d'abord accessible du côté de son sujet, qui la pense et la vit, non du côté de son objet, qui peut être aimé ou aimable sans se rapporter d'aucune façon au sentiment dont il reste précisément l'objet.[53]

Derrida is making an argument here that leads to the claim for an 'instability' in the love-relation, such that the very equality on which it is ostensibly based reveals itself as a hierarchy, an inequality. The inequality in question fundamentally depends on a *temporal* priority: the lover (and her or his establishment of freedom, *à la* Montaigne) is *in advance of* the loved: friendship is an affair of the

---

52   Montaigne, *Essais*, i. 236.
53   Derrida, *Politiques de l'amitié*, 26.

lover *before* it is an affair of the loved. Though we need not make a foundational philosophy from this principle (as Derrida notes in the passage just cited), nonetheless this temporal priority makes friendship, the love-relation, or, indeed, sociality itself, basically a relation dependent not upon the 'spatial' (non-secular, non-temporal, non-historical) relations between two subjects facing each other *at the same time*, but rather a relation dependent upon the fact of an incommesurability between these subjects who must *necessarily and axiomatically* occupy different times or different moments insofar as their relation is predicated upon friendship, love, sociability. As Derrida has it, in his gloss on Aristotle, one cannot love and be loved *à la fois*[54].

It is this very temporality of friendship—now also a temporality of the social—which is troubling for the lover precisely because it introduces instability into the relation of lover to loved, and even of lover to herself or himself, threatening the durability that is the marker of perfect ethical friendship for Aristotle. If, as Derrida has it, 'la *philia* commence par la possibilité de survivre',[55] then it follows that love itself may—in time, in that time which is of the essence of its very condition and possibility in the first place—end, may bring to an end the autonomy and freedom of the subject-in-love. If love is thus conditioned by temporality (by its intrinsic debt to narrative according to which it has a beginning and thus also the possibility of an ending); and if, further, truth is considered as something fundamentally immutable; then it follows that there is now a fundamental divergence between the ethical demands of love and the ethical demands for truth. Molière's comedy is symptomatic of a politics of friendship which deals with this anxiety about time by trying to think the social in spatial—geographical, geopolitical, *national*—terms, as I can now argue.

Given Montaigne, and Derrida's gloss on Montaigne's use of Aristotle, we can now ask a fundamental question first of *Le Misanthrope*: what happens when the *object* of love—the loved—is identical with the *subject* of a loving intention—the lover? What happens to the love-relation when it is shaped by the lover's regard for *his own* singularity, as in the case of Alceste? The answer is that there is a necessary foreclosure of time, a denial of the temporal priority—the *beforeness*, with its concomitant

---

[54] Ibid. 27–8.   [55] Ibid. 31.

unpreparedness—now proposed as the very condition of love, friendship or the social. For Alceste, love becomes a matter of spatial relations. In his closing speech, he reveals that he thinks of love and truth as, effectively, non-secular: truth, like love, is to be unchanging. And if that cannot be the case *here*, if his here is one in which the now cannot persist unchanged forever, then he must seek some other place, some *alibi*, where the persistence and consistency of truth can be guaranteed. The eradication of time, the erasure of the possibility of temporal difference, leaves Alceste with what is fundamentally a *spatial* predicament: what should, in fact, be an anxiety about time (or history and change) becomes an anxiety about place, and allows Alceste the tactical refuge of 'exile' (displacement of the self in space rather than in time) as a way of remaining 'true-to-himself'. Given, however, that 'truth-to-the-self' (or the self-regard in which the object of love is identical with its subject) is axiomatically the foreclosing of a sociability that normally rests on the uncertainties and instabilities of time, it follows that Alceste's ostensibly free choice of exile as a strategy is not at all free, but is rather already determined by his characterological constitution. That is to say, his character is determined by a 'humour' in what is now becoming the older sense of that term: by having his misanthropic character as an *essential* quality constitutive of the self, Alceste becomes merely an object: he is incapable of assuming the position of the subject-in-love, for such a position requires an openness to time and to the social (and hence a threat to any truth considered as immutable). In this play, the exigencies of truth actively deny freedom and autonomy to the truth-teller, Alceste, reducing him to the status of an object (to be pursued at the end of the play) precisely at that moment when he believes himself to be most fiercely asserting his subjectivity.

This takes an explicitly political turn in *Le Bourgeois gentilhomme*, in which it is not the self-regard of a character for himself that is at stake, but rather the self-regard of various nation-states eager to constitute themselves as a harmonious Europe set against an excluded Turkey. Having used the Turkish language at various moments throughout the play to provoke a significant part of its laughter, the play closes with a multilingual song-and-dance, involving Spanish, Italian, and French musicians and dancers, each doing a set piece in their own languages and finally, 'Tout cela finit par le mélange des trois nations',[56] in which they sing together that the joy of this spectacle is greater than that enjoyed by the gods. The songs they sing are songs of a plaintive love; and set against this is an idealized love demonstrated by the harmonious song of birds. Singing together, at the end, the three nations form themselves into a harmony which is, like that of the birds, guiltless, painless, care-free—or careless—regarding the silence of the nation whose language has not been included: Turkey, which now sets the borders of a Europe based on mutual 'love' or harmony. This condition of a 'culture of benevolence' is what we must now further examine.

[56]   Molière, *Oeuvres complètes*, 541.

SECTION II

THE SUBJECT OF DEMOCRACY

3

Culture and Benevolence

I

At the close of Molière's *Le Bourgeois gentilhomme*, then, we see the emergence of a troublesome vision of 'Europe', in the form of a theatrical chorus comprising the cultures of France, Spain, and Italy, singing together in the face of a suddenly silenced Turkey. This 'Europe', produced aesthetically, constitutes a political state of affairs, in which Europe is formulating itself in terms of internal affinities between obviously different cultures; but where such 'friendship' between cultures, even between cultures whose languages are mutually incomprehensible, requires a common or shared sense of enmity elsewhere. That elsewhere is here conveniently provided by the yet more linguistically troublesome eastern border of Europe, Turkey, whose language, satirized during the play, is in the end effectively silenced by a now identifiably European chorus of mutual assent and mutual benevolence.

As Derrida has recently pointed out, this would hardly be the whole story of the emergence of the European 'autre cap'. The three nations whose mutual benevolence is celebrated at the end of Molière's play form a Mediterranean Europe, certainly; but Derrida, who draws attention to his own roots in the 'rivage méridional de la Méditerranée' and who holds himself to be 'une sorte de métis européen sur-acculturé, sur-colonisé', attends to Europe's own self-memorialization (or historical self-consciousness), the effect of which is to take Europe into another geopolitical direction:

Dans sa géographie physique et dans ce qu'on a souvent appelé, comme le faisait Husserl par exemple, sa *géographie spirituelle*, l'Europe s'est toujours reconnue elle-même comme un cap, *soit* comme l'extrême avancée d'un continent, à l'ouest et au sud (la limite des terres, la pointe avancée d'un Finistère, l'Europe de l'Atlantique ou des bords greco-latino-ibériques de la méditerranée), le point de départ pour la découverte, l'invention et la colonisation, *soit* comme le centre même de cette langue en forme de cap, l'Europe du milieu, resserrée, voire comprimée suivant un axe greco-germain, au centre du centre du cap.[1]

In considering Europe thus, Derrida notes also the peculiar position—that is to say, the absence—of England and Englishness; and by thus noting it, presents and includes this absence as a problem for our understanding of what constitutes 'Europe'. In later texts, Derrida further ponders an 'ethics' of this Europe. In his address to the first 'congrès des villes-refuges' held in Strasbourg in March 1996, *Cosmopolites de tous les pays, encore un effort!*, Derrida inserted himself in a logic indebted to the work of Arendt and Benjamin, and proposed an extremely forceful political argument making the case for an identification of ethics as such with a 'law of hospitality' to outsiders. He ponders the phrase, *cultiver l'éthique de l'hospitalité*, and argues:

Cultiver l'éthique de l'hospitalité, ce langage n'est-il pas, de surcroît, tautologique? Malgré toutes les tensions ou contradictions qui peuvent la marquer, malgré toutes les perversions qui la guettent, on n'a même pas à cultiver une éthique de l'hospitalité. L'hospitalité, c'est la culture même et ce n'est pas une éthique parmi d'autres.[2]

In this chapter, I shall be exploring this condition of 'hospitality' as an ethical demand, and its relation to the political formation of Europe, specifically with reference to the position or non-position within Europe of England; for it is historically this rather odd attitude of England that will be seen to have been at stake at the turn of the eighteenth century when aesthetics and culture were themselves shaping the idea of the nation state and its emergent ideologies.

[1] Jacques Derrida, *L'Autre cap* (Minuit, Paris, 1991), 24–5.

[2] Jacques Derrida, *Cosmopolites de tous les pays, encore un effort!* (Galilée, Paris, 1997), 42. Derrida further relates the concept of hospitality back to the Bible, especially *Numbers*, 35: 9–32, and *Chronicles*, 6, 42, and 52, and follows a logic of medieval polity according to which the great cities found their specific identities upon the ways in which they severally inflect the 'grande Loi de l'hospitalité, cette Loi inconditionnelle, singulière et universelle à la fois, qui commanderait d'ouvrir les portes à chaque un et à chaque une, à tout autre, à tout arrivant, sans question, sans identification même, d'où qu'il vienne et quel qu'il soit' (p.46). See also Anne Fourmantelle et Jacques Derrida, *De l'hospitalité* (Calmann-Lévy, Paris, 1997).

When Molière presents a version of a foreign policy based upon a proto-orientalist exclusion of Turkey from the mutual benevolence or hospitalities in which France, Italy, and Spain can occupy the same cultural terrain, he is demonstrating a philosophical issue that was to be worked through in more explicitly philosophical detail by Shaftesbury in England broadly in the period between the 1688 Revolution and the 1707 Act of Union with Scotland. Where, for Derrida, especially in *L'Autre cap*, one of the presiding questions confronting and constituting 'Europe' is to be formulated in the question of 'responsibility', for Shaftesbury at the turn of the eighteenth century, this question was to be raised in the form of a contest between, on the one hand, the powers and political attractions of a Hobbesian/Mandevillian egocentricity in which self-regard or self-love is the motor of history and, on the other hand, what Shaftesbury saw as the necessity of the social as a precondition of the very existence of the self and thus the consequent attractions of a culture based on attitudes of mutual benevolence among subjects or citizens in a polity. The result, in Shaftesbury's highly influential thinking, was the production of an idea of the culture of 'politeness' in which aesthetic and political attitudes meshed with each other to produce what was, in effect if not by explicit intention, a 'national character' of 'Englishness'. Interestingly, in political terms, Shaftesbury formulated his cultural position—indeed, his very attitude to foreign policy while he served in Parliament—partly in explicit opposition to the model of French politics and French culture, as Klein has persuasively argued:

Shaftesbury's earliest extant political statements concern the [1688] Revolution, which he praised for having frustrated three great objects of Whig distrust—Stuart absolutism, Catholicism, and France . . . he was hostile to the memory of the Stuarts and to the example of absolutist France. On the other hand, he regarded the Dutch as firm defenders of liberty and so as natural allies of Britain.[3]

Questions of national identity at the turn of the eighteenth century are clearly tied up with questions regarding philosophy, culture, and ethics. For Shaftesbury, benevolence is not simply a desirable attitude leading to a form of pleasant social comportment, it is also a founding condition of that very political enfranchisement that he

[3] Lawrence E. Klein, *Shaftesbury and the Culture of Politeness* (Cambridge University Press, Cambridge, 1994; repr. 1996), 133.

supported as the desirable condition of being an English gentleman.
While for Derrida, as we saw in the previous chapter, the relation
of *l'aimant* to *l'aimé* need *not* be foundational, for Shaftesbury, following more conventionally a neo-Aristotelian line, not only *can*
benevolence be foundational, but also *and insofar as one is*
'*English*' *and a* '*gentleman*'—that is to say, insofar as one is an
autonomous subject or agent— it *must* be thus foundational.

My collocation of Shaftesbury with Derrida here testifies to the
validity of Derrida's well-substantiated proposition that the subjects of 'cultural identity' and of 'European identity' are not novel,
not a new question. This 'subject', he writes,

'garde peut-être un corps vierge. Son nom ne masquerait-il pas quelque
chose qui n'a pas encore de visage? Nous nous demandons dans l'espoir, la
crainte et le tremblement à qui va ressembler ce visage. Ressemblera-t-il
encore? Et à celui de quelque *persona* que nous croyons connaître, Europe?
Et si sa non-ressemblance avait les traits de l'avenir, échappera-t-elle à la
monstruosité?[4]

Such an image of a 'masked' Europe has a very clear precursor in
Shaftesbury's 1709 essay on 'Sensus communis', subtitled the
'Freedom of Wit and Humour', where Shaftesbury hypothesizes the
scene of a 'masked' Europe confronted by its other: in this instance,
the other is not precisely the *métis* such as the Algerian Derrida, but
rather the Ethiopian. In the essay, Shaftesbury is considering the
question of cultural specificity or relativity in humour or comedy:
what one culture finds amusing may simply puzzle another. More
widely, the issue at stake for Shaftesbury is one more immediately
recognisable to us as that of cultural value and its status in the face
of that relativism which demands that, in justice, that which is specific to a culture be judged in terms appropriate to that culture and
not by other standards. For Shaftesbury, as for us, this wider issue
of relative evaluation impinges directly upon the question of how
we evaluate propositions made in the interest of their supposed or
claimed truth-content. Shaftesbury asks us to imagine the
Ethiopian who visits Europe during a time of masquerade or during one of those carnivalesque rituals of proto-Bakhtinian comic
masking in which social regulation is ostensibly called into question while actually being reinforced. The Ethiopian, he suggests,

---

4   Derrida, *L'Autre cap*, 12.

will laugh alongside the Europeans at the sight of the masks worn by the participants in the carnival; but, asks Shaftesbury, what if he laughs all the more when the European unmasks, and reveals a fair complexion which the Ethiopian takes to be not the true self of the European but rather—and to the Ethiopian, obviously or self-evidently—another mask, one equally amusing as the first? At this point, Shaftesbury makes his claim for some kind of absolute standard, and asks

wou'd not he [the Ethiopian] in his turn become ridiculous? By carrying the Jest too far; when by a silly Presumption he took *Nature* for mere *Art*, and mistook perhaps a Man of Sobriety and Sense for one of those ridiculous Mummers?[5]

Had Shaftesbury or his audience seen *Le Bourgeois gentilhomme*, they would have witnessed precisely such an example of one who takes nature for mere art, in the figure of Jourdain, duped precisely by people who 'act' their 'real' selves at the close of the play. Shaftesbury's intention, however, is to widen his example into a more general principle regarding truth and a foundational principle for epistemological enquiry:

Nor is the Face of Truth less fair and beautiful, for all the counterfeit Vizards which have been put on her ... we must remember withal our ETHIOPIAN, lest by taking plain Nature for a Vizard, we become more ridiculous than the People whom we ridicule.[6]

This possibility of the 'theatricalization' of the self is an important issue for Shaftesbury and for subsequent cultural politics. Modernity, as I argued earlier in this book, is conditioned partly by this very notion of theatricality: for the modern, 'authenticity' is

---

5 Shaftesbury, 'Sensus communis; or, an essay on the Freedom of Wit and Humour' (1709); repr. in Shaftesbury, *Characteristicks of Men, Manners, Opinions, Times* in 3 vols. (4th edn., 1728), i. 83. Fundamentally, Shaftesbury is here questioning the notion of absolute standards of taste set against cultural relativity of judgements. The same question was raised vigorously by Dryden in his preface to his *All for Love*, when he criticizes French writers, and then argues 'I desire to be tried by the [critical and aesthetic] laws of my own country; for it seems unjust to me, that the French should prescribe here, until they have conquered' (James Kinsley and George Parfitt, eds., *John Dryden: Selected Criticism* (Clarendon Press, Oxford, 1970), 55–6). Dryden asks explicitly in terms appropriate to the nation-state the same question that Shaftesbury poses more diplomatically and philosophically.

6 Shaftesbury, *Characteristicks*, i. 84–5.

complicated by the necessity of a 'hypocrisy' or by the necessity that the subject 'acts' or 'enacts' selfhood. Clearly, Shaftesbury's propositions for a society based upon 'politeness' might appear to be exactly a part of such theatricality in which the social will be regulated by masks and by social forms or etiquette. It is important here to note, however, that such a version of politeness is far-removed from what Shaftesbury actually advocated.

As Klein has argued, Shaftesbury essentially set out to codify and legitimize the cultural and political rulership of the gentleman class in England after 1688. 'Politeness', in these terms, is certainly not a matter of hypocritical etiquette, but is rather an affair of lived and material social relations. At its base, there lies a culture of 'sociability' in which the erstwhile exclusivist and specialist bureaucratic rule of both Church and State is contested by way of advancing the rule of a relatively well-educated, but non-specialist, English gentleman class. Shaftesbury's politics represent the attempt to legitimize the well-informed amateur over the professional or the 'expert' (that is, over people like Molière's 'doctors'), and thereby to widen the politico-cultural franchise, to open the workings of Church and State to informed criticism and even to informed participation. His philosophy is an instance of the advancement of an 'interested' class —that is, a class that is economically and culturally interested, a class with a 'stakeholding' interest in society—in the name of a version of a fledgling bourgeois democracy.

In these terms, Shaftesbury can be seen to be endorsing that Aristotelian conception of friendship, according to which friendship—or, in Shaftesbury's terms, benevolence—is the bond which holds societies together. 'Politeness' is seen more clearly thus to be founded upon a politics of alterity for Shaftesbury, in which the very foundation of the possibility of the existence of society lies in a proto-Levinasian benevolent disposition towards the other, whose ethical demand on me constitutes the ground of the social bond as such. Inasmuch as it constitutes a politics, Shaftesbury's 'politeness' is what we can call a 'strong philosophy': to subscribe to it intellectually or rationally is also to live it empirically, and hence politeness is no mere ritual or theatrical etiquette.

It follows from this that, for Shaftesbury, right thinking is allied to good breeding. This is the relation that was explored in Molière; and it is one of the primary relations that brings aesthetics and politics together in the formation of something that we now recognize as 'culture' itself. When Derrida argued that the phrase 'cultiver l'éthique de l'hospitalité' is tautological because ethics *is* hospitality, I can now add here that for Shaftesbury, culture itself *is* hospitality. In Shaftesbury, philosophy is allied to good breeding in that both are concerned with human relations and with their regulation into formal patterns. As Klein has it, 'The desire for a normative grasp of human interactions issued in ethics and the desire for a normative grasp of forms issued in aesthetics.'[7] Seen in this way, sociability, friendship, or benevolence is what makes the discourses of both ethics and aesthetics possible; and both of these are dependent upon a prior condition of the acceptance of a strong philosophy of polite ('English gentlemanly') behaviour.

Shaftesbury faces a major problem in his philosophy if it is to counter effectively the prevailing tendency to 'theatricality' and to a vacuous formality in which the merest social etiquette replaces the more profound condition of real, lived or empirical sociability. That issue is, in many ways, at the very core of Enlightenment, for it can be expressed in terms of the problematic question of the relative weight to be given in human identity-formation between the rival claims of autonomy and—and this is not the opposite of autonomy but rather its concomitant—the claims made for the historical mobility or 'plasticity' of the self. It is the issue of the relative priorities to be given to *being* over and against *becoming*, essence against existence, transcendence against historicity. In short, if one embraces the conditions of autonomy, one must simultaneously be arguing for a core of self-same selfhood (one's autonomous identity or the 'being' that drives history) while yet also entertaining the possibility that such selfhood is based upon the possibility of change in one's historical being and thus that one's identity is based upon difference (one's autonomous history or 'becoming'). In Shaftesbury's case, the benevolent and sociable self is advanced against the Hobbesian or Mandevillian egoistic self, certainly; but in its very plasticity or 'becoming'—its openness to change in the light of social discussion or friendship among gentlemanly equals endowed with attitudes of mutual benevolence—such a self threatens the self-same identity or 'being' of the gentleman class—and, by extension, of the 'English' national character—itself.

7 Klein, *Shaftesbury*, 35.

Shaftesbury's negotiation of this problem is instructive. He seeks a *via media* between two forms of sociability, a 'third way' which will not be identifiable with either of the extremes between which this middling way is to be found. This third way is to be located between two modes of friendly sociability: on the one hand, facile and superficial sociability (the theatricality of social decorum and empty ritual) which presents the self dishonestly, 'masked'; on the other hand, a gravity and austerity regarding the self's autonomy and integrity that leads to an Alceste-like isolation of the self from actual social encounter. Shaftesbury sought a sociability 'that was neither so sociable that it sacrificed integrity nor magisterial in a way that repelled others';[8] and the consequence of this is a form of mixed discourse, in which the serious and the jocular are combined to give the self in the form of the detached ironist. This ironic self—sociable without being entirely described by or encapsulated in its social being—is, of course, precisely the 'Spectator': the self which, although a constitutive part of the social, nonetheless detaches itself from any precise commitment to the very social formation of which it is a constitutive element precisely by means of expressing a commentary upon the social, remaining thus detached precisely for the duration of such a critical commentary. In short, Shaftesbury's philosophy produces one identifiable version of the 'spectating-theorist', in the form of the Stoic pragmatist who can mock—or simply be critical of—a society of which she or he is a part while yet remaining aloof through a discourse marked by an irony which refuses any precise or explicit commitments.[9]

Shaftesbury thought through his position largely while he had withdrawn from public life, in a form of early retirement in the Netherlands. Amid the fraught politics of the Netherlands at this time, the thinking of the son of some other émigrés, Spinoza, had

---

    8   Klein, *Shaftesbury*, 96.
    9   For a gloss on this version of the theorist as 'spectator', see Patrick Parrinder, *The Failure of Theory* (Harvester Press, Brighton, 1987), 14. A good contemporary example of this kind of theorist is Terry Eagleton, a significant part of whose critiques (especially those carried in the journalistic public domain, in reviews and the like—but also in some of his academic work) consists of suppositious remarks, unproved hypotheses, mocking negative comments with no clearly posited alternatives (other than an extremely vague, but always claimed, Marxism). The rhetorical result of such 'theory' is often broad agreement on the part of his reader, but no clear sense of what it is that is being agreed with, other than a vaguely 'friendly' mood or disposition, leading to a shared sense of a communal superiority over whatever position it is that is the object of the mocking or satirical 'critique'.

taken root. Spinoza's parents, as is well known, fled from Portugal, where they had been forced to live as 'marranos', observing all the rites subscribed to by converts to Catholicism even though they had been born Jewish. What they fled was exactly that mode of 'politeness' that was based on the vacuities of the formal observation of empty ritual. Spinoza, himself excommunicated from Judaism, had proposed a philosophy which, to a large extent, depended upon an understanding of the force of emotion and its effects upon the social. For Spinoza, the social does to some acknowledged extent condition the self. For example, he makes as Proposition 22 of Part III of *The Ethics* the observation that:

If we imagine that someone is affecting with pleasure the object of our love, we shall be affected with love towards him. If on the other hand we think that he is affecting with pain the object of our love, we shall likewise be affected with hatred towards him.[10]

Shaftesbury would, on one hand, have welcomed such a thought in that it acknowledges the centrality and even determining force of the effects of love upon the social; but he would have been extremely disturbed by the negative consequence of the latter half of the proposition, in which a form of hatred is a logical corollary—indeed, is the underside—of the very benevolence upon which his own philosophy of sociability is based. It is left to the philosopher whose work effectively saved Shaftesbury for modernity—Hutcheson—to come to terms with the social effects of love and its potentially negative consequences in social and political enmity; and it is to his work that I shall now turn attention.

II

In 1711, when Shaftesbury's *Characteristicks* was published, Hutcheson matriculated at Glasgow University, an institution to which he would return to take the Chair in Moral Philosophy in 1729, election to which was partly in recognition of the importance of work written in his native Ireland and published in London in

---

[10] Baruch Spinoza, *Ethics; Treatise on the Emendation of the Intellect; Selected Letters*, ed. Seymour Feldman (trans. Samuel Shirley; Hackett, Indianapolis, 1992), 116.

1725, *An Inquiry into the Original of our Ideas of Beauty and Virtue*. The Scotland he found in 1711 was very different from the Scotland that had existed when Hutcheson was born in Drumlanrig some seventeen years earlier; for by 1711, Scotland had, of course, been recently united with England in a supposedly 'benevolent' act of union. The conditions for union, as is well known and documented, had been hardly self-evidently propitious. In 1695, William Paterson, the Dumfries merchant who had helped found the Bank of England, launched the disastrous Scottish colonial exercise of the Darien expedition, as part of a bid to re-establish for Scotland those colonial powers it had lost when Charles I had sold Nova Scotia to the French. The Darien expedition put Scotland in explicit—if not entirely intentional—opposition to the English; for at the time when it was launched, William had been forging an alliance of England with the Spanish who actually controlled the isthmus of Darien. Tension between Scotland and England intensified in 1704 when Scotland passed the Act of Security demanding—among other important measures such as a say in the issue of the succession to the throne—equal trading rights between the two countries; and, partly consequential upon this Act, Scotland was now providing legal conditions for the duty-free import of French wine into the island territory. All this at a time when the English were formally at war with the French. England—and with it English national and cultural identity—thus faced pressures not simply or even primarily from the French, as Colley has argued; but also, and in a kind of pincer-movement, from the Scots.[11] It was in these circumstances that the Act of Union was formulated in 1707. In political terms, this Act was presented to the Scots as an act of cultural, political, and economic 'benevolence' (and was indeed accepted by many as such); but the real politics of the situation—and the philosophy of that politics—is described most adequately not by Shaftesbury but rather by his arch-opponent, Mandeville.

Mandeville, a Dutchman who would make his name in England through his satirical attack on the English (following thus that path already laid by the Frenchman, Sorbière) in his 1714 *Fable of the Bees*, went on to write the more philosophically exacting essay, 'A Search into the Nature of Society' in 1723, an essay that played its part in prompting Hutcheson to write his riposte to Mandevillian

---

[11]   See Linda Colley, *Britons* (Pimlico, 1992).

and Hobbesian egoism. In the 1723 essay, Mandeville draws attention to the ways in which individuals forge located cultural and even explicitly national identities:

> Two Londoners, whose Business oblige them not, to have any Commerce together, may know, see and pass by one another every Day upon the Exchange, with not much greater Civility than Bulls would: Let them meet at Bristol they'll pull off their Hats, and on the least opportunity enter into Conversation, and be glad of one another's Company. When French, English and Dutch meet in China or any other Pagan Country; being all Europeans, they look upon one another as Countrymen, and if no Passion interferes, will feel a Natural Propensity to love one another.[12]

That—essentially modern—identification of society with nation and state is partly established as a consequence of the cultural attention to otherness or foreignness already forged by the artists and philosophers. It reiterates, for example, Molière's closing sequence for *Le Bourgeois gentilhomme* already discussed above. As Mandeville knows, however (long before an acknowledged prophet of the modern, Rimbaud), such identifications are themselves already tainted by a specifically interior otherness, the *autre* to be found within the *je*. As the passage just cited shows, Mandeville knew well that national character was not necessarily identical with geographic or geo-political boundaries. The otherness of the French to an Englishman, for example, could be easily elided when it suited the English self to form an alliance with a French other when both are in the presence of someone who could be stigmatized as 'exotic' or other to a higher degree, such as a Chinese person. An 'act of union', then, is in some circumstances a means of forgetting mutual difference and enmity in the face of a threat, while never properly homogenizing the heterogeneity that constitutes two fundamentally different politics or states, be they those identified as England and France or, more pointedly in 1723, England and Scotland. This version of 'national identity' must, of necessity, be based upon a *myth* of the nation-state, or, indeed, upon a mythic nation. Such a nation, not necessarily subscribed to by all its participants, is therefore unstable, culturally and politically fragile.

In short, and to put this in slightly more philosophical or abstract

---

[12] Mandeville in *The Fable of the Bees*, ed. Phillip Harth (Penguin, Harmondsworth, 1989), 345–6.

terms, for Mandeville, alterity is a founding condition of located identity in the first place. The question arising from this is whether the would-be autonomous agent within such a polity acts primarily in her or his own interests (i.e. egocentrically), or whether those very interests are themselves preconditioned or given by the necessity of a sociability based in an ethical benevolence with regard to the other who is seen as determining the self in the first place. For Mandeville, deepening the Hobbesian position, this is easily answered by the fact that this other was always already within the self, and therefore that the egoistic position is morally defensible. For Hutcheson, following Shaftesbury, such sophistry offers an insufficient response to the problem—as the political case of Scotland's assimilation to England makes abundantly clear. Scotland—as England's other, internalized in the Act of Union—offers an exemplification of the power-structures involved in cultural benevolence, and allows Hutcheson to deepen Shaftesbury's ethical and politico-cultural analysis. In what follows, I shall begin the exploration of this through a consideration of the differing cultural pedagogies of Scotland and England. This will offer an initial exploration of the relation between aesthetics and democracy in the emergent nation-state and its academic apparatus, accompanied by an understanding of Hutcheson's formative and influential position in the history of aesthetics (with an aesthetic philosophy that pre-dates Baumgarten).[13]

III

There has long been an acknowledged difference in the pedagogical priorities of the Scottish and the English educational systems, governed as they are by two fundamentally different sets of ideological, social, and cultural priorities.[14] That difference is relevant

---

[13]   This question of the academic institution and the institutionalization of aesthetics is discussed more fully in Ch. 7.

[14]   For a fuller examination of the brief account which I offer here, see George Davie, *The Democratic Intellect* (1961; repr. Edinburgh University Press, Edinburgh, 1982); Davie, *The Crisis of the Democratic Intellect* (Polygon Press, Edinburgh, 1986); Andrew Lockhart Walker, *The Revival of the Democratic Intellect* (Polygon Press, Edinburgh, 1994); and cf. some accounts, engaging more critically, by Craig Beveridge and Ronnie Turnbull, in their two books on *The Eclipse of Scottish Culture* (Polygon Press, Edinburgh, 1988), and *Scotland After Enlightenment* (Polygon Press, Edinburgh, 1997).

to any consideration of Hutcheson, most of whose influential work was carried out through his daily activities as a teacher in Glasgow. The difference is most clearly articulated in the well-known argument advanced by Davie and others, according to which it is claimed that a Scottish tradition of 'generalist' education, open to wide participation within the community precisely because it is generalist and not over-burdened with narrower specialist 'expertise' within restricted disciplines, presents a grounding 'democratic intellect' whose subjects and agents have an awareness of foundational philosophy and of questions of primary intellectual importance. This democratic intellect, it is argued, has come under threat (since at least 1707) from an 'alien' English tradition of specialization which, by implication at least, is 'undemocratic' and 'unintellectual' (even anti-intellectual), and concerned with the production and legitimization of a bureaucratic elite whose interests are not necessarily shared by a people at large. In this account, the Scottish student may not learn how to execute the most intricate manoeuvres in mathematics, say, nor might she or he have a thorough and well-rehearsed acquaintance with the precise linguistic equivalents between Greek and Scots (or English) words; yet she or he will nonetheless be forced to consider and to develop an understanding of the fundamental rules pertaining to mathematical computation (a philosophy of number, say) or to linguistic study in general (a philosophy of linguistics, semantics, translation, and so on). The result is the production of a highly informed intellect capable of turning to virtually any problem with which it may be confronted, while not necessarily (even if possibly) excelling in the minutiae of any specific narrow discipline. Against this model of the well-informed 'clever' and adaptable participant in society is set a hypothetical English student, endowed, it is supposed, with a hypothetical 'knowledge' of facts which, though available to the student, is not based on any fundamental awareness of the basic issues at stake in the production of those facts or, indeed, on any awareness of issues fundamental to the discipline within which she or he disposes of such factual knowledge. For example, according to this account, the English student might have a greater facility in proffering linguistic equivalents between Greek and English words, say, being thus capable of providing an acceptable translation between the two tongues; but she or he will remain unaware of and indeed uninterested in the problems of the cultural specificity of linguistic terms, in the arguments associated with cultural normativities and their inscription within languages, in relativism, in the problem of translation between historical moments, and so on. For this student, *agape* is 'love'; and no questions are raised about how benevolent affections are actually lived in and through *agape* and how they are lived in and through 'love'.[15]

This contest is clearly one with its own history, to which I have been adverting in my presentation of Shaftesbury above. Shaftesbury's 'gentleman', suspicious of the specialist and mystifying discourses in which Church and State legitimize the politico-cultural norms of eighteenth-century society, can be clearly—if surprisingly and paradoxically—allied with what is hypothesized as an inherently 'Scottish' democratic intellect.[16] When Hutcheson takes on the mantle of Shaftesburian benevolence during his times in Glasgow, he is addressing not simply a matter of philosophy (the desire to found a philosophy upon ethical first principles which are altruistic and not based in egoism), but also a matter of cultural or civic politics. He is, as it were, negotiating 'love' (or benevolence) and its associated 'acts of union' in terms of the tension between Scotland and England in the aftermath of 1707.

We can now identify an underlying tension, shaping Hutcheson's thinking, between two basic drives. First, we see a drive towards 'abstraction' (the drive towards the exploration of first philosophical principles implied in any question, therefore attending less to the specifics of any individual problem or case), and this we might identify as a drive governed by 'theory' or the general primacy of whatever principles shape our perceiving consciousness itself; second, we

---

[15] This, indeed, can probably be tested in any English university seminar on, for example, 'Shakespeare'. For many if not all students, the term 'love' in Shakespeare presents no problem of comprehension; many remain unaware of and uninterested in how the term operated in Shakespeare's day, as one indicating 'affiliation' sometimes tribal affiliation, and not as a marker of erotic interest. If such an awareness is offered, it still does not provoke a meditation on semantics.

[16] The surprise—even shock—to those who defend a 'democratic intellect' on some avowedly or politically nationalist grounds is surely in the indebtedness of the model of the hypothetical Scottish student generalist to the English gentleman. In Davie's initial work on the democratic intellect, which admittedly focuses directly on the nineteenth century, neither Shaftesbury not Hutcheson are acknowledged as explicit influences; and only Walker, among those cited in footnote 14 above, mentions Shaftesbury, and then only in the briefest passing note acknowledging his influence on Hutcheson. My point here is that, even if one subscribes to a version of the cultural differences between the two modes of education (as I do), it is nonetheless a mistake to account for that difference on ethnic nationalist grounds.

see the impetus towards 'distraction' (in which the thinker allows herself or himself to be 'distracted' and distrained—or delayed—by the particularity of the individual case, ignoring the general grounds which may shape the conditions of that case in the first place), and this we could identify as a drive exhorting us to see the object of enquiry 'as in itself it really is', the *Ding-an-sich*, to put this in Kantian terms.[17] In this division, Hutcheson foreshadows the twentieth century's cultural and pedagogical contests between 'theoretical' and 'practical' criticisms; but in Hutcheson's contemporary terms in the eighteenth century, the questions at stake are marked not just by philosophy but also by national politics.

For Hutcheson, our question is necessarily articulated by attempting to adjudicate the priorities between, on the one hand, seeing the particular as something that exists in a dialectical relation to an ostensibly pre-determining general state of affairs and, on the other hand, seeing the particular as something determined by its relation to its subject, the 'I' in relation to which it gets its meaning. The former priority entails questions about the ontological conditions of objects of our contemplation (their beauty or their virtue, intrinsic or otherwise, say); the latter priority considers the real to be a matter of the 'appropriation' (or ownership) of objects (or property, in every sense of the term) by knowledgeable and legitimate subjects, subjects of consciousness and subjects of the State, philosophical and political subjects legitimized by their cultural knowledge and location.

This is the tension, in short, between the (Scottish) philosophical subject and the (English) bourgeois or mercantile, property-owning, landowning subject. Indeed, Alasdair MacIntyre offers a useful additional location in which we can see precisely the same opposition at work. In a brief passage in *Whose Justice? Which Rationality?*, he compares and contrasts the principles of *The Institutions of the Law of Scotland* (1681; revised 1693) by James Dalrymple (Viscount Stair) in Scotland with William Blackstone's 1765 *Commentaries on the Laws of England*, produced in Oxford. Having shown how essential the ownership of property is for the English subject who would participate in the dominant social structures, MacIntyre writes:

[17] See, in passing, Walker, *Revival of the Democratic Intellect*, 158, 166 on Kant's Scottish connections.

Blackstone unsurprisingly absolutizes the rights of property. What obligations individuals have depends almost, if not quite entirely, upon their place within established property relationships. Stair by contrast makes the treatment and the status of obligations prior to the treatment and the status of property. So obligations are imposed upon and constrain the property owner.[18]

This tension—more and more clearly a tension based in conceptions of national character and the nation-state—reveals itself fully in what becomes for Hutcheson a major guiding principle in all his thinking on aesthetics, ethics, and the socio-political. The principle in question is one which strives to effect a reconciliation between the demands of the general and those of the particular, and it is articulated in terms of the discovery, within whatever he contemplates, of 'uniformity amidst variety', the precise degree of which (or absence of which) allows for the computation, quantification, and thus evaluation of beauty and of virtue. In the second section of his *Inquiry Concerning Beauty, Order, Harmony, Design*, he writes, in a formulation which determines virtually everything else in his aesthetics and ethics:

The figures which excite in us the ideas of beauty seem to be those in which there is *uniformity amidst variety*. . . . what we call beautiful in objects, to speak in the mathematical style, seems to be in compound ratio of uniformity and variety: so that where the uniformity of bodies is equal, the beauty is as the variety; and where the variety is equal, the beauty is as the uniformity.[19]

This gives Hutcheson a first principle from which he is able to establish a dialectic between the general (uniformity among any group of ostensibly different phenomena) and the singular (that variant which distinguishes one phenomenon from those others comparable with it), leading to a vocabulary for the analysis of the quality of beauty in art or virtue in morals; and it also gives him a model for the computation and measurement of the quantity of beauty and, subsequently, of virtue as well. In this quantification

---

[18] Alasdair MacIntyre, *Whose Justice? Which Rationality?* (Duckworth, 1988), 230.
[19] Hutcheson, *Philosophical Writings*, ed. R. S. Downie (Everyman, 1994), 15. In all citations of Hutcheson, I have collated this easily available edition with the separate first editions of the work.

of benevolence, virtue and beauty, Hutcheson includes what has become a famous conception of number, which will be of importance in what follows regarding the constitution of a democratic aesthetics or politics. He writes:

In comparing the moral qualities of actions, in order to regulate our election among various actions proposed, or to find which of them has the greatest moral excellency, we are led by our moral sense of virtue to judge thus; that in *equal degrees* of happiness, expected to proceed from the action, the virtue is in proportion to the *number* of persons to whom the happiness shall extend (and here the *dignity*, or *moral importance* of persons, may compensate numbers); and in equal *numbers*, the virtue is as the *quantity* of the happiness, or natural good; or that the virtue is in a compound ratio of the *quantity* of good, and *number* of enjoyers. In the same manner, the moral evil, or vice, is as the degree of misery, and number of sufferers; so that *that action* is *best*, which procures the *greatest happiness* for the *greatest numbers*, and *that worst*, which, in *like manner*, occasions *misery*.[20]

This mathematization is clearly an effect of Hutcheson's cultural and historical position, in which he is thinking through the tension between theory and practice, generality and particularity or specialism, the English gentleman and the (now politically assimilated but still recalcitrant) Scot or democrat. Virtue now becomes a matter of counting and accounting; but it is a matter in which the philosophy of number does not necessarily depend upon simple arithmetic. Hutcheson acknowledges that some persons may be more equal than others, that the dignity of one person might make her or him count for more than one other less-dignified individual. The parenthesis in the passage cited here offers a very important qualification of what has frequently been taken in simple arithmetical or formal terms to mean that the quality of a virtuous act—indeed of any act—can be quantified simply by counting the bare number of persons made happy by it.

Although Hutcheson proposes a means of evaluating or quantifying virtue or beauty, he does so in a fashion that seems simultaneously to assert the primacy of mathematical computation (basic arithmetic) while yet also rejecting the idea that $1 + 1$ *must* $= 2$, as of necessity. The point of the parenthesis to which I draw attention is that, in some cases, where the quality or 'dignity' (worth) of one

[20]   Ibid. 90.

of the individuals to be aggregated is already excessive, 1 + 1 might come to a great deal more than 2. In short, thus, one is not always one. Any bourgeois version of democracy—and we should of course recall that it is *only* bourgeois versions of democracy that could be in question at this time, immediately after Locke and Shaftesbury—requires of necessity that arithmetical counting and accounting be the final arbiter of any disputed power, authority, or legitimation (and even, in extreme instances, of truth itself). For this kind of democracy to work and to secure the agreement of its participants, one plus one *must* equal two; three *must* be acknowledged as greater than two; and so on. Were we to disregard Hutcheson's parenthesis in which he introduces the idea of the 'dignity' of some individuals over others, Hutcheson would appear to have formulated a means of generating and sustaining the evaluative and normative conditions—and thus the foundations—of a bourgeois democracy in which aesthetic evaluations or judgements regarding beauty can map directly on to the establishment of political norms through the medium of pragmatic and mathematical evaluations of 'what is better qualitatively and for most people in the way of belief'. In this, paint, music, literature or any aesthetic activity can become politics through the medium of an aesthetic evaluation which is always inherently moral, and in which moral value is quantifiable in terms of the production of social happiness and of consensus. In such a state of affairs, we have a '1 + 1 = 2' democracy, according to which norms of value (and thus power itself) become the domain of the greater number, of the higher arithmetical aggregate. Every singularity ('1') implies a possible wholeness ('2' or more), and such a wholeness (or uniformity) is greater than singularity (or varieties). Yet something peculiar happens to the functioning of such arithmetic, for if the 'two' (as a wholeness) is constitutively greater than the summation of the hypothetically equal 'one's or singularities—inasmuch as their being in a 'two' has transformed their status from being merely singulars to being participants in a generality—then it must follow that one plus one cannot equal *merely* two (for two is supposedly only an aggregate). Oddly, therefore, one plus one equals already something greater than two, a whole which exceeds the sum of its aggregated singular parts. Hutcheson gives, and simultanouesly disqualifies, the basis for a bourgeois democracy.

Such a problem persists in contemporary philosophy. Badiou,

for instance, a thinker who has placed benevolence (or love) at the core of his philosophy, tries to contemplate the relation of such benevolence to arithmetic. He hypothesizes a state of affairs which bears a remarkable similarity to Lyotard's concept of the *differend*.[21] In any given encounter (that is, in any social situation conditioned by ethics or benevolence), there are two subject-positions. These two positions are, in principle, absolutely disjunctive with regard to each other (and it is their incommensurability—or simply their mutual *unavailability*—that makes this state of affairs akin to a differend). Further, there is no third position available, no transcendent subject-position or location which could overcome or supersede the disjunction between the two positions, reconciling them and their separate domains. Given that there is no such third position, argues Badiou, we would have to reformulate our opening gambit: it cannot be the case that there are 'two' positions, for to identify them as two would, of necessity, presuppose a third position, external to the two, from which the two could be identified and aggregated—and there is no such third position. Now, therefore, we do not have 'two'; rather we have a position 'one' and another position 'one'. This is a one plus one that cannot equal two: it is a one plus one that recognizes the absolute singularity of each several one while yet also acknowledging the social requirement that we could not even be aware of such singularity without also being in a situation where there is mutual regard among each several or different singularity, and thus without also being aware of the necessity (and difficulty) of homogenizing the participating singulars into a universal or general condition.

What this constitutes, for Hutcheson two centuries prior to Badiou and in a very specific historical and national situation, is a problem concerning the establishment of the social and, perhaps more pointedly, the impossibility of effecting a reconciliation between his two competing impulses: ('Scottish') generality and ('English') singularity. Yet Hutcheson himself avoids such a pessimistic conclusion: he prefers the view that such reconciliation is possible. Reconciliation between uniformity and variety is not a straightforward dialectic; for reconciliation is already contained *within* the terms that are to be reconciled. Uniformity (in that

---

[21] See Jean-François Lyotard, *Le Différend* (Minuit, Paris, 1983); and cf. Alain Badiou, *Conditions* (Seuil, Paris, 1992), ch. 5.

'uniformity' as understood by Hutcheson is another term for 'reconciliation') is itself already the establishment of generality; and Hutcheson's argumentation is therefore clearly already prejudicially disposed in favour of a priority for the general over the particular. Given the political substratum of this, as reflected in the different educational priorities of Scotland and England, what this means, in effect, is that Hutcheson is in the business of mediating the Act of Union not as the overwhelming and colonization of Scotland by England, but rather precisely the contrary: the possibility of 'celticizing' the English. This will allow me to consider now the question of the nation more clearly, insofar as it silently inhabits Hutcheson's formative and influential aesthetics. In the first instance, however, we might conclude in this chapter that the culture of benevolence is one which enables Scottish theory to provide a legitimization of nationalism, a conclusion that is obviously highly paradoxical. The nationalism in question in the Act of Union is, in political terms, one in which the English nation effectively subsumes the Scottish; yet the philosophical foundation for this rests itself in the specifically 'Scottish' generalist, theoretical, mentality; hence Scotland can be offered the (false) solace that the Union is a union of equals, a 'one plus one'. The one that is English, however, is different constitutively from the one that is Scottish; and Hutcheson's philosophy, indebted to the English gentleman class as characterized in Shaftesbury, conceals this as it endorses it. In the following chapter, I shall explore more fully the stakes of these paradoxes, especially in relation to the temporal condition of aesthetics or of benevolence.

4

Democracy Time and Time Again

I

In the establishment of a culture of benevolence, as I argued in the last chapter, there is a corollary 'place-logic', according to which the temporality that is a primary condition of friendship or benevolence is circumvented: the ethical relations that shape the social are seen to be matters of location, of how and where we stand in relation to each other, and not matters of history or of our temporal being with regard to each other. In this chapter, in which I shall explore further the philosophy of Hutcheson and its influence on our own contemporary aesthetics or culture, I shall trace out the implications of this evasion of temporality for an aesthetics that would be democratic.

Hutcheson starts from the proposition that philosophy up until now has prioritized reason over sense, utilizing, as he claims, 'some trite arguments' to do so.[1] While rational knowledge might add to the pleasures and pains of the senses, knowledge itself as such offers a *mediated* relation to the world, while sense offers a more *immediate* experience of it. Hutcheson's task is thus not simply to reverse what he perceives as the existing priorities of reason over sense in philosophy, but rather to give sense its due in order to allow him to promote not only an aesthetic sensibility but also an ethical sensibility which can attend to the empirical facts of experience. This will enable the production of an ethics which is not dependent simply upon reason or upon rationally principled argumentation, and which will not yet fall into irrationality through a

---

[1] Francis Hutcheson, *Philosophical Writings*, ed. R. S. Downie (Everyman, 1994), 3.

wilful ignoring of reason. Hutcheson's ethics will be sensible, certainly; but they will also be 'sense-ful'.

Marx famously opens the *Eighteenth Brumaire* with the observation that 'Men make their own history; but they do not do so under conditions of their own choosing',[2] thus opening the problem of autonomy when the possibility of human agency is situated in a history that pre-exists and predetermines the possibilities of individual and specific human agents or subjects. About a hundred years prior to this, Hutcheson too had pondered the question of autonomy in relation to the moral choices we might make, moral choices which are fundamentally conditioned by our general aesthetic capacities, our powers of perception. He acknowledges that, in matters of our perceptual and cognitive relation to the world, whilst we might be able to be active in our engagements with objects, those objects are there *before* us and they do not allow us to make and to shape the world as we please: 'Objects do not please us according as we incline they should. The presence of some objects necessarily pleases us, and the presence of others as necessarily displeases us'.[3] The relation between objects of perception and their subjects is a tense one, in which objects can resist the desire that subjects may have for untrammelled power over them, and in which subjects must find ways of negotiating that resistance such that they are not overwhelmed by objects or by the environment in which they are located. For Hutcheson, the mind can also act on these objects of perception, having the power to be active inasmuch as it has the capacity to compound numbers of ideas that it receives separately, to compare objects, to get the proportions and relations between objects, and to distinguish complex sensations into simple ones. This capacity should properly be described as that power of 'abstraction' that I characterized in the previous chapter as a facility for 'theorization'; it allows the human subject to counter her or his otherwise entirely passive reaction to singularity, to single objects whose very singularity would itself resist comprehension were it not for our theoretical mind. Without such theory, all experience would approximate to a condition now diagnosed as a form of 'schizophrenia', in which

---

[2] Karl Marx, *The Eighteenth Brumaire of Louis Bonaparte* (Foreign Languages Press, Peking, 1978), 9.
[3] Hutcheson, *Philosophical Writings*, 4.

each moment of experience is radically disjunctive with regard to all other moments of experience and in which, consequently, human identity—and the potential for human agency—is called into question.[4] Before Marx, then, Hutcheson was considering the problem of how we deal with an environment that has to some extent predetermined our engagements with it, or which has shaped the very possibilities of our experience of it in the first place. How can we both respect history (the environment which we 'inherit' in its determinant given-ness *before* us, its anteriority to us), while not being entirely enslaved by it or fully determined by it?

Hutcheson's response to this problem depends on his argument for recasting our understanding of the senses as such. He widens the concept of the senses to go beyond what operates in his day as a Hobbesian norm in which senses react to external material forces playing on the body; and he adds to these 'material' or physical senses what he calls an 'internal sense', which will allow him to incorporate the metaphysical—and the moral—as itself a 'material' sense. Having added his 'sixth sense', he divides sensibility into two modes. The division yields not, as one might have expected, the opposition of internal to external; instead it subtends a relation between an internal sense (associated with aesthetic matters, being as it is 'our power of perceiving the *beauty* of regularity, order, harmony') and a moral sense (concerned with virtue, being 'that determination to approve affection, actions, or characters of rational agents, which we call *virtuous*').[5] Given this, it becomes a simple move for Hutcheson to proceed towards what I shall call the 'aestheticization of ethics', in which he can claim that 'The Author of nature has ... made virtue a lovely form, that we might easily distinguish it from its contrary, and be made happy in the pursuit of it'.[6] Such an aestheticization of ethics, in which morality will be as self-evidencing as beauty, involves also an Optimistic attitude to history; and it is this that now requires fuller exploration.

---

[4] For this version of 'schizophrenia'—by no means identical with clinical schizophrenia—especially as it has been understood, via Lacan, in contemporary theory, see especially Fredric Jameson, *Postmodernism* (Verso, 1991), 26–7. In these terms, schizophrenia describes a temporal predicament, in which propositions do not flow consequentially or fluently one from the other: each proposition inhabits a discrete 'present' tense, whose links with other such 'present' moments are entirely contingent.

[5] Hutcheson, *Philosophical Writings*, 5.   [6] Ibid.

II

Hutcheson's basic principle, from which all else in his work follows, is that which I have already described in the previous chapter: the discovery of 'uniformity amidst variety'. This is the key to
beauty, not just in nature (where it constitutes what he calls
'absolute' beauty) or in art (where it is 'relative' beauty),[7] but in
everything. The aesthetic principle in which we are able to look at
a specific object and place it into a network of relations permitting
us to ascertain that it is not simply single, but is rather comparable
with and commensurable with other ostensibly different objects,
becomes a foundational key for all of Hutchesonian philosophy.
Starting from a consideration of art, Hutcheson claims that 'we
find ourselves pleased with a regular form, a piece of architecture
or painting, a composition of notes'; and, if we ask ourselves
whence we derive this pleasure, we find that 'the pleasure arises
from some *uniformity, order, arrangement, imitation* and not from
the simple ideas of *colour* or *sound* or *mode of extension* separately considered'.[8] Insofar as the perception of beauty is intrinsically
dependent upon the perception of *relation*, then, it follows that to
perceive the beauty of some singular entity, we must see it not as a
simple singular, but either as a single entity comprising related
internal elements or as an entity single in itself but immediately perceived as a single only insofar as it relates to other such discrete singulars, and thus as part of a whole which transforms its identity.

Given this, it becomes possible for Hutcheson to see beauty
everywhere, and not simply in the realm of art; and, importantly, it
is possible to perceive beauty even when the external physical senses are not in play. For instance, he argues for the perception of
beauty in theorems, where particular truths, though different and
various, remain consistent all with the uniformity of the general
theorem. Such would be the case, say, of the isosceles triangle, of
which there is an infinite variety of examples, all of which observe
the same general principles consequent upon being a triangle two
of whose sides are of equal length: there is no need to *see* any particular isosceles triangle before assenting to the general principles

---

[7] For the distinction between absolute and relative beauty, see Hutcheson,
Philosophical Writings, 13.   [8] Ibid. 4.

(indeed, it would be impossible to claim to have seen all such possible examples), and to the beauty of the theorems applicable to this geometric form. From this, we can claim a theory of beauty that is not solely dependent upon a sense-perception, where the sense in question is one of those described by Hutcheson as 'external' (sight, hearing, taste, smell, touch).[9] That the mode of this perception is still sense-perception is given, to Hutcheson, because the pleasure we receive in the perception of beauty is *immediate*, not dependent upon the *passing* of time, which is the proper realm of those pleasures associated with knowledge and not the senses:

This superior power of [aesthetic] perception is justly called a *sense* because of its affinity to the other senses in this, that the pleasure does not arise from any *knowledge* of principles, proportions, causes, or of the usefulness of the object, but strikes us at first with the idea of beauty. Nor does the most accurate knowledge increase the pleasure of beauty, however it may superadd a distinct rational pleasure from prospect of advantage, or from the increase of knowledge.[10]

Knowledge is here distinguished from pleasure or beauty: where beauty is immediately apparent, and is given for immediacy or for the moment, knowledge is explicitly a matter of time, and specifically of the future in which we may glimpse, courtesy of knowledge, a 'prospect of advantage'.

There is a geo-political aspect to this as well, explicitly addressed in Hutcheson. He is alert to the question of the relativity of evaluations of beauty: that is, he is aware that what constitutes beauty for one culture or nation may be a learnt response cultivated through the modes of education specific to particular nations. In allowing for this, Hutcheson nonetheless wants—in his benevolence—to allow the perception of beauty to all nations, while yet arguing for the absolute standard of value to be held by none. He

---

⁹ This relates to the question of the philosophical understanding of the operations of consciousness. In the eighteenth century, the question is raised in the terms which remain appropriate to more recent investigations in Diderot's *Lettre sur les aveugles* (1749). How could one blind from birth have a concept of colour, say? In more recent philosophy, the work which alludes most directly to Diderot is that of Derrida in his *Mémoires d'aveugle* (Louvre, Paris, 1990); but the same issue is addressed, for example, in recent work on the nature of consciousness such as Daniel Dennett's *Consciousness Explained*. See Hutcheson, *Philosophical Writings*, 40, for an incidental comment relevant here: 'Did ever blind men debate whether purple or scarlet were the finer colour, or could any education prejudice them in favour of either as colours?'   ¹⁰ Hutcheson, *Philosophical Writings*, 12.

considers the Goths, known to his time for, among other things, a reputed barbarism towards the Romans. In arguing for a universality of a sense of beauty, he writes:

A Goth, for instance, is mistaken when from education he imagines the architecture of his country to be the most perfect; and a conjunction of some hostile ideas may make him have an aversion to Roman buildings, and study to demolish them, as some of our reformers did the popish buildings, not being able to separate the ideas of the superstitious worship from the forms of the buildings where it was practised. And yet it is still real beauty which pleases the Goth, founded upon uniformity amidst variety. For the Gothic pillars are uniform to each other, not only in their sections, which are lozenge-formed, but also in their heights and ornaments. Their arches are not one uniform curve, but yet they are segments of similar curves, and generally equal in the same ranges ...[11]

The universality of the sense of beauty among human subjects is claimed here, but in such a way as to deny that there can be any single absolute standard realized in any single specific nation-state. It is as if there is an unrealized or unpresentable ideal *uniform* (or universal) standard, and that all actual evaluations of beauty, from wherever they emerge, are but representations or *variant* versions of that ideal. The fact of the existence of the ideal is attested to by the fact of the variety of imitations of it; but none can directly represent the ideal as such. In taking what is effectively such a Neoplatonic line on this, Hutcheson endorses his basic principle, for he is able to claim that the fact of the variety of standards of beauty among different nation-states, combined with the fact that all nation-states have such standards at all, is yet further evidence of a variety of particular nations within one uniform—and now universal—system. The very philosophy in which he articulates a theory of beauty ('uniformity amidst variety') is itself beautiful, according to the terms of that definition of beauty: all particular states contribute to the beauty of the system that gives them their individuality. The political is therefore alluded to, but slightly circumvented here, in the manner of Shakespeare's Miranda in *The Tempest* who, confronted with foreign bodies for the first time proclaims:

> O wonder!
> How many goodly creatures are there here!

---

[11]   Hutcheson, *Philosophical Writings*, 34.

> How beauteous mankind is! O brave new world,
> That hath such people in't.

Yet that politics (as in Shakespeare) instantly returns ("'Tis new to thee'). Immediately following the passage I have just cited, Hutcheson goes on to address cross-cultural affairs that are slightly more immediate for his day than the example of the Goths and Romans:

> The very Indian buildings have some kind of uniformity, and many of the Eastern nations, though they differ much from us, yet have great regularity in their manner, as well as the Romans in theirs. Our Indian screens, which wonderfully supply our imaginations with ideas of deformity, in which nature is very churlish and sparing, do want indeed all the beauty arising from proportions of parts and conformity to nature; and yet they cannot divest themselves of all beauty and uniformity in the separate parts. And this diversifying the human body into various contortions may give some wild pleasure from variety, since some uniformity to the human shape is still retained.[12]

Even in the face of ugliness, then, Hutcheson is still able, with his principle, to recuperate the availability of beauty. By this stage, a culture of benevolence, when directed towards an other whose very alterity is such that it defies comprehension ('our Indian screens'), is turning steadily into something else: Optimism.

The anxieties about the supposed universality of beauty—anxieties apparent in Hutcheson's increasingly implausible attempts to recuperate beauty either from ugliness (grotesques) or from simple incomprehensibility (Indian screens whose pictorial content observes codes of signification not immediately familiar to an Irishman writing in Dublin or Glasgow)—lead Hutcheson towards an ambivalent attitude towards that temporality which Montaigne reveals—and which Derrida will much later endorse—as a condition of benevolent friendship. Benevolence, as a condition of aesthetics and of ethics or politics, leads Hutcheson, in his own politically contradictory position, to a premature acceptance of the easy availability of the perception of beauty with its corollary immediate perception of moral (and, further, state-political) worthiness. The conditions governing what I am calling his Optimism—and particularly the relation of such Optimism to

---

[12] Ibid. 34.

Hutcheson's thinking on time and space/place—require further identification here.

The presiding principle of uniformity amidst variety establishes in Hutcheson's aesthetics a basic relation between singularity and wholeness, or particularity and generality (as it is more usually considered). It should be clear by now that my preferred terms for this relation are, on the one hand, historical specificity (what I referred to earlier as 'distraction') and, on the other, formal theory ('abstraction'). The former of these terms—specificity—would seem to be profoundly temporal, historical, marked by its instant or moment in time and 'distracting' the perceiver by playing on her or his senses, and thereby giving a *content* to the moment of perception. The latter abstracts from various moments of time to establish a more general state of affairs or set of relations in which various moments of time can all be abstracted from their specific instant for the purposes of comparison (and giving a *form* to time), thus taking both object and subject of perception ostensibly out of the flow of experiential time, or time as it is given to the physical senses; and this latter is more obviously 'spatial' than temporal. In short, thus, Hutcheson's aesthetic establishes a relation between time and space, in which beauty is discovered always in a principle associated with our capacity for abstraction or theory—which is space. The philosophy enacts thus a triumph of (spatial, abstract) form over (temporally specific) content; and the elaboration of Hutcheson's argument leads to the more or less silent assumption that wholes prefigure singles, for the singularity (or oddity, specificity—and potential ugliness) of any particular case is always open to explanation—in allowing others to have a perception of its intrinsic beauty—through its relation to a grander scheme in which it assumes merely exemplary status or of which it is a constituent part. In other words, form precedes content in any aesthetic (or moral) perception. In the previous chapter, I aligned this explicitly with the political condition in which Hutcheson finds himself; and in which the Act of Union can be sustained in Scotland once we accept the priority of 'Scottish' theory over 'English' property. Here, I want to widen my concern with the politics of Hutcheson's position, and to see how he copes with the inherent attractions of a sense-perception given to seduction by the singularity of a specific object and, simultaneously, the demands of a reason that grounds the perception of the beauty of such singularity in grasping its relation to a general or theoretical state of affairs.

III

There is, in Hutcheson's texts, a series of oppositions which could be easily tabulated. On one side, we have reason; on the other, sense. Aligned with reason, we have form and space; with sense, we have content and time. Now, experience or sense-perception—at least since Descartes—has been the locus of ambiguity, uncertainty, doubt; against this, reason has been considered to be the arena in which thought can be more pure, and can exist untrammelled by ideology or by the vagaries of the individual senses. Reason, considered thus, is hardly self-evidently 'democratic' (in an admittedly weak sense of the term), for reason is the privileged possession of those who are able to speak in a specific way, of those who conform to the legitimate discourses whose purpose is to ground a social formation in norms recognized by those discourses, and to permit the negation of any other ways of thinking or representing the world. In Hutcheson's day, those discourses—the discourses which regulated and organized the social as such—were those of the established Church and State. The attempt in his philosophy to rehabilitate sense against this rampant 'reason' is thus not just some kind of assertion of the somatic joys to be had from sensation, but is rather also part of a political project in which the franchise is to be widened, and in which legitimacy can be given to those who have sense while not necessarily speaking the languages or rhetorics of reason.

In the opposition of sense to reason, sense is marked by immediacy, in that our sensible response to objects is unmediated, a kind of pure present moment or intensity in which our response can never be prepared for or programmed ('Objects do not please us as we incline they should'). This is the central distinction between sense and reason to be borne in mind here: reason would allow us to determine whether we should like or dislike objects, and would thus distort our actual experience (would perhaps even destroy our sensible experience) of them. To see the world 'reasonably' is to see the world through a veneer of a specific discourse—that of Church and State—which bars most of us from a more direct and unmediated experience of our present moment. For Hutcheson, then, the assertion of the importance of sense-perception as a guide to values (aesthetic and moral) is allied with a democratizing impulse in which he wants to legitimize the experience of those who do not possess the rhetorics of 'reason'. When I aligned Hutcheson with Marx at the start of this chapter, it was precisely to stress that both these thinkers are formed by their anxiety about autonomy: how can we shape a future when we, as agents, are to a large extent already *given* or determined by the past—or by the institutions—that shaped or shape us? It follows now that the opposition of sense to reason does not lead, for Hutcheson, to an implied deeper opposition between immediacy and mediation. Rather, what is now at stake is a profound opposition between immediacy (sense) on the one hand and autonomy (reason) on the other: between experience of the other—of the singularity of a world which is the other of the subject of sense-perception, and given to that subject through the *body*-in-time, on the one hand (in which we might see this particular other as ugly, say); and experience of the world through *language* and its capacities for abstracting from the singular (and also to attend to the beautiful, a beauty which is at least latent, in computable degrees, in all alterity), on the other.

In that opposition, immediacy is clearly marked by the temporality of the instant; but autonomy would also be marked by a temporality, in fact. Reason/autonomy would be marked by temporal *difference* (the ability to interact with history such that the future is not entirely given by the past which shapes the subject or agent), rather than temporal *identity* (the sensuous being-in or being-for the moment of sensible perception). In that Hutcheson requires the reassertion of the importance of sense-perception to give credence to the political legitimacy of sense-experience, he needs to establish a philosophy of identity; yet in that his benevolence leads always back to a grounding principle of abstract theorisation as the foundation of beauty (and thus of ethics), he also requires a philosophy of difference. In short, Hutcheson clearly wants to attend to the intensity of present experience while allowing also for that intensity to shape the possibility of the subject's agency and thus to enable the autonomy of the human agent.

It is obvious that this philosophy is marked by a determination to see a temporal element inserted into the practice of criticism; and yet, paradoxically, this is exactly what does not happen. Having established the centrality of these anxieties about time to criticism,

Hutcheson then sets about regulating and controlling such a temporality back under the sign of space. Another way of putting this would be in the terms more appropriately associated with Kantian philosophy: how can we move from 1) the *fact* that I, as a subject experiencing the world, *like* a given art-work, to (2) the establishment of a *norm* allowing me to state that *intrinsically*, the artwork therefore is *good*, and thus (3) on to an ethical demand that, insofar as you too are a rational subject, *you* too *should like it*? How can we establish *consensus*, the consensus necessary for political being and social co-operation, on grounds that are not exclusive with respect to those participants in the social formation who are not privy to its modes of theoretical abstract reasoning and their attendant rhetoric?

For Hutcheson, this problem is associated with time in the aesthetic. In Hutcheson's assertion that there exists a moral sense cognate with the aesthetic sense, he proposes a philosophy in which morality will be self-evidencing, and therefore just as immediate as our aesthetic response to beauty. Having analysed the senses into two different kinds (those which are, as in Hobbes, purely *physical* and those which are susceptible to the aesthetic *and* moral good), Hutcheson must now reconcile them. In the resulting aestheticization of ethics, his task is not that of Keats, to claim that beauty is truth; rather, he limits himself for the moment to the argument that beauty is good, good beautiful. The rationale for this identification of the good with the beautiful, already half-given by his consideration of both in terms of the internal (non-physical) sense, lies in his claim that 'The Author of nature has . . . made virtue a lovely form, that we might easily distinguish it from its contrary, and be made happy by the pursuit of it.'[13] Here, the good is as immediately apparent as aesthetic beauty: indeed, it is just such an aesthetic beauty. It is important to note here that Hutcheson does not just aestheticize the ethical, for that would simply allow us to perceive the good; additionally, for this to be a genuinely ethical philosophy, he requires us to pursue the good as well, and not just to come across it. That is an important qualification: were he content to allow us simply to come across the good, or to be subjected to it as a series of unmediated (immediate) sensible phenomena, he would be subscribing to a philosophy whose effect would be to exclude

[13]   Hutcheson, *Philosophical Writings*, 5.

reason, and with reason, to exclude autonomy. Reason, we recall, is that which allows us to compare—and therefore to recall or to project, to narrate or to predict, and so to govern—autonomously—a future; and without such reason, life would become a rather schizophrenic chain of intensities, in which no two events could ever configure themselves into an 'experience' and in which the subject would exist only as an effect of an instance of aesthetics or of perception as such, the content of her or his identity at any given instant being dependent upon whatever it is that constitutes the object of perception. Such a subject, lacking the directive powers of autonomy, could not be free, but could only be subjected and constrained by a history that gives her or him an identity; and against this, in order to have the possibility of an ethics at all, Hutcheson requires that the subject be free, autonomous, capable of *becoming different* instead of just *being an identity*.

One would imagine, then, that Hutcheson's view of history would fully entertain the temporality necessary to the aesthetic as such. However, when he attends to history, he argues differently. First, he claims that we can get a specific type of pleasure from what he calls 'comparative beauty', a beauty associated with acts of representation, figurative art and so on (different, thus, from 'absolute beauty', which is of the province of the given world or nature). In comparative beauty, we can observe with pleasure that 'some works of art acquire a distinct beauty by their correspondence to some universally supposed intention in the artificers', and so beauty here is the site in which we remark the correspondence between an implicit form of art and its particular execution (once more, consistent with a Neoplatonism, but here understood in the terms of a variant execution of a uniform or universalizable norm). He goes on:

This beauty arising from correspondence to intention would open to curious observers a new sense of beauty in the works of nature [usually an absolute beauty], by considering how the mechanism of the various parts known to us seems adapted to the perfection of that part, and yet in subordination to the good of some system or whole.[14]

Each part, thus, is internally 'differential', because its local specifics, while absolutely appropriate to itself, are yet subordinate

---

[14] Hutcheson, *Philosophical Writings*, 25, 26.

to some greater whole or system not given as such in the specific entity under consideration: that is, the singularity of the part, though complete in itself, is yet subservient to the whole of which it is a constituent. This, of course, is an explanation of philosophical Optimism, in which the local gets its meaning, *sub specie aeternitatis*, as something not immediately given (hence deferred) and as something not self-evidencing (hence different).[15] As if this were not enough, Hutcheson then makes the implication of the philosophical position absolutely explicit when he claims that History too exhibits beauty, because History has a uniformity of design with a variety of incidents:

Everyone knows how dull a study it is to read over a collection of gazettes, which shall perhaps relate all the same events with the historian. The superior pleasure then of history must arise, like that of poetry, from the manners: when we see a character well drawn wherein we find the secret causes of a great diversity of seemingly inconsistent actions; or an interest of state laid open, or an artful view nicely unfolded, the execution of which influences very different and opposite actions as the circumstances may alter. Now this reduces the whole to an unity of design at least; and this may be observed in the very fables which entertain children, otherwise we cannot make them relish them.[16]

History itself, thus, is one universal story with varieties of incidents; and thus History too is a site of beauty. This, however, is the case only if we prioritize form over content: that is, only if we do precisely the contrary of what it is that Hutcheson ostensibly sets out to do when he wishes to reinstate sense-perception over against the formalizing capacities of reason. Hutcheson asserts the unification of sense and reason, claiming that, although they have different modes of operation, they are nonetheless mutually consistent. The effect of that is to take the temporality out of aesthetics, to *regulate* the time-experience of sense-perception under the *spatializing* tendency of reason and theory, both of which are concerned to locate the subject outside of her or his present moment in which she or he identifies with a singular and specific object of perception.

---

[15] The formulation here is intended to draw attention to a covert similarity between Optimism and deconstruction, specifically in deconstructive *différance*—a differing and deferral—as constitutive of meaning.

[16] Hutcheson, *Philosophical Writings*, 35.

For Hutcheson, it is imperative that God has made sense and reason mutually consistent in this way:

> For were it not so, but on the contrary, if irregular objects, particular truths and operations pleased us, beside the endless toil this would involve us in, there must arise a perpetual dissatisfaction in all rational agents with themselves, since reason and interest would lead us to simple general causes while a contrary sense of beauty would make us disapprove them. Universal theorems would appear to our understanding the best means of increasing our knowledge of what might be useful, while a contrary sense would set us on the search for particular truths.[17]

Hutcheson is now also constrained to argue that God acts by general laws, and not by attending to particulars; but he argues this in a way that relates this prioritization of theory or the general over specificity to time itself:

> For were there no general laws fixed to the course of nature there could be no prudence or design in men, no rational explanations of effects from causes, no schemes of action projected, or any regular execution. If, then, according to the frame of our nature, our greatest happiness must depend on our actions, as it may perhaps be made appear it does, the universe must be governed not by particular wills but by general laws upon which we can found our expectations and project our schemes of action.[18]

If we are to have autonomy, then, we must be in a position to regulate time. Whilst beauty is a matter of immediacy, nonetheless our autonomy as agents or subjects depends upon our ability to be absolutely—sensibly—*in* the moment of aesthetic perception while not yet being fully *of* that moment. The immediacy of sense perception—that continuous present tense of the sensual in which the present moment has a *content* given by the relation of whatever emerges as a subject to whatever constitutes that subject's object of perception—here gives way to the absolute primacy of the 'historical'—which, because it gives priority to the *form* of history over the specific content of any of history's single moments, is paradoxically the very refusal of time and of temporality itself. The historical, as can now be seen, is for Hutcheson a matter of prediction, or of theory in its formalist sense. With this kind of time, there can be *talk* of events and even the *narration* of events, but there can be no events that are experienced by sensible subjects. In the light of

[17] Hutcheson, *Philosophical Writings*, 43.   [18] Ibid, 44.

this, and given Hutcheson's supposed drive for the legitimation of those who may be possessed of sense but not yet of reason, what happens to the democratizing impulse in the aesthetic theory itself? To understand the answer to this, we need to turn to more recent arguments in political theory, specifically some arguments concerned with democracy in relation to a project called modernity.

IV

The arguments relevant here are explored in twentieth-century theory; but, as I shall show, some of our most vibrant debates over the relation of aesthetics to politics in these closing years of the twentieth century are indebted to the (usually unstated) legacy of Hutcheson and Shaftesbury. I have argued elsewhere that what we take as the issue of 'postmodernism' has its roots in arguments within the Frankfurt School.[19] Now I am in a position to align one of postmodernism's foremost analysts, Fredric Jameson, with the much earlier precursor that is Hutcheson.[20] Hutcheson's uncomfortable position, trying to adjudicate continuously between the requirements of the particular and the demands of the general, is reiterated, albeit in a different lexicon, by Jameson in his consideration of the 'antinomies of postmodernity', in *The Seeds of Time*. The first of these antinomies, he argues, relates to time and speed, with their corollary of 'rates of change' in our contemporary societies. An obvious paradox emerges right away:

the paradox from which we must set forth is the equivalence between an unparalleled rate of change on all the levels of social life and an unparalleled standardization of everything—feelings along with consumer goods, language along with built space—that would seem incompatible with just such mutability. It is a paradox that can still be conceptualized, but in

---

[19] See my *Postmodernism: A Reader* (Harvester-Wheatsheaf, Hemel Hempstead, 1993), 'Introduction'.

[20] I am being careful here to describe Jameson as an *analyst* of postmodernism, following his own comments and discriminations in the final chapter of his *Postmodernism*, 297–8 et seq. in which he distinguishes his carefully described *taste* for some postmodern art from his *analysis* of that art, and both of these from *evaluation* of the postmodern. It is a mistake to see Jameson as being simply 'for' or 'against' postmodernism. The distinctions he makes, especially that between taste and analysis, maps fairly readily on to the eighteenth-century distinction between sense and reason.

inverse ratios: that of modularity, for example, where intensified change is enabled by standardization itself, where prefabricated modules, everywhere from the media to a henceforth standardized private life, from commodified nature to uniformity of equipment, allow miraculous rebuildings to succeed each other at will, as in fractal video. The module would then constitute the new form of the object (the new result of reification) in an informational universe. ...[21]

What follows from this is that particular antinomy in which we live through absolute change which results in no change at all: the so-called 'end of history' or that state of affairs in which 'absolute change equals stasis'.[22] In short, what appears to be absolute difference (or what Hutcheson would have called variety) turns out to be absolute sameness (or Hutchesonian uniformity). Where the eighteenth century finds uniformity amidst variety, the twentieth finds sameness (or identity) lurking within difference (or alterity) as difference's real condition.[23] Jameson writes through an anxiety about the ways in which corporate capital has effectively disenfranchised the human agent. The fear is that the subject has no autonomy for the simple reason that the subject's history—or time—has not begun, and indeed cannot begin: any proposal for change or for a future that has not been entirely predicted from a past that gives the subject-as-such is simply impossible—and nowhere more so than in the realm of absolute change, that 'revolution' whose effect will be to promulgate absolute stasis.[24]

---

[21] Fredric Jameson, *The Seeds of Time* (Columbia University Press, New York, 1994), 15–16.   [22] Ibid. 19.

[23] For a fuller investigation of how this evasion of difference occurs precisely in those critical theories whose avowed aim is to celebrate or discover difference, see my study, *Alterities: Criticism, History, Representation* (Oxford University Press, 1996).

[24] This, in fact, is what lies behind the supposed 'nihilism' of Jean Baudrillard, who argues that, within any governing system, the possibility of critique of that system is always already accommodated by the system, with the effect that the exercise of a 'negative' criticism upon the system serves, paradoxically, to strengthen the system itself. See, for example, his arguments concerning Watergate, and Disneyland, in his *Simulations* (trans. Paul Foss, Paul Patton, and Phillip Beitchman; Semiotext(e), New York, 1983); and cf. my commentary on this in my *After Theory* (Edinburgh University Press, Edinburgh, 1996), esp. ch. 9, where I also trace Baudrillard's development from conventional Marxism through to his more recent challenging positions. My argument here should also allow us to hear Jameson's famous injunction, 'Always historicize!', at the opening of *The Political Unconscious* (Methuen, 1981), 9, in a slightly different way, to mean something like 'Always strive to get history started'.

Jameson's concern for autonomy can thus be seen to be grounded in a philosophy of time, in which he shares with Hutcheson (never acknowledged as such) an interesting view of 'the present'. In Hutcheson, there is a lingering influence of Augustine which will be seen to be persistent even through to our contemporary moment. Augustine famously pondered the issue of time in both his *Confessions* and *City of God*. In both texts, Augustine effectively evacuates the present moment of content. Consider here the most often-cited passage on this from the *Confessions*: 'What, then, is time? I know well enough what it is, provided that nobody asks me.' Insofar as time is *experienced* for Augustine, it cannot be the object of a *knowledge* (or, in Hutcheson's terms, it is the object of a sense-perception, not of a rational observation). Augustine goes on:

Of these three divisions of time [past, future, present], then, how can two, the past and the future, *be*, when the past no longer is and the future is not yet? As for the present, if it were always present and never moved on to become the past, it would not be time but eternity. If, therefore, the present is time only by reason of the fact that it moves on to become the past, how can we say that even the present *is*, when the reason why it *is* is that it is *not to be*? In other words, we cannot rightly say that time *is*, except by reason of its impending state of *not being*.[25]

The present here—and it is in this that Hutcheson and, later, Jameson, will agree with Augustine (though Jameson's reference-point for this is more likely to be Derrida, of course)—is a moment characterized in a seemingly self-contradictory fashion. On the one hand, it is characterized by a *content* constituted by mutability (the Jamesonian 'absolute change' that is also our Hutchesonian 'sensible' response to what is given before us—our history or our environment); and the effect of this is to make the subject in the present an 'accident' or an effect of time. On the other hand, the present is also characterized by *form*, giving absolute stasis (Augustine's 'eternity'; Hutcheson's 'theory' or reasoned abstraction from the distraction of the sensible present; Jameson's 'modularity'), regardless of content and perhaps giving the present as vacuous, empty—*only* form. What is at stake in this is a contest between our capacity to be absolutely 'singular' in our

²⁵ Augustine, *Confessions* (trans. R. S. Pine-Coffin; Penguin, Harmondsworth, 1961; repr. 1982), 264 (Bk. xi, ch. 14).

lived (if 'schizophrenic') relation to the intensity of a sensibly experienced present moment (a present full of content), and our capacity to be 'representative' or to universalize our experience of the intensely sensible present through the operations of abstract reasoning, whose effect is to evacuate the present of content, but to give it a form which will make our own experience (the content of the present) available to other rational agents. What is at stake, thus, is the category of 'representation'; and it is this category that is constitutive of modernity's construction of a 'democratic' attitude. Kant will lay out the terms of the argument rather formally: how can we legitimately universalize a normative objective standard from an experientially-given subjective fact? Hutcheson, in laying out this question in pre-Kantian terms— how can we attend to an abstract or rational uniformity while acknowledging the variety of sensible experience—allows for the placing of temporality at the centre of this modern aesthetics, for his question is actually asking how we can reconcile the present moment as experience with the present moment as knowledge. Jameson's formulation—how can absolute difference also be absolute identity—is simply a reworking of that same problem, but one which can recuperate the temporal problem at the core of the aesthetic and political issue.

Given the centrality of the problems of representation and of legitimation to this, we can see that the derivation from Shaftesbury via Hutcheson raises explicitly political questions concerning the availability, within aesthetics, of representative 'democracy', a political category, itself. Shaftesbury's philosophy is proposed in tandem with a politics whose project is to establish the hegemony of the English gentleman and thereby to widen the political franchise; Hutcheson finds himself in a situation in which questions of cultural and political autonomy are raised because one nation has assimilated the citizens of another. In both cases, not only is an ethical culture of benevolence at stake, but also the relation between such friendship or polite conversation and time. It is when Marxism takes the linguistic turn, most obviously in the work of Habermas, that we see the direct relevance of Hutcheson and Shaftesbury for an aesthetic that would be both 'modern' and 'democratic'.

In what has to be a central essay in any contemporary analysis of democracy, Habermas, in 1993, proposed 'Three Normative

Models of Democracy'.²⁶ He identifies the three models as the 'liberal', the 'republican', and the discursive or 'deliberative' (his own preferred term). The liberal model, often identified as the only modern model of democracy by the nations of the developed West, derives from Locke. In this liberal democracy,

the democratic process accomplishes the task of programming the government in the interest of society, where the government is represented as an apparatus of public administration, and society as a market-structured network of interactions among private persons.²⁷

According to this model,

the citizen's status is determined primarily according to negative rights they have vis-a-vis the state and other citizens. As bearers of these rights they enjoy the protection of the government, as long as they pursue their private interests within the boundaries drawn by legal statutes.²⁸

In political terms, this translates into what is now a 'negative' right of 'free speech' as a means of participation in the formation of a government, for example by voicing one's support for a specific party which then has the obligation to represent the voice or vote of the supportive subject. The 'republican' model adds to this basic liberal position the complication consequent upon the introduction of the concept of 'solidarity' and what Habermas calls the 'orientation to the common good' as a third source of the social integration sought in liberal or Lockean democracy. In this mode,

political rights—preeminently rights of political participation and communication—are positive liberties. They guarantee not freedom from external compulsion but the possibility of participation in a common praxis, through the exercise of which citizens can just make themselves into what they want to be—politically autonomous authors of a community of free and equal persons.²⁹

As can be seen, these two models are both fundamentally indebted to Locke, and especially to Locke's great 'modern' political text, the *Two Treatises of Government*. Shaftesbury had been taught by Locke but, although thus intimate with him, he nonetheless rejects his thinking. Klein sees that rejection (in which

²⁶ Jürgen Habermas, 'Three Normative Models of Democracy', in Seyla Benhabib (ed.), *Democracy and Difference* (Princeton University Press, Princeton, 1996), 21–30.
²⁷ Ibid. 21.   ²⁸ Ibid. 22.   ²⁹ Ibid.

Locke is surprisingly aligned with Hobbes by Shaftesbury) as some kind of quasi-Oedipal struggle in which Shaftesbury manages to avoid the excessive influence of his forebear and thus to consolidate his sense of himself as an original author delighting in his own autonomy. One need not search for a psychological explanation such as this, however, when a political one will suffice. Shaftesbury's rejection of Lockean democracy lies in two fundamental facts. First, Locke's political theory assumes the precondition that the social is an aggregate of 'private persons', and that such privacy exists prior to the social within which it can be maintained; secondly, given that one's rights in such a state of affairs are 'negative' (in Habermas's terms), they thereby shrink in authenticity, becoming merely legalistic rather than fully legitimate. In the first case, Shaftesburian theory (especially as developed by Hutcheson) cannot accept that the social is an 'aggregate' of individuals (a '1 + 1 = 2' model); and in the second case, legal authority (that of Church and State) is precisely what Shaftesbury sees as an authority (albeit a legal one) in need of legitimation (by the English gentleman class). Although distrustful of the institutionalized powers of the eighteenth-century establishment, Shaftesbury did not yet have fully open to him the possibility of the republican gesture; yet it is clear that he would have been attracted by its more positive participatory emphases and by its 'orientation to the common good' as the fulcrum of a social solidarity which makes autonomous individuated life possible and meaningful.

It is Habermas's third model, the 'deliberative' model of democracy elaborated from the linguistic and discursive turn taken by Habermas in the 1980s, that looks most clearly akin to the Shaftesburian legacy with which Hutcheson had to work. For Habermas, this third model takes from both the preceding models. Its most significant difference from them is that it operates with— indeed it provides—an image of the state as *decentred*: 'This concept of democracy no longer needs to operate with the notion of a social whole centered in the state and imagined as a goal-oriented subject writ large.'[30] This distancing of the deliberative model from the liberal and republican models is extremely pertinent to the condition of Britain in 1707, when the relation of centre to periphery

---

[30]   Habermas, 'Three Normative Models', 27.

within what is imagined as the single state is up for negotiation: 1707 marks the formulation of a distinction between centre and periphery in which Scotland, until then a nation with its own centre and periphery, becomes entirely constituted as the periphery of another state, the entirety of which can now be constituted as 'central' and as the centre of legitimation. The corollary of this kind of structure, for Habermas's contemporary theory, is that deliberative democracy consists largely in the establishing of a wide-ranging network of discourses, all of which seek influence, but all of which act, at best, interdependently with each other, forming nonce 'centres' of legitimation, 'local' regimes which can operate both as centres and as peripheries with regard to other localities. The image of the social here is one of a 'federalism', in which participants relate both to their immediate situation or community and also to a wider set of interests and a more widespread imagined community called the nation.[31] Solidarity here does not coalesce into a socio-political programme in which the State can be considered allegorically as a subject whose single and autonomous intentionality drives it towards pre-determined goals; rather, solidarities—in the plural—prefer to influence the social more *informally*. Shaftesbury's position, imagining polite conversation as the source of nonce-legitimations, is clearly close to that of Habermas, and is the very source of that version of the modern 'intellectual' whose business is imagined not just to be a form of teaching but also a form of influence.[32]

In brief, Shaftesbury's position initiates the practice of the cultural critic whose most earnest wish is that her or his criticism will have a social or political effect of some grand consequence. It is precisely the position satirized by Stanley Fish in *There's No Such Thing as Free Speech* and, more directly, in his Clarendon lectures, published as *Professional Correctness*, whose argument he concludes by disintricating literary criticism firmly from political intentionality. He writes there that 'each practice [including, centrally here, literary criticism] is answerable to the norms implicit in its own history and conventions', and that literary interpretation 'has

---

[31]   The implicit reference here is, of course, to Benedict Anderson's *Imagined Communities* (rev. and expanded edn.; Verso, 1991), although Anderson's interest lies explicitly, in that book as in many of his other writings, outside of Europe, in Asia.

[32]   This position of the intellectual comes under closer scrutiny in Ch. 7.

no purpose external to the arena of its practice'.[33] Insofar as Shaftesbury can be identified as the source of precisely the kind of criticism identified as logically impossible by Fish here, he can also be identified as the source of a liberal tradition of the intellectual. There are thus two paradoxes associated with this: first, the 'English gentleman' turns out to be at the root of what has been hypothesized as a Scottish 'democratic intellect'; secondly, the 'English gentleman' is at the root of that critical consciousness—a leftist consciousness—that would see the English national and nationalist gentleman class as being among its prime enemies.

Hutcheson, clearly, is in a difficult situation when he takes on the mantle of benevolence, for its effects far exceed the intentions of its primary advocate. Hutcheson faces a moral dilemma occasioned by the political and cultural situation in which he finds himself. On the one hand, his sympathy lies with a philosophy based on benevolence, whose corollary is broadly republican (which translates, in Hutcheson's terms, an 'orientation to the common good' into an orientation towards the *general* based upon the altruistic disposition towards the other); on the other hand, the political reality of his time, together with his own intellectual formation (a formation which left him much more sympathetic to Locke than was Shaftesbury himself), requires a cultural and social practice based upon the negative rights of property (which, in Hutcheson's terms, translates into the prioritization of *singularity* over the general). His mathematical adjudications between uniformity (the general) and variety (the singular) are thus also adjudications between Scotland and England, between the power of philosophy and the power of property, between the intellectual who has power only in the sphere of the intellect and the landowner who has power beyond the ownership of a specific land.

The philosophy informing Hutchesonian politics, which he would prefer to be modelled on what we can now identify as a Habermasian 'deliberative democracy' with its attendant *decentred* state, is complicated by the desire to reconcile absolute difference (variety) with absolute identity (uniformity). As Jameson's formulation of this above now allows us to see, this is fundamentally a

---

[33] See Stanley Fish, *Professional Correctness* (Clarendon Press, Oxford, 1995), 112, 113; and cf. Fish, *There's No Such Thing as Free Speech* (Oxford University Press, 1994).

problem of temporality at the core of what seems ostensibly to be a spatial problem: the relation between two nations. I can now show that, although he lacked the terminology with which to express the position in his own time, Hutcheson was concerned to establish an ethics which was 'occasionalist', an ethics which was primarily a matter of temporal 'events' rather than of facts, formulations, or spatial and geopolitical conditions. For Hutcheson, democracy becomes consistent not precisely with any of Habermas's three normative models, but rather with the modification of those recently proposed by Sheldon Wolin, who argues for 'fugitive democracy' or what Benhabib calls an 'agonistic' version of democracy.[34]

For Wolin, democracy is not a state of affairs, but rather something that happens from time to time. It is less a condition and more an event. Accordingly, it follows that it is best considered not in terms of our spatial or hierarchical political relations with each other in a social network, but rather under the much more troubling sign of the temporality of our relations—such as that temporality governing friendship or benevolent altruism—or even of the temporariness of our social arrangements (including, one might suggest, colonial or national arrangements). In outlining his position, Wolin writes:

I shall take the *political* to be an expression of the idea that a free society composed of diversities can nonetheless enjoy moments of commonality when, through public deliberations, collective power is used to promote or protect the well-being of the collectivity. *Politics* refers to the legitimized and public contestation, primarily by organized and unequal social powers, over access to the resources available to the public authorities of the collectivity. Politics is continuous, ceaseless, and endless. In contrast, the political is episodic, rare.[35]

For Wolin, further, democracy is 'a project'. It was also, I claim, a project for Hutcheson, and one in which 'the democratic' was, like 'the political', episodic and rare. Hutcheson's dilemma is that he is torn between what I have been calling 'abstraction' and 'distraction', between philosophy and property; and this becomes for him a matter of the relative priorities to be given to space and time. The

---

[34] All of the argumentation on democracy here relates to Benhabib's collection of essays, *Democracy and Difference*, in which Wolin's article 'Fugitive Democracy' is to be found.　　[35] Sheldon S. Wolin, 'Fugitive Democracy', 31.

crucial space in question is that of the boundary of 'the nation'; the time that of '1707'. The question is whether the moment that is 1707 has any 'content', and therefore whether the Union has any legitimacy other than a purely formal one.

The twentieth-century thinker whose work opened this meditation, Jameson, can now also help us close it. Although addressing a matter entirely different from these issues relating to Hutcheson, Jameson might have been addressing his case precisely, for what Hutcheson is concerned with is the shaping and identification of a landscape and of what it signifies—that of Scotland, England, Ireland, Britain—at a particular moment in its history. When Jameson considers landscape in art in *The Seeds of Time*, he describes it as—in its secular version at least—a very recent phenomenon; and he finds it to be the elaboration of 'a space that is somehow meaningfully organized and on the very point of speech'. He notes the shift from land-tenure to land ownership in the history of capital; and, while tenure involved care (to the point of distraction), ownership involves abstraction in which land becomes effectively nothing more than a sign (as a landscape or map). After 1707, this is not merely a philosophical issue, but rather one touching directly on politics and democracy. It is the Hutchesonian confrontation of England with Scotland, property with philosophy. Capital has the power, argues Jameson, to homogenize space; and he writes of:

the effects that result from the power of commerce and then capitalism proper—which is to say, sheer number as such, number now shorn and divested of its own magical heterogeneities and reduced to equivalencies—to seize upon a landscape and flatten it out, reorganize it into a grid of identical parcels, and expose it to the dynamic of a market that now reorganizes space in terms of an identical value. The development of capitalism then distributes that value most unevenly indeed, until at length, in its postmodern moment, sheer speculation, as something like the triumph of spirit over matter, the liberation of the form of value from any of its former concrete or earthly content, now reigns supreme and devastates the very cities and countrysides it created in the process of its own earlier development.[36]

Property reduces variety to uniformity: it is the condition of an Act of Union in which the different content of two nation states can be

---

[36]   Jameson, *Seeds of Time*, 25.

formally—but only formally—reconciled in a supposed uniformity. In this triumph of form over content, we have a triumph of the abstractions of space over the particularities or intensities of moments in time; and it follows from this that '1707', as such a moment in time, is evacuated of content. It may have a *formal* existence, but its existence is thus only like that present moment described by Augustine:

the only time that can be called present is an instant, if we can conceive of such, that cannot be divided into even the most minute fractions, and a point of time as small as this passes so rapidly from the future to the past that its duration is without length. For if its duration were prolonged, it could be divided into past and future. When it is present it has no duration.[37]

In having no duration, it has no content; and in having no content, whatever 'happens' in that present moment cannot be attested to by Hutchesonian 'sense', and thus cannot be legitimized, given that the legitimacy of an event depends, for Hutcheson, upon the possibility of reconciling our sense of it with our reasoning about it. Thus, the Union has no content, and thus no temporal existence, and thus no historical legitimacy. Its vacuity rests on its attitude to precisely that false 'democracy' of $1 + 1 = 2$, in which the incommensurability of each '1' with regard to the other '1' is ignored in the interests of the formality of 'sheer number', number 'divested of heterogeneity'. Thus stated, the Union is antipathetic to democracy inasmuch as it cannot attend to the temporality of sense or of the aesthetic. It offers the form of democracy, or democracy as a condition; but not democracy as an 'event' or as an experienced lived reality. For this, an aesthetic attitude which favours 'singularity' or which at least does not dissolve singularity under 'representation' or the homogeneity of space, is required. And on this matter, Hume and Rousseau will have a great deal to say, as my next chapter shows.

[37] Augustine, *Confessions*, 266 (Bk. xi, ch. 15).

5

The Politics of Singularity

Writing in 1940, Walter Benjamin famously argued, in his seventh thesis on the philosophy of history, that 'Whoever has emerged victorious participates to this day in the triumphal procession in which the present rulers step over those who are lying prostrate. According to traditional practice, the spoils are carried along in the procession. They are called cultural treasures'; and it follows from this, in the oft-cited phrase, that 'There is no document of civilization which is not at the same time a document of barbarism'.[1] Almost two hundred years before this, we can find a similar sentiment, uncannily prescient of Benjamin in its rhetoric and theoretical persuasions, in Voltaire. On 24 October 1766, Voltaire wrote a letter, subsequently published, to David Hume, in which he argued that:

The particulars of the most bloody wars perish with the soldiers that were the victims. Even the critics of new theatrical pieces, and particularly their elogiums, are the next day buried in oblivion with them, and the periodical pamphlets that treat of them. Nothing but Keyser's sugar-plums have been able to keep their ground a little.[2]

Unlike Benjamin, Voltaire is not pretending here to engage in any deep philosophical argument about time, about memory, forgetting, and history: rather, his letter is one advising Hume that the

---

[1] Walter Benjamin, 'Theses on the Philosophy of History', in *Illuminations*, ed. Hannah Arendt (trans. Harry Zohn; Fontana, 1973), 258.

[2] Voltaire, letter to Hume dated October 24, 1766, (trans. from French; S. Bladon, London, 1766), bound within *An Account of the Controversy between Mr Hume and Mr Rousseau* (trans. from French; T. Becket and P. A. De Hondt; London, 1766), 15–16 (separately paginated).

recent spat between Hume and Rousseau is threatening to get out of all proportion, and that the best way to deal with Rousseau is simply to ignore him. Yet time (with its corollaries: memory, forgetting, history), as my previous chapter has shown, is itself exerting a pressure on the question of aesthetics in Europe at this moment. Voltaire's letter—usefully if certainly inadvertently—brings together the issue of time and justice in a further complication of the intimacy now operative between time and judgement: justice will be served, Voltaire argues, through the passage of time and in an act of forgetting (that act which, much later, Benjamin will associate with a form of violence and barbarity). The rupture between Hume and Rousseau, into which Voltaire's letter interleaves itself, is not as well documented or as well remembered as the antipathy between Voltaire and Rousseau; but it is worth outlining in a little detail, for it is grounded in a philosophical difference central to my argument.

The circumstances are simple, if a little convoluted. Rousseau and Hume had initially made contact with each other in 1762, when Rousseau was under siege in Montmorency, just outside Paris, after the publication of *Emile*. Hume had been alerted to Rousseau's difficulties through the mediation of Mme de Boufflers, and was prepared to arrange a refuge for him in England or Scotland. Two things conspired to delay the formal meeting of Hume with Rousseau at this time, however. First, as Rousseau put it, 'I have never liked England or the English; and all Mme de Boufflers' eloquence, far from overcoming my repugnance, served for some reason to increase it';[3] second, and perhaps more importantly, among Rousseau's friends in Montmorency, the threat from the civic authorities at this time was not taken entirely seriously, it seems. Describing the events in the *Confessions*, Rousseau implies as much when he notes an odd discrepancy in the supposed time of the issuing of the warrant for his arrest:

There was nothing left but to think of departure. The officers of the law should have come at ten o'clock. It was four in the afternoon when I left, and they had not yet arrived. ... Between La Barre and Montmorency I passed four men in black in a hired coach who saluted

³ Jean-Jacques Rousseau, *Confessions* (trans. J. M. Cohen; Penguin, Harmondsworth, 1954), 537.

me with smiles. From the description which Thérèse afterwards gave me of the officers' appearance, the hour of their arrival and their way of behaviour, I have never been in any doubt that it was they [the arresting officers]; especially since I subsequently learnt that instead of the warrant being issued at seven o'clock, as I had been told, it had not been ready till midday ...[4]

The implication is clear: as long as Rousseau was prepared to leave, he would not seriously be pursued by the law. However, the matter of timing—more precisely, the matter of time itself —will be seen in a moment to be of much greater significance for Rousseau, for it constitutes a major predicament in the formulation of his aesthetic ideology or in his attempts to articulate fully the relation between culture and politics.

For the moment, though, it is important simply to note that Hume's offer of benevolent assistance to a writer in trouble was not taken up until 1765, when Rousseau was again under attack; and Hume, having escorted Rousseau to England, found a refuge for him in the house of Richard Davenport in Wootton in Derbyshire. The arrangement appears to have been broadly congenial, and a sentimental friendship was established, even if Rousseau was—perhaps predictably—a little prickly with the neighbours, ostensibly being typically protective of his intense privacy:

The minister of the parish came to see me yesterday, who, finding that I spoke to him only in French, would not speak to me in English, so that our interview was almost a silent one. I have taken a great fancy to this expedient, and shall make use of it with all my neighbours, if I have any. Nay, should I even learn to speak English, I would converse with them only in French, especially if I were so happy as to find they did not understand a word of that language. An artifice this, much of the same kind with that which the Negroes pretend is practised by the monkeys, who, they say, are capable of speech, but cannot be prevailed upon to talk, lest they should be set to work.[5]

Rousseau's simian artifice or pretence here seems jocular; but, as I shall later show, it has a serious component in his thinking, in which the truth of action (but not of theatrical acting) is often set against the falsehoods of speaking (including theatrical speaking:

---

[4] Rousseau, *Confessions,* 538–9.
[5] Letter from Rousseau to Hume, March 29, 1766, in *An Account of the Controversy between Mr Hume and Mr Rousseau,* 16.

the rehearsal, reiteration, recital).[6] The predicaments of temporality and of theatricality complicate Rousseau's much-vaunted desire for that very sincerity or integrity which is axiomatic to his claims for a democratic sociality, as I shall show in this present chapter. Yet, despite any such philosophical problems, for the moment at least, relations between Hume and Rousseau appear to have been good, sweet and affectionate.

These amicable relations persist in this way until a letter, purporting to be in the hand of Frederick, the King of Prussia, appears in the *St James's Chronicle*, no. 793 (dated Tuesday April 1–Thursday April 3, 1766). The letter is a satire on Rousseau, describing him as a man who seeks out persecution and misery, and who is overly concerned about his own singularity and difference from the rest of humanity: 'Vous avez fait asses parler de vous par des Singularités peu dignes d'un grand Homme; démontrez à vos Ennemis que vous pouvez avoir quelque fois du bon Sens. ... Si vous persistez toujours à creuser l'Esprit pour trouver de nouveaux Malheurs, choisissez les tels que vous voudrez; Je suis Roi, Je puis vous en procurer au gré de vos Désirs'.[7] Although Rousseau explicitly claims just such a difference when he comes to write the start of his *Confessions* some years later, claiming as his opening gambit in that text that 'I am made unlike any one I have ever met; I will even venture to say that I am like no one in the whole world. I may be no better, but at least I am different',[8] he nonetheless reacted very badly to a satire in which he is presented to a 'polite' English educated public as an Alceste-like misanthropic caricature, writing to the *Chronicle* to demand a retraction, in a letter published by the paper in no. 796 (dated Tuesday April 8–Thursday 10 April 1766).

To put this in terms that would have been familiar to Rousseau himself, Rousseau's *amour-de-soi* (which is a good thing, concerned as it is with a proper self-regard required for self-preservation) veers straight into *amour-propre* (which is a bad thing, concerned as it is

---

[6] Rousseau's attitude to the relation between truth and theatre uncannily prefigures the thinking of Artaud. See Antonin Artaud, *Le Théâtre et son double; suivi de Le Théâtre de Séraphin* (Gallimard, Paris, 1964); and cf. also the relatively early work of Jacques Derrida on Artaud in *L'Écriture et la différence* (Seuil, Paris, 1967), ch. 6, 'La Parole soufflée', and ch. 8 'Le Théâtre de la cruauté et la clôture de la représentation'.

[7] *St James's Chronicle, or, the British Evening Post*, no. 793, Tues. 1 Apr–Thurs. 3 Apr., 1766. Is that date significant? Is the letter a *poisson d'avril*?

[8] Rousseau, *Confessions*, 17.

with a self-evaluation derived from how one imagines one appears to others).[9] From this point, relations between Rousseau and Hume are soured beyond repair, for suddenly Rousseau assumes—or pretends to assume—that Hume is complicit with the writers and publishers of this letter, who must of course be Rousseau's malevolent enemies.

It is not that Rousseau believes himself to have fallen from favour with Frederick, his protector (along with the émigré Scotsman, Lord George Keith), when he had taken refuge in Motiers, Neuchatel (at that time under the control of Prussia) in 1762. Rather, he knows the letter to be a forgery, and assumes it to be part of his 'persecution' at the hands of—among others in what he called 'the Holbach clique'— d'Alembert, with whom his relations had already taken a turn for the worse on the occasion of d'Alembert's article on 'Geneva' for the seventh volume of the *Encyclopédie* in October 1757. Like Rousseau, d'Alembert believed in the cultural power of theatre, and in the famous excursus in the middle of his article, he suggested that, provided the occasionally dubious morals of individual actors could be curbed by good laws, Geneva could benefit greatly, morally, spiritually—culturally—from the establishment of a vigorous theatre in the polity:

Par ce moyen Genève auroit des spectacles et des mœurs, et jouiroit de l'avantage des uns et des autres: les représentations théâtrales formeroient le goût des citoyens, et leur donneroient une finesse de tact, une délicatesse de sentiment qu'il est très difficile d'acquérir sans ce secours. La littérature en profiteroit, sans que le libertinage fît de progrès, et Genève réuniroit à la sagesse de Lacédémone la politesse d'Athènes. ... Le séjour de cette ville, que bien des François regardent comme triste par la privation des spectacles, deviendroit alors le séjour des plaisirs honnêtes, comme il est celui de la philosophie et de la liberté.[10]

---

[9] For a fuller description of this subtle but telling distinction between *amour-de-soi* and *amour-propre*, see Gerard Mairet's note in his edition of Rousseau's *Écrits politiques* (Livre de poche, Paris, 1992), 480–1, in which he quotes directly from Rousseau's own footnote XV added to the *Discours sur l'inégalité*: 'L'amour de soi-même est un sentiment naturel qui porte tout animal à veiller à sa propre conservation et qui ... produit l'humanité et la vertu. L'amour-propre n'est qu'un sentiment relatif, factice et né dans la société, qui porte chaque individu à faire plus de cas de soi que de tout autre, qui inspire aux hommes tous les maux qu'ils se font mutuellement et qui est la véritable source de l'honneur.'

[10] Jean le Rond d'Alembert, 'Genève', repr. as appendix in Rousseau, *Lettre sur les spectacles*, introduction de L. Brunel (5th rev. edn.; Hachette, Paris, 1910), 209–10.

One might well have expected Rousseau to be in broad agreement with such an argument, especially if one notes (as it was certainly noted at the time) that he himself was a great frequenter of plays and that he had indeed previously written for the theatre (a sketch, *Narcisse*, in 1731; the opera, *Muses galantes*, 1745; a reworking of the opera by Voltaire and Rameau called *Fêtes de Ramire*, also in 1745). Yet the response to the article was his fractious *Lettre à d'Alembert sur les spectacles* (1758).

According to the account given in the *Confessions*, Rousseau had been alerted to the article by Diderot, who told Rousseau that it 'was part of a plan concerned with certain Genevese of high rank for the purpose of setting up a theatre in the city, as a result of which certain measures had been taken, and it would not be long before it was carried out'.[11] Rousseau then saw the excursus on theatre in d'Alembert's article as part of a wider campaign on behalf of none other than Voltaire, whose plays were being acted in Voltaire's own house in Ferney which, though actually in France, was just outside the city boundaries of Geneva. Voltaire, of course, was Rousseau's enemy, at least since the publication of the *Discours sur l'origine et les fondements de l'inégalité* in 1755, to which Voltaire had responded rather contemptuously—and satirically—in his letter of 30 August 1755, describing it as 'votre nouveau livre contre le genre humain'.[12] The mutual contempt of the two men was firmly established by the time of Voltaire's great poem on the Lisbon earthquake, with its austere rejection of Optimism, provoking Rousseau to claim that:

Though Voltaire has always appeared to believe in God, he has really only believed in the Devil, because his so-called God is nothing but a malicious being who, according to his belief, only takes pleasure in doing harm. The absurdity of this doctrine leaps to the eye, and it is particularly revolting in a man loaded with every kind of blessing who, living in the lap of luxury, seeks to disillusion his fellow-men by a frightening and cruel picture of all the calamities from which he himself is exempt.[13]

---

[11]   Rousseau, *Confessions*, 459.

[12]   Letter, cited in Jean-Michel Raynaud, ' "Rousseau Jean-Jacques, que j'aurais pu aimer" ', in *Le Magazine littéraire*, no. 357 (Sept. 1997), 23. It is worth noting Raynaud's observation, argued in this article, that the object of Voltaire's critique is actually the first discourse (*Le Discours sur les sciences et les arts*), and not the second.

[13]   Rousseau, *Confessions*, 399.

Rousseau, of course, took the view that he himself was better qualified to speak of disaster, having himself supposedly suffered it continually. What emerges from this is a perhaps surprising pusillanimity in the relations between these two, a pusillanimity which, in fact, is hardly made any more dignified if we choose to rephrase it in terms more comfortable to the present day by saying that in the relations between these two, the political is avowedly the personal. Rousseau's *Lettre à d'Alembert*, then, is part of a larger action of Rousseau's, in which he situates himself as the personal enemy of the Holbach clique, and in which he believed that the encyclopaedists were using their cultural authority and power corruptly, sleazily, in the service of personal advancement.

And now Rousseau, still confounding the political with the personal, sees Hume as complicit with his enemies in this act of betrayal, satirizing Rousseau among an intellectual public who, as Rousseau points out, are the bearers of a 'polite' education and who therefore can be counted on to read and take seriously what they read in papers like the *St James's Chronicle*.[14] Hume, however, claims that the offending letter was a simple instance of 'raillery', that it was written by Horace Walpole, and that it had circulated in manuscript copies in Paris purely as a light comic item before its unfortunate publication. Interestingly, Hume's account of this, published in his *Account of the Controversy*, is extremely similar in its wording to the explanation given in the *St James's Chronicle*. Both accounts describe it as a 'harmless piece of Raillery' and an 'imposture' that was 'innocent'.[15] Hume provides the evidence for his account, in a letter (dated 26 July 1766) from Walpole in which this latter acknowledges his authorship of the satirical parody, and states—with Rousseauvian frankness—that 'I have a hearty contempt for Rousseau, and am perfectly indifferent

---

[14] See David Hume, *A Concise and Genuine Account of the Dispute* in *An Account of the Controversy*, 60: 'The people in England read the public papers, and are in no wise prepossessed in favour of foreigners', according to Rousseau in this account.

[15] The comparison of the *St James's Chronicle*, no. 796 (8–10 Apr. 1766) with Hume's *Concise and Genuine Account* is instructive and suggestive, for the newspaper introduces Rousseau's letter in words that are strikingly similar to those given by Hume in his own 'genuine' account, so much so that the contemporary eye suspects what we might call plagiarism—or what Rousseau's eye would have seen as insincerity. Did Hume simply copy the version given by the *St James's Chronicle*; how close was he to the editorial line, and did he in fact influence it?

what any body thinks of this matter',[16] and in another undated letter from d'Alembert denying authorship and stating that he would
not have written such a satire on Rousseau on the grounds that 'we
ought not to ridicule the unfortunate'.[17]

What is significant in this ostensibly rather trivial spat which,
according to Voltaire is best forgotten (and we might well agree
that its personal element is indeed unworthy of serious consideration), but some of the intricacies of which I am endeavouring to
recall here, is the different theoretical and philosophical attitudes of
Hume and Rousseau to the affair. More precisely, what is important is their different attitudes to what we might call the singular or
the particular. For Rousseau, particulars are important in a very
specific way: they signify and have a meaning which exceeds their
ostensible being. That is to say—and here we can see a clear overlap with Leibnizian Optimism—all particular events hang together
in some pattern or plot; and the insertion of any specific singular
event into a plot inflates and transforms the value and meaning of
the event. This attitude is laid most bare, perhaps, in that section
of the *Confessions* in which he details, at great length and with
almost baroque intricacy (indeed, with a paranoiac intricacy worthy of the plotting of Pynchon, whose novelistic consciousness is
perhaps distantly related to that of Rousseau), the controversies
around the publication of *Emile*, in which the matter especially of
the timing of the issuing of the warrant for his arrest becomes of
great significance. He apologizes for the detail, but explains:

It is not for no purpose that I have dilated, in the tale I have just told, on
all the circumstances which I have been able to recall. Although they do
not seem very enlightening in themselves, once one seizes the thread of the
plot they will shed light on its development; and although they do not iso-
late the essentials of the problem I am going to outline, they offer considerable help in solving it.

If we suppose that my removal was absolutely necessary for the execution of the conspiracy against me, for it to be successful everything had to
happen much as it did. But if, instead of letting myself be frightened by
Mme de Luxembourg's nocturnal ambassador and disturbed by his warn-
ings, I had continued to hold out as I had begun, and if, instead of remaining at the Chateau, I had returned to sleep quietly in my bed till morning,

---

[16] Horace Walpole, letter of 26 July 1766 cited by Hume in his *Concise and
Genuine Account*, 88.

[17] Letter from d'Alembert, undated, cited by Hume, ibid. 90.

would the warrant have been put into execution just the same? A big question upon which depends the solution of many others; and as we examine it there is some point in noting the hour at which the warrant was to have been issued according to my warning, and the hour at which it really was issued. *A crude but impressive example of the importance of minor detail when setting out the facts, if one is looking for their secret causes in order by induction to explain these facts in their entirety.*[18]

A minor and even incidental detail, once seen in relation to a grander scheme of things, becomes of major significance. A singular event, under the sign of history, finds its meaning and value transformed by the consciousness which is able to see it not just as a single event but as part of a transcending whole. That is to say, the meaning or value of the event is transformed by that consciousness which is able to see it as an event that occurs *in time*, subject therefore to having its meaning revealed by the passage of time; and, insofar as the event happens *in time*, it cannot be, for Rousseau, an event happening in a state of nature. As Starobinski puts this, Rousseau hypothesizes a 'fall' which is actually a fall into history or time itself:

Rousseau transporte le mythe religieux dans l'histoire elle-même; il la divise en deux âges: l'un, temps stable de l'innocence, règne tranquille de la pure nature; l'autre, histoire en devenir, activité coupable, négation de la nature par l'homme.[19]

Hume, by contrast, took a rather different view of the importance of the singular event. Before Rousseau wrote his first great *Discours*, the *Discours sur les sciences et les arts*, he had begun his own meditation 'Of the Rise and Progress of the Arts and Sciences' by making a distinction between chance events and determined events; and the claim is that there is an intimate link between singularity and chance on one hand, and between generality and determination on the other:

The distinguishing between chance and causes must depend upon every particular man's sagacity in considering every particular incident. But if I were to assign any general rule to help us in applying this distinction, it would be the following: *What depends upon a few persons is, in a great measure, to be ascribed to chance, or secret and unknown causes: what*

[18] Rousseau, *Confessions*, 542–3; stress added.
[19] Jean Starobinski, *Jean-Jacques Rousseau: la transparence et l'obstacle* (Gallimard, Paris, 1957; new edn., 1971), 24.

arises from a great number, may often be accounted for by determinate and known causes.[20]

Broadly, while we may see in Rousseau an aspect of paranoia better explained (that is, explained in philosophical rather than personal terms) as Optimism, in Hume we see a more open acknowledgement of inexplicability, an awareness that things or events in the world might not be there 'for' our consciousness, that they might exist 'secretly' or independently, and that it would therefore be an error to reduce their 'being' to their 'meaning' or to accommodate them—Optimistically—in a meaningful and organized world or history, a world or history whose organization and significance is guaranteed by the surveillance of some form of absolute knowing (or God). It follows from this that Hume has a fundamentally different attitude to time from that which underlies Rousseau's thinking, and one which we might call more genuinely historical. Hume, in accepting inexplicability as a possibility, not only accepts that the world is not necessarily centred on any unifying consciousness (absolute knowing or God); he also accepts thereby the possibility of an *unpredictability* in events. He accepts that the future may not either explain the present or past, and furthermore that it cannot be predicted, for 'pre-dictability' implies a situation in which history is simply reiterating an already written pathway; and Hume's agnosticism (the scepticism regarding absolute knowing) leaves open the possibility of the future as a conflict between different dictions or discourses. This is what Lyotard will much later describe as a 'paganism' which is set against the subscription to a universal history or a single history implicit in the Optimistic attitude.[21]

We can now see why Benjamin's seventh thesis is an appropriate

[20] David Hume, 'Of the Rise and Progress of the Arts and Sciences' in Hume, *Selected Essays*, ed. Stephen Copley and Andrew Edgar (Oxford University Press, Oxford, 1993), 56–7

[21] See Jean-François Lyotard, *Rudiments païens* (Christian Bourgois, et 10/18, Paris, 1977), and *Instructions païennes* (Galilée, Paris, 1977) for one of Lyotard's early attempts to counter the prevailing historicist subscription to a universal history, and in which he validates the pagan, the thinking from the *pagus*, as a form of 'local' knowledge set against universal knowledge. See also Lyotard's essay on 'Universal History and Cultural Differences' in *The Lyotard Reader*, ed. Andrew Benjamin (Blackwell, Oxford, 1989), 314–23. For a different approach to the question of such universalism, see Alain Badiou, *Saint Paul* (Presses Universitaires de France, Paris, 1997).

place in which to open our consideration of this eighteenth-century conflict, a conflict at the very root of the questions concerning aesthetic ideology which constitute our modernity. The conflict as I have outlined it fundamentally has to do with the possibility (or otherwise) of the agency of a subject who may yet also be the victim of a history with which she or he is complicit. Both Hume and Rousseau lack the concept of ideology to explain their varied stances regarding the organization of the social. As a consequence, Hume comes close to accepting that what is taken for granted among a generality—that is, what has broad consensus—might be open to rational investigation such that its significance can be explained to the consciousness of any subject who either forms part of that consensus or who opposes it. Accordingly, in Hume, the subject can act in the knowledge of what she or he is doing and with a certain degree of assurance regarding the moral rectitude of the subject-agent. In this case, there can be a perfect alignment between how one acts and how one speaks of or describes that action: representation—as that which reconciles being and meaning—in general terms, is possible and is subject to verification through this nascent form of 'ideology-critique'. On the other hand, Rousseau, prioritizing the specific over the consensual, produces a subject who is at the mercy of plots contrived by others; and it is the task of that subject to attend to the 'minor detail' in order to locate herself or himself in history—but now as a victim of history rather than as an agent of it: representation is precisely the area in which *discrepancies* between being and meaning, between acting and speaking if you will, become not only possible but entirely inevitable. 'Critique'—in the form of a critical act of consciousness leading to the possibility of historical agency—is not possible here; and Rousseau's position, as I describe it, is limited to the verbal criticism of a victim of history directed against his supposed (or real) oppressors. However, such a criticism disables historical agency, or at best reduces that agency to the status of the verbal action: the Alceste-like or misanthropic complaint. For Hume, what we call ideology becomes a matter of moral agency; for Rousseau, it becomes a matter of psychoanalysis and paranoia. A sentimental friendship between these two positions is simply impossible, for they are completely antipathetic the one to the other: hence the necessity of a break, initiated by Rousseau to the puzzlement of Hume. In what follows in the present chapter, I shall explore more fully the terms of this inevitable rupture and its consequences for the antinomy between the autonomy of the subject (as manifested in 'taste' or in a judgement which, though ostensibly aesthetic, is actually informed by ethics and justice) and the establishment of a democracy based precisely upon such autonomy (and in which, therefore, the regulation of taste—ostensibly a matter for individual subjects—relates to the political state).

II

It is a commonplace of philosophical history that Hume's *Treatise of Human Nature*, published in 1739, did not have an immediate effect or find a ready and listening audience. Many have accepted Hume's own disappointment at its reception, as reflected in the oft-cited remark from *My Own Life* (1777) that 'Never literary attempt was more unfortunate than my Treatise of Human Nature. It fell *dead-born from the press,* without reaching such distinction, as even to excite a murmur among the zealots.'[22] Yet its effect on his own career was fairly quickly evident for, as Bruce Lenman puts it, 'Hume's *Treatise* was alive enough by 1745 to lose him the succession to the Chair of Moral Philosophy in the University of Edinburgh,'[23] the very Chair which had been offered to (but declined by) Hutcheson, with whom Hume had entered into a brief correspondence at the time of making his *Treatise*. Lenman is being slightly disingenuous here, for the struggle over the appointment to that Chair involved local as well as national politics, alongside the more respectable and conventional considerations of the academic qualifications of likely candidates; but Hume's own rather conservative politics were viewed as not quite conservative enough by the local council, some members of which feared the possibility of a man of avowedly agnostic persuasion giving lectures in morals—as the Professor had to do, for the duties of the occupant of the Chair 'specifically implied a commitment to the validity of the Christian Revelation'[24]—to the youth of the University.

---

[22] David Hume, *My Own Life* (1777; repr. The Mill House Press, Stanford Dingley, 1927), 6.

[23] Bruce Lenman, *Integration and Enlightenment: Scotland 1746–1832* (Edinburgh University Press, Edinburgh, 1981), 26.

[24] Ibid. 26. It is useful to compare Lenman's account of this episode with that advanced by Alasdair MacIntyre, in his chapter on 'Hume's Anglicizing Subversion' in *Whose Justice? Which Rationality?* (Duckworth, 1988), 281–99, esp. 286.

The conventional view on the matter is that the council effectively mistook his intellectual radicalism for social and political radicalism; and in the period around the Jacobite rebellion, such a confusion could matter a great deal in British academic affairs. Some six years later, Hume made a further attempt to gain an academic position, this time rather half-heartedly nominating himself for the Chair of Logic (or Moral Philosophy) in the University of Glasgow. This again came to nothing, and Hume settled in Edinburgh where, as keeper of the Advocates' Library, he began work on his monumental historical works, and where he wrote many of his occasional essays. It was these latter writings, especially his essays, that brought him the wider public—precisely that 'polite' public of Shaftesburian politics—that he had wanted in writing his *Treatise*, and he used the occasion of these essays to develop and explain aspects of his philosophy for that wider public. To some extent, thus, it could be said that the tactic of the polite essay, in place of the established legitimacy and authority of an academic position, as a means of effecting a strategic political and cultural shift or movement—in which a democratized 'general audience' constituted a community with some autonomous power—worked well in the case of Hume: he found an audience of generalists even as he failed to find—at least momentarily—his preferred audience of scholars or technical specialists.

It is in these essays that one finds the ideas of Hume regarding what we can call 'aesthetic ideology' expressed in a form that was not only popular but also influential. In a series of essays, he pondered what we have come to regard as some great modern questions—questions whose very articulation and determination are constitutive of modernity itself. Primarily, the greatest of these—regarding the validity of general or objective legitimation claims based upon the primacy of subjective judgements—is now more firmly associated with Kant, and especially with the Kant of the *Critique of Judgement* (1790). The foundations for that critique, however, lie in the earlier quarrels whose terms are laid out in the terrain between the Scot and the Genevan—monarchist and republican—in the 1750s; and the terms of those debates continued the reflections started explicitly by Hutcheson, but with roots in an earlier century's socio-cultural struggles (articulated in ostensibly arcane arguments about tragedy and comedy) over the establishment of legitimate nation-states. In what follows here, I shall examine more fully the ways in which the issue of history—or of temporality—exerts further pressure on those discourses which are trying to combine aesthetics with politics; and, more precisely, I shall turn attention more fully to the ways in which a pressure for democracy is felt to intrude upon the question of taste and of human subjectivity.

First, Hume. Hume makes a distinction between what he characterizes as two types of 'delicacy': delicacy of passion, on the one hand, and delicacy of taste, on the other. He argues that there is an intimate relation between these two delicacies. Both are modes of responsiveness to the world: a delicacy of passion makes those possessed of it 'extremely sensible to all the accidents of life' and therefore susceptible to extremes of joy and of grief; while a delicacy of taste 'produces the same sensibility to beauty and deformity of every kind' as the delicacy of passion produces to prosperity or adversity.[25] By this formulation, Hume has already divided the world up into two realms: a realm of what he calls 'accidents' which corresponds broadly to the material or historical world of contingency; and a realm of aesthetics which may overlap with this former but which remains nonetheless a special aspect—a special case privileged by intentionality—of materiality. Hume proposes a nearly mathematical relation between the two sensibilities, claiming that a delicacy of passion is bad for you, but that it can be healed (or reduced in its effect) through the cultivation or expansion of the corresponding delicacy of taste:

delicacy of taste is as much to be desired or cultivated, as delicacy of passion is to be lamented, and to be remedied, if possible. The good or ill accidents of life are very little at our disposal; but we are pretty much masters what books we shall read, what diversions we shall partake of, and what company we shall keep. . . . I am persuaded that nothing is so proper to cure us of this delicacy of passion, as the cultivating of that higher and more refined taste, which enables us to judge of the characters of men, of the compositions of genius, and of the productions of the nobler arts.[26]

In this argument, Hume is indirectly making an argument in favour of a special arena for human autonomy: if we cannot control our history fully (those 'good or ill accidents of life'), then at least we can learn how to negotiate terms with it such that it will not throw us into strange fits of passion, for such passion will have been

---

[25] Hume, *Selected Essays*, 10.   [26] Ibid. 11.

accommodated by—and acclimatized to—taste, to the kinds of taste and judgement or response we make to aesthetic objects, such as books or other artistic 'diversion'. The political world—that historical realm of material objects whose very contingency proposes a threat to human mastery or agency—will have been controlled or predetermined to some degree by the aesthetic world, the world in which the human subject does appear to exercise—in and through her or his taste—some high degree of autonomy or mastery.

In early versions of this essay, Hume also inserted a passage in which the 'considerable connexion' between the two forms of delicacy is demonstrated. In the passage, Hume argued that once the taste of *women* is pleased (and, apparently, it is pleased more readily than that of men), then their affections will be more readily engaged. To present oneself 'tastefully' or in a manner liable to stimulate the delicacy of taste positively—that is, beautifully—is to affect the response to oneself in the world of material or real human relations—that is, historically. Leaving aside the question of gender for the moment (to be returned to when I focus on Rousseau below), we can see some clear primary consequences for Hume's logic. Aesthetics, it would follow from his argument, affects—and even *determines*—history; yet Hume excised this passage in later editions of his essays, seemingly unwilling to accept or to face this logical corollary of his own argumentative position.

One passage which does remain in all editions, however, is a passage which is uncannily prescient of the terminology and rhetorical lexicon of a much later figure not usually associated with what we can call an 'agnostic critical disposition', Leavis:

A greater or less relish for those obvious beauties which strike the senses, depends entirely upon the greater or less sensibility of the temper. ... In order to judge aright of a composition of genius, there are so many views to be taken in, so many circumstances to be compared, and such a knowledge of human nature requisite, that no man, who is not possessed of the soundest judgment, will ever make a tolerable critic in such performances. And this is a new reason for cultivating a relish in the liberal arts. Our judgment will strengthen by this exercise. We shall form juster notions of life.[27]

---

[27] Hume, *Selected Essays*, 11–12. It is particularly in the final sentence quoted here that one hears the clearest premonition of Leavis; but the rest of the passage is almost equally transparently a harbinger of the combination of aesthetic or intellectual sensitivity and a strong moral sense that one will find in the twentieth-century's

It is not for nothing that Hugh Macdiarmid, writing in 1962, and seeing then the abiding presence and relevance of Hume, 'undoubtedly the greatest Scotsman of them all', could describe himself as 'struck by how prophetic he was, how up-to-date, how applicable to all that has happened since and is happening now'.[28]

As he pondered further the relation between delicacy of passion and delicacy of taste—between the relative claims of aesthetic judgement (which would be subject to regulation) and of contingency (which would not)—Hume modified his position. Far from curing us of all passion, the cultivation of taste would enable us to enjoy more fully those pleasant and positive passions in a more intense experience of life, with a greater sense of what we might call—after Leavis, of course—the 'felt life' (or, indeed, what we might call—after the Lyotard and the Deleuze of the 1970s—libidinal 'intensities').[29] Such more tender passions are explicitly identified as those associated with love and friendship, or with what Hutcheson (following Shaftesbury) called benevolence and what Rousseau would call *bienfaisance*.

For Hume, such love and friendship is not at all 'social', not concerned with matters of community or with the polity; rather, it is a love or friendship dependent upon judgement, upon making fine, nice discriminations among the many people who could constitute valid objects of our affection such that we will actually narrow down our range of affections, thereby more precisely focusing our love more intensely on one individual or one small number of individuals to the positive *exclusion* of a wider community. He writes:

influential—and extremely 'English'—critic. On the Englishness of Leavis's criticism, see Ch. 7.

    [28] Hugh Macdiarmid, *The Man of (almost) Independent Mind* (Giles Gordon, Edinburgh, 1962), 7, 9. This essay was privately published by Gordon—who had commissioned it for inclusion in the journal *New Saltire*—after Gordon's co-editors had rejected it.

    [29] The work referred to here is, most obviously, Jean-François Lyotard's *Economie libidinale* (Minuit, Paris, 1974), and Gilles Deleuze's work with Felix Guattari, especially the first volume of *Capitalism and Schizophrenia*, the *Anti-Oedipe* (Minuit, Paris, 1972). Both Deleuze and Lyotard wrote out of a frustration at the inefficacy of a contemporary Marxism; and the thrust of my comparison here is intended to suggest that, in their attention to 'intensities', they were re-working the old contest between the claims of reason (as advanced in the scientistic Marxisms they were then rejecting) and those of sense. Lyotard more explicitly still attends to this rehabilitation of sense in his *Discours, figure* (Klincksieck, Paris, 1971). In both cases, an attention is given to the body; and I shall later argue that there is an indebtedness here to Schopenhauer (for which, see Ch. 6).

'a delicacy of taste is favourable to love and friendship by confining our choice to few people, and making us indifferent to the company and conversation of the greater part of men.'[30] Such affection or benevolence, therefore, is here to be aligned with a kind of 'critical election', enabling the evaluation of singularity among the generality of a community. A benevolent attitude *à la Hume*, developed from the cultivation of increasingly sensitive responses to the arts, now becomes a rather more *private* affair than had been anticipated by Shaftesbury or Hutcheson; or, to put this more firmly in the preferred terms of the present study, love for Hume is a matter of singularities in which singularity is marked by the divorce from the social. Humean love—in which aesthetic judgements are mapped onto contingencies of material history—is, paradoxically, a non-social affair.

Yet for Hume, this is certainly not the end of the story. He is not an advocate of those principles that would legitimize the validity of the judgements made about private affections on the purely pragmatic or empirical grounds that people know their own affections and are therefore enacting a truth whenever they state their feelings or act in conformity with them. He would have difficulty in understanding a text that begins by stating that:

My purpose is to display to my kind a portrait in every way true to nature, and the man I shall portray will be myself.

Simply myself. I know my own heart ...[31]

The text, of course, is Rousseau's *Confessions*. For Hume, such private affection as this is tied up intimately with the very sociality it needs to exclude. He comes to a fuller engagement with the problem—the problem, as I have suggested above, constitutive of our very 'modernity' and more generally known in Kantian terms as the problem of how one might legitimate a general judgement from the starting-point of a subjective intense feeling—in his essay 'Of the Rise and Progress of the Arts and Sciences'. In this essay, he begins his meditation from an observation that one must always, in one's thinking, distinguish between the accidental or aleatory on one hand and the determined or caused on the other. This is, of course, already predictive of Kant's famous distinction in the third *Critique* between 'reflective' and 'determining' judgements. Hume's

---

[30] Hume, *Selected Essays*, 12.   [31] Rousseau, *Confessions*, 17.

rather loose rule (to which I have alluded already) is that what is singular is likely to be aleatory, while that which is more general is likely to be determined by comprehensible causes. As he puts it: 'What depends upon a few persons is, in a great measure, to be ascribed to chance, or secret and unknown causes: what arises from a greater number, may often be accounted for by determinate and known causes.'[32] It is important to note, in passing here, that he is not subscribing to any simplistic equation between a sensus communis and truth; rather, he is making it clear that what is held commonly to be the case is susceptible to examination, criticism, and understanding (which will reveal either its truth or its falsity).

He then continues the argument in such a way as effectively to modify it, claiming that those who are gifted in the taste required for the manifestation of an artistic competence are small in number; yet also claiming that it would be an error, despite this fact and despite his rule-of-thumb, to suggest that their being was entirely chance-given, accidental, and not amenable to understanding. In fact, the contrary is the case; for these artists do not live in isolation, but have some (determinate) relation with the masses from whom they distinguish themselves through the exercise of their sensibility: 'The mass cannot be altogether insipid from which such refined spirits are extracted,' he writes.[33] This enables a most significant turn or inflection in the argument, for it follows from this that the discussion of the place of the arts and sciences is not simply a matter regarding personal or individual being or the *Bildung* of individuals; rather, it is a matter concerning a community, and, for Hume, this community is rapidly identified as a *national* community. His essay turns out to be the beginnings of a meditation on national character:

The question, therefore, concerning the rise and progress of the arts and sciences is not altogether a question concerning the taste, genius, and spirit of a few, but concerning those of a whole people, and may therefore be accounted for, in some measure, by general causes and principles. . . . I am persuaded that in many cases good reasons might be given why such a nation is more polite and learned, at a particular time, than any of its neighbours ...[34]

Hume moves rather abruptly, then, from a consideration of sensibility as a marker of individual capacities for human social relations

---

[32] Hume, *Selected Essays*, 56–7.   [33] Ibid. 58–9.   [34] Ibid. 59.

to aesthetic sensibility as a marker of national character. More than this, he constructs a rationale for such national character based upon what can only be called national cultures, about whose differences he writes elsewhere, as when he claims in 'The Sceptic' that 'You will never convince a man, who is not accustomed to ITALIAN music, and has not an ear to follow its intricacies, that a SCOTCH tune is not preferable.'[35]

Once this question of the nation is in place, it follows inexorably that an argument that might have promised the prioritization of aesthetic sensibility as a determinant of political reality should now be reversed; and Hume indeed makes the explicit claim that the flourishing of the arts and sciences is dependent upon the preconditions established by modes of government: the political determines the very possibility of the aesthetic in the first place, in short. Hume argues that people must exist under a 'free government' if the arts and sciences are to flourish. The character of this government is not, as Rousseau might have wished it, republican; rather, and on the contrary, it is for Hume a 'civilized monarchy' that produces the best conditions for the flourishing of the arts and for the healthy development, therefore, of personal (social) character. His logic is simple:

in a republic, the candidates for office must look downwards to gain the suffrages of the people; in a monarchy, they must turn their attention upwards, to court the good graces and favour of the great. To be successful in the former way, it is necessary for a man to make himself *useful* by his industry, capacity, or knowledge: to be prosperous in the latter way, it is requisite for him to render himself *agreeable* by his wit, complaisance, or civility. A strong genius is best in republics; a refined taste in monarchies ...[36]

The civility thus established, however, has its darker and more threatening side. In another prefiguration of Benjamin's seventh thesis to which I have already alluded in the present chapter, Hume shows the ways in which civilization and barbarism are imbricated one with the other:

As nature has given *man* the superiority above *woman*, by endowing him with greater strength both of mind and body, it is his part to alleviate that superiority as much as possible, by the generosity of his behaviour, and by

---

[35] Hume, *Selected Essays*, 98.   [36] Ibid. 68–9.

a studied deference and complaisance for all her inclinations and opinions. Barbarous men display this superiority, by reducing their females to the most abject slavery; by confining them, by beating them, by selling them, by killing them. But the male sex, among a polite people, discover their authority in a more generous, though not less evident manner, by respect, by complaisance, and, in a word, by gallantry.[37]

Gallantry such as this would be seen by the Alceste-like Rousseau as precisely the hypocritical cover of barbarity. The Genevan would see such gallantry as part of the rule-governed theatricalization of everyday life, and as such a clear demonstration and realization of our capacity for distancing ourselves from the hypothetical state of nature. For Hume, though, politeness not only acts as a cover for barbarity, but also effectively marks our social and civilised progress as we move away from those primitive conditions in which violence organizes relations. Art, thus, in the form of the educated sensibility, enables us to progress socially to an ameliorated condition. Further, art deals with violence—and also with the *unpredictability* associated with violence—by the establishment of a new stability based on the acceptance of codes, conventions, regulations; but—and this is the key element in this for Hume—such an artistic sensibility, such an aesthetic, is dependent upon a monarchy, and monarchies are essentially hierarchical. That hierarchy is codified here in terms of a primary hierarchy, based in the body, of gender.

It should now be clear why Hume had to excise the passage in his essay 'Of the Delicacy of Taste and Passion' in which he associates the progressive (or at least remedial) delicacy of taste with women, finding in women a primary identification with such aesthetic sensibility. That argument, as I noted above, would have led Hume to the uncomfortable position in which not only would it be the case that aesthetics determines history, but also—and much more uncomfortably—women would be seen to be the primary agents of such a history, superior in this to men who would thus be relegated to the position of being the Rousseauvian victims of history. Politeness is the key that gives Hume access to what is required for the deconstruction of this relation between the genders. The consequence of the deconstruction, however, is that attention is diverted from the primacy of social relations based on

[37] Ibid. 73–4.

an aesthetic sensibility that would predicate the social as an effect of love or benevolence; and instead, Hume forces a focus on the primacy of the nation state as the determinant of the possibility of aesthetics (and thus implicitly now as the guarantor of security for the potential victims of history, now—courtesy of the deconstruction, or, as we may put it, courtesy of courtesy itself— women rather than men). Women as agents of history sit too comfortably with republicanism or with the questioning of a monarchy and its hierarchies for Hume, for women are too intimately related in this thinking with inexplicability or singularity, and hence with the very unpredictability of time—history—itself. Hume's problem, thus, is that he opens the possibility of a critique in which the human subject can assume a responsibility for its actions and can determine the shape of its history; but that subject is one that is gendered female.

Hence the importance of another excised passage, this time from the essay 'Of the Rise and Progress of the Arts and Sciences'. Hume has just argued the case for gallantry at the core of the social, asking 'What better school for manners than the company of virtuous women' which acts as a guarantor of refinement, education and decorum.[38] Early editions of the essay then add the aside:

> I must confess, that my own choice rather leads me to prefer the company of a few select companions, with whom I can, calmly and peaceably, enjoy the feast of reason, and try the justness of every reflection, whether gay or serious, that may occur to me ...[39]

The deconstruction effected by Hume, in which men swap positions with women as the agents of history, has the corollary effect of shifting attention almost entirely away from gender (and with it the primacy of the aesthetic sensibility as a determinant of the social or of politics) to the issue of the nation-state, an issue that was extremely vibrant in the years after the Act of Union, and which came to a head in the near eradication of all markers of Scottish national character after 1745. When Hume was a candidate for his academic positions, one fear was that his perceived radicalism aligned him with the Jacobites; but Hume's essays give him the chance to demonstrate the contrary.

Hume was very aware of the issues surrounding the descriptions

---

[38] Hume, *Selected Essays*, 74.   [39] Ibid. 353.

of national characters, not only in the seemingly incidental example I have already cited from 'The Sceptic' which asserts that the Scot has difficulty in appreciating Italian music. His interest in the question becomes extremely apparent in his essay 'On Civil Liberty', which seems to organize itself almost entirely around this series of brief caricatural versions of national characters:

the most eminent instance of the flourishing of learning in absolute governments is that of FRANCE, which scarcely ever enjoyed any established liberty, and yet has carried the arts and sciences as near perfection as any other nation. The ENGLISH are, perhaps, greater philosophers; the ITALIANS better painters and musicians; the ROMANS were greater orators; but the FRENCH are the only people, except the GREEKS, who have been at once philosophers, poets, orators, historians, painters, architects, sculptors, and musicians. With regard to the stage, they have excelled even the GREEKS, who far excelled the ENGLISH. And, in common life, they have, in a great measure, perfected that art, the most useful and agreeable of any, *l'Art de vivre*, the art of society and conversation ...[40]

This celebration of diversities between national characters, in which different evaluations of peoples becomes possible, is endorsed in the essay 'On National Character'; but there the argument takes a significantly different turn. Differences in national character exist, he writes, explaining the reasons why he believes that such differences have primarily moral rather than physical causes: a 'sympathy or contagion of manners' within a community—in short, a *sensus communis* based upon mimesis or representation in which the human subject learns to insert herself or himself into the community through (theatrical, ritualized) conformity—establishes a mode of living which establishes a general behaviour for a specific community: and this is national character. Yet, as he ponders this, Hume makes the extraordinary claim that England offers a special case. The characters of governments determine national characters or the typical behaviour of the population (that is again to say that governments determine the very possibility of the existence of an aesthetic sensibility and shape its performance). The English government, however, is rather indeterminate, being 'a mixture of monarchy, aristocracy, and democracy'. It follows from this plurality or diversity, argues Hume, that 'the ENGLISH, of any people in the universe, have the least of a national character, unless this very singularity may pass for such'.[41] That is to say: the English have no national character and, at the same time, their national character is precisely marked by this inexplicability or ineffability, this lack of a determined national character. England thus becomes the degree zero—the *absolute* or *universal* ground or foundation—of the standards of taste and of the standards of civil society: the Scot eliminates Scotland in an act of union complicit with the eradication—or, more precisely, delegitimization—of Scotland as a nation-state; and, of course, as with Scotland, so also with any other nation-state when placed alongside England. England's sensibility becomes the *sensus communis* of the world. (How, we might ask, could the burghers of Edinburgh have been fooled?)

This national standard replaces philosophical standards or foundations for Hume. In his essay 'Of the Standard of Taste', he outlines what is emerging as the fundamental question regarding the legitimizing powers of aesthetic sensibility in the middle of the eighteenth century. That question is one we now know as the great modern question of autonomy: not only how can the subject act *in freedom*, but also how can the subject legitimize her or his action as being consistent with the best interests of a community (even when the community might not appreciate its benefits in the first instance), such that we could legislate to make the action of the subject not just a *fact* but also a *norm*. In short, how can we move from the *fact* that 'I like it' to the *normative validity* of the statement 'and *therefore* you *should* like it'; or, how can the personal *become* the political? How can we legislate for the generality of a community from what is in its essence the singular response of a particular sensibility in a specific situation; and how can we do this while safeguarding the freedom of the subject? The problem is well put when Hume outlines the position against which he will range himself:

The difference, it is said, is very wide between judgement and sentiment. All sentiment is right; because sentiment has a reference to nothing beyond itself, and is always real, wherever a man is conscious of it. But all determinations of the understanding are not right; because they have a reference to something beyond themselves, to wit, real matter of fact; and are not always conformable to that standard.[42]

---

[41] Hume, *Selected Essays*, 119.   [42] Ibid. 136.

This 'principle of the natural equality of tastes' is, of course, forgotten when it suits us: as for example when someone asserts the equality of Ogilby with Milton.[43] As Ferry elegantly phrases it:

Le problème principal de l'esthétique moderne, du début du XVIIe siècle jusqu'à la fin du XIXe, est encore de concilier la subjectivisation du beau (le fait qu'il n'est plus un 'en soi' mais un 'pour nous') avec l'exigence de 'critères', donc d'un rapport à l'objectivité ou, si l'on veut, au monde.[44]

Hume has now found a way out of these troubling difficulties, by reversing the terms of the questions. The 'legitimacy' of the 'non-nation nation-state' gives the norms that explain the specific instances or individual cases (I paint or sing in this way because I *am* Italian; I like this music because I *am* Scottish; and so on). 'England'—in all its semantic vacuity, or foundational inexplicability— becomes normativity for Hume; and the political therefore shapes the personal. This is at once both his radicalism (in which he foreshadows Marx), yet also his conservatism (for the normative politics he legitimizes in his writings is that of the hierarchical monarchy which wards off the threats of historical change proposed by the feminine aesthetic sensibility, or love).

Hume is thus forced into a rather restrictive position. Sensibility, if fully exercised, might become a democratizing force; but that would go hand-in-glove with the disruption of the 'natural' order of things in which men were superior to women or in which hierarchies were firmly established. Hume the conservative does not want this, yet does not want either to abandon the aesthetic. The consequence is that for Hume, the aesthetic becomes a force which contributes to the happiness of the individual within an already established polity: the enhancement or cultivation of sensibility will make us more alive to the pleasures and joys to be experienced under a civilized monarchy. By extension, as my argument has shown, the aesthetic also becomes a *consolation* for those (Scots and subsequently other victims of English imperialist nationalism) whose national character lacks the normative force of 'England'. As Benjamin was much later to put it:

Fascism attempts to organize the newly created proletarian masses without affecting the property structure which the masses strive to eliminate.

---

[43] Ibid. 137.
[44] Luc Ferry, *Homo Aestheticus l'invention du goût à l'age démocratique* (Grasset, Paris, 1990), 20.

Fascism sees its salvation in giving these masses not their right, but instead a chance to express themselves.[45]

The relation of the aesthetic to democracy in Hume is one in which the varieties of alterity (the different cultures of the non-English world) are equal in their subservience to the normativity of an English 'civilized monarchy'. Republicans, Jacobins, Jacobites might want a different politics or a different history; Hume allows them their artful expressions of this desire. Hume's astute establishment of a norm where there was only a fact (the English monarchy as a foundational standard) actually forestalls the movement of history itself. This is Hume's own 'state of nature'.

III

They organize these matters differently in France, however. In that 'state of culture' much admired by Hume, the *Encyclopédie* was beginning to attract its own version of the polite audience. At this same time, Rousseau was also beginning to find his voice, and his audience; or, as we might now put it, he was beginning to construct a community responsive to his expressly occasional writings. In 1750, he responded to the Académie de Dijon—when the question *mise au concours* was 'Si le rétablissement des sciences et des arts a contribué à épurer les mœurs'—by writing his first great essay, the *Discours sur les sciences et les arts*. The great success of this paper, the polemical response to which legitimized Rousseau's name as a powerful authority, encouraged Rousseau to write his next work, the *Discours sur l'origine et les fondements de l'inégalité parmi les hommes*, again prompted by the Académie de Dijon, although this time Rousseau was rather contemptuous of the technical requirements of the *concours*.

In these great discourses, in which Rousseau begins to articulate what is to become his avowedly 'democratic' cultural theory, he finds an abiding problem for human society of what we should now call 'theatricality'. For the social as we know it to exist at all, 'politeness' appears to be required; but for Rousseau, it is in such politeness that we see the emergence of an insincerity in human

---

[45] Benjamin, 'The Work of Art in the Age of Mechanical Reproduction', in *Illuminations*, 243.

relations, and, more importantly, a dissociation of the subject from itself: a state of affairs we have since learnt to think of in terms of the Eliotic 'dissociation of sensibility' (though the difference between Rousseau and Eliot on this is substantial).[46] In such a dissociation, it is not simply the case that the subject is able to watch herself or himself 'at a distance', as if the subject exists like some puppet-master pulling the strings of a Lacanian mannequin whose function is to represent the subject there where she or he is not (although this is a more or less adequate description of what Eliot had in mind when he 'invented' this dissociation). More telling than this is the fact that for Rousseau, such a dissociation of the subject with respect to itself introduces into the very constitution of the subject a *temporal* difference or distance, such that the being of the subject is now marked by temporality rather than by the essentially timeless continuous present tense of existence in a state of nature. The subject-in-time (a *sujet-en-procès*, as Kristeva will much later formulate this[47]) is one which cannot actually sensibly experience anything: its very interior temporality effects a rupture in the 'now' such that the subject can never be found *in* a present moment. Politeness, it follows, might be necessary for the social; but it denies the possibility of experience *of* that very social in the first place. The social is thus an empty space, surrounded by now vacuous subjects (subjects whose condition is that they are continuously 'becoming') in search of a being.

Politeness, for Rousseau, then, is a form of 'technology', with mechanistic rules that have to be learnt and codified (a mode of living, therefore, subject to 'mechanical reproduction' through a theatrical rehearsal of conventions); and although such technology might bring what we call civilization, it also weakens the human subject and leaves her or him increasingly dependent upon the technologies which she or he has invented. Better, according to Rousseau, 'de se porter . . . toujours tout entier avec soi'.[48]

---

[46] On the 'dissociation of sensibility', see T. S. Eliot, 'The Metaphysical Poets', in *Selected Essays* (3rd edn., 1951; repr. Faber and Faber, 1980), 287–8. See also below, Ch. 6, in which I align Schiller with the idea of such a dissociation. In an earlier study, I have aligned this concept with an exploration of irony in de Man's most celebrated essay, 'The Rhetoric of Temporality'. See Thomas Docherty, *After Theory* (Edinburgh University Press, Edinburgh, 1996), ch. 4.

[47] This concept appears early in Julia Kristeva's work, and yields its greatest fruit in the much later study of Proust, *Proust et le temps sensible* (nrf, Gallimard, Paris, 1994). [48] Rousseau, *Écrits politiques*, 81.

In these two great discourses, we can see already a logic that is steadily driving Rousseau to write his polemical *Lettre sur les spectacles* against d'Alembert (and behind d'Alembert, Voltaire), such that the ostensibly personalist aspect of his break with Hume will take on a more philosophical cast and find its rational foundation. As Rousseau writes his way towards his avowedly 'democratic' cultural theory in the articles of the 1750s, he begins to articulate an argument that sees theatricality—even representation— as an abiding problem in human social and cultural affairs. The logic, however, is only rather shakily forming itself; and is therefore not entirely straightforward, hence requiring some consideration here.

For Rousseau, there is a fundamental contradiction at the very heart of the social itself. He asserts the primacy of ethics as a kind of foundational philosophy, proposing that a sentimental ethics is anterior to all reason, ranging himself explicitly against Hobbes in this.[49] Having looked at the disagreements among the scholars regarding the question of fundamental human rights, and seeing the confusion that seems to reign among ancient and modern thinkers alike on the question of the foundation of the social, Rousseau decides to leave all scholarship aside:

Laissant donc tous les livres scientifiques qui ne nous apprennent qu'à voir les hommes tels qu'ils se sont faits, et méditant sur les premières et plus simples opérations de l'âme humaine, j'y crois apercevoir deux principes antérieures à la raison, dont l'un nous intéresse ardemment à notre bien-être et à la conservation de nous-mêmes, et l'autre nous inspire une répugnance naturelle à voir périr ou souffrir tout être sensible et principalement nos semblables.[50]

The tactic deployed by Rousseau here, of ostensibly abandoning the best that has been thought and said on a subject, should not in fact be very shocking by this point in European cultural history, for it is a cliché whose roots lie at least as far back as the late European Renaissance. The poetic trope that evokes sincerity, as in Sidney's closing line in the first sonnet of *Astrophil and Stella*, ' "Fool," said my muse to me; "look in thy heart and write" ' is already even at

---

[49] See Rousseau, *Écrits politiques*, 99–100. One should recall here Derrida's argument, in *Of Grammatology* (1967; trans. Gayatri Chakravorty Spivak; Johns Hopkins University Press, Baltimore, 1974), 172–3. There, Derrida argues (in his best scholarly fashion) that Rousseau's 'Essay on the Origin of Languages' pre-dates the Second Discourse, where pity—as an ethics—is not quite so primary.

[50] Rousseau, *Écrits politiques*, 69.

that time a cliché in poetry; and its philosophical equivalent is none other than Descartes's abandonment of scholarship to rest his philosophy upon what can be derived immediately from the contents of his own consciousness. By the age of Rousseau, it certainly does not designate sincerity; rather, it demonstrates the mastery of a rhetoric, an ability to imitate and to write by the conventional rules—an ability to *pose*, somewhat theatrically—and it is already, therefore, a tactic which calls into question precisely the sincerity it is supposed to establish.[51]

Further, the ethical foundation as it is proposed by Rousseau for human being is not itself entirely novel. In its attention to the intimacy felt between the self and its other, and most specifically the other who is 'mon semblable—mon frère', it is an attitude that we have seen already in the tragic theory of Corneille: the second instance, therefore, of theatricality in a writing that is attempting to eschew theatre in favour of direct self-expression. Not only all this, but the primacy of this ethic advocated by Rousseau depends, vitally, upon access to a state of nature which we no longer have:

ce n'est pas une légère entreprise de démêler ce qu'il y a d'originaire et d'artificiel dans la nature actuelle de l'homme, et de bien connaître un état qui n'existe plus, qui n'a peut-être point existé, qui probablement n'existera jamais, et dont il est pourtant nécessaire d'avoir des notions justes pour bien juger de notre état présent.[52]

When Rousseau himself acknowledges that this state of nature might never have any real existence, past or future, he is acknowledging that it is at best a myth and at worst a theatrical model that will allow for sure judgement by establishing normative standards against which we can measure our present predicaments: a third theatricalisation, therefore, threatening the purity of his sincerity. What is lamented in all of this is the lack of that which we can *imagine* once having: the transparent relations of human to human in a simple state of nature:

Avant que l'art n'eût façonné nos manières et appris à nos passions à parler une langage apprêté, nos mœurs étaient rustiques, mais naturelles; et la différence des procédés annonçait au premier coup d'œil celle des caractères. La

---

[51] See Philip Sidney, *Selected Poems*, ed. Katherine Duncan-Jones (Clarendon Press, Oxford, 1973), 117. On sincerity, see what is still the most interesting study: Lionel Trilling, *Sincerity and Authenticity* (Oxford University Press, Oxford, 1972),
[52] Rousseau, *Écrits politiques*, 66–7.

nature humaine, au fond, n'était pas meilleure; mais les hommes trouvaient leur sécurité dans la facilité de se pénétrer réciproquement, et cet avantage, dont nous ne sentons plus le prix, leur épargnait bien des vices.[53]

Given the impossibility of transparency in anything other than an imagined community, the yet more fundamental issue for Rousseau is the very theatricality he requires to formulate his position of non-posturing sincerity or integrity, a theatricality whose irruption into his discourse establishes a distinction between *être* and *paraître* precisely at the moment when his discourses are ostensibly claiming a self-presence of *être*.

The determination 'to be' rather than 'to appear' (or not to be) in Rousseau may be surprising in a character who described himself as a man modelled on fictions. Rousseau is a prime example of the malady that Flaubert was to analyse much later in his Emma Bovary, or that Jane Austen was to satirize in *Northanger Abbey*. By his own admission in the *Confessions*, Rousseau was formed by the novels left to him by his mother and which he read avidly as a child. As Starobinski puts it, 'Sans doute n'est-il pas sans importance que la conscience de soi date pour Jean-Jacques de sa rencontre avec la "littérature".'[54] Working from this insight, Starobinski is able to discover a certain theatricality or romanticization in Rousseau's relations with Hume.

In Rousseau's bizarre account of his relations with Hume, he tells of Hume staring fixedly and silently at him with a gaze that evokes a terror:

As we were sitting one evening, after supper, silent by the fire-side, I caught his eyes intently fixed on mine, as indeed happened very often; and that in a manner of which it is very difficult to give an idea; at that time he gave me a stedfast, piercing look, mixed with a sneer, which greatly disturbed me. To get rid of the embarrassment I lay under, I endeavoured to look full at him in my turn; but, in fixing my eyes against his, I felt the most inexpressible terror, and was obliged soon to turn them away. The speech and physiognomy of the good David is that of an honest man; but where, great God! Did this good man borrow those eyes he fixes so sternly and unaccountably on those of his friends![55]

The scene is uncannily prefigurative of Hogg in Rousseau's account; and it is related, by Rousseau, to his further anecdote

53 Rousseau, *Écrits politiques*, 27.
54 Starobinski, *Jean-Jacques Rousseau*, 17.
55 Rousseau, in *A Concise and Genuine Account*, 52–3.

about Hume's dream in which Rousseau overhears the 'four terri-fying words' spoken by Hume in his sleep: 'Je tiens J-J Rousseau'. The fixed stare provokes Rousseau to an overwhelming emotion, however, and one in which he feels intense remorse at thinking ill of Hume:

Bientôt un violent remords me gagne; je m'indigne de moi-même; enfin, dans un transport que je me rappelle encore avec délices, je m'élance à son cou, je le serre étroitement; suffoqué de sanglots, inondé de larmes, je m'écrie d'une voix entrecoupée: Non, non, David Hume n'est pas un traître; s'il n'était le meilleur des hommes, il faudrait qu'il en fut le plus noir ...[56]

As Starobinski points out, this description of the scene between Hume and Rousseau is uncannily similar to that in which Saint-Preux begs pardon from Milord Edouard in *Julie; ou la Nouvelle Héloïse*:

Imaginez en quel état je me trouvais après cette lecture, qui m'apprît les bienfaits inouis de celui que j'osais calomnier avec tant d'indignité. Je me précipitai à ses pieds: et, le cœur chargé d'admiration, de regret et de honte, je serrais ses genoux de toute ma force sans pouvoir proférer un seul mot.[57]

Rousseau's clearest literary antecedent, however, is Molière's Alceste. It will be recalled from Chapter 2 that Alceste takes his desire for truth and sincere integrity to the extreme point where he is prepared to lose a judgement in court, and thus to the point where his integrity will lead to his very disintegration. Set that against the passage in the *Confessions* in which Rousseau describes his situation when facing the possibility of a court-action over *Émile*. Madame de Boufflers, who tried to mediate between Rousseau and Hume and to persuade Rousseau to flee to England, points out to him that if he stays and is arrested and interrogated, he will have to mention his relations with Madame de Luxembourg. He ought therefore to think carefully about his deci-sion so as not to have to do anything that would risk compromis-ing the reputation of Madame de Luxembourg. Rousseau recounts this in the following terms:

[56] Ibid. 54; cf. 78; also cited by Starobinski, in *Jean-Jacques Rousseau*, 163.
[57] Rousseau, *Julie; ou la Nouvelle Héloïse* ed. Michel Launay (Garnier-Flammarion, Paris, 1967), 154.

I replied that she could be confident that under such circumstances I should never compromise Madame. She answered that such a resolution was more easily made than carried out. And there she was right, especially in my case, since I was quite determined never to perjure myself or to lie to the judges, however dangerous it might be to speak the truth.[58]

In this situation, Rousseau establishes, like Alceste, a specific relation to truth, the paradox of which is that the absolute identification with truth is based upon a pose or a posture—a mere representation—of integrity. Truth is seen as a danger to the self, but a danger which is to be welcomed by the self; for if the self survives the telling of truth, its integrity is secure and standfast, and thus a normative standard against which to measure all that is external to the self, all otherness or alterity. Paradoxically, thus, to speak the truth in such a way as to allow for the explosive revelatory power of truth, one must actually lie. This is the case not just in the banal sense that, for example, for the basic trope of the *Confessions* actually to *work* in his text, Rousseau has implicitly (and, on many occasions explicitly) to assert that what we thought was truth before was actually lies, revealed now as such even to the shame of Rousseau himself (but this self-shaming acts, of course, as further testimony to an essential and stable truth at the core of Rousseau's self: when he was living, he was in a state of 'becoming', permeated with lies; now that he writes, he is in a state of 'being', flush with truth). It is so also in a more serious sense: presence—the *être* desired by Rousseau—requires, as I have argued above, representation—the *paraître* which is always at odds with *être* and which threatens its integrity with dissociation; and for representation to be mimetically adequate, it must be absolutely 'singular', a representation of some single entity in all its *thisness*; which means, in turn, that it cannot be anything that is *recognizable* as a representative case of something more general, and is therefore *necessarily* a *misrepresentation*—a lie. Truth, therefore, is lies for Rousseau. To put this less extremely, we might say that as with Alceste, the standards of truth are measured and quantified in terms so extreme that not only the self but also truth itself is threatened: it is almost a homage to the absoluteness of truth to claim that its revelation will threaten pain or even threaten the very existence of the self at

---

[58]   Rousseau, *Confessions*, 534.

all as a unified (integrated) being, a being capable of speaking truth at all.[59]

In Rousseau, there is an opposition set up between speech and action, in which action is seen as the repository or as the sign of genuine truth, while speech is the arena in which lies, vacillation, instability and uncertainty can operate. Action operates in the realm of being: it is transparent, in that its 'value' is immediately self-evidencing. Speech, on the other hand, is the arena in which the Rousseauvian subject finds itself marked by the temporal predicaments of becoming: here it is axiomatic that value cannot be self-evidencing, for the ontological value of some entity or action evidences itself not through itself but precisely through another medium entirely, that of language. Action, we might say, is 'singular'; speech is inherently representational or theatrical in that it involves a doubling and thus a potential duplicity: action is 'natural' in its self-presencing, whereas speech is temporal.

A fuller understanding of this situation requires an investigation into Rousseau's attitudes to language itself. In what follows, I shall take for read Derrida's work in *Of Grammatology*, concentrating attention here specifically on the attitude to the origins of language as expressed in the second *Discours*. There, Rousseau claims that the first language is some kind of 'cri de la nature';[60] and from this observation there follows an imitative or mimetic theory of language in which the speaker tries to accommodate the world outside the self by a language emanating from inside which somehow represents that world. The consequence of this is, unsurprisingly, a form of nominalism; but what is of interest for my present argument is that this nominalism expresses a specific attitude to singularity:

Chaque objet reçut d'abord un nom particulier, sans égard aux genres, et aux espèces, que ces premiers instituteurs n'étaient pas en état de distinguer; et tous les individus se présentèrent isolés à leur esprit, comme ils le sont dans le tableau de la nature. Si un chêne s'appelait A, un autre chêne s'appelait B: de sorte que plus les connaissances étaient bornées, et plus le dictionnaire devînt étendu ...[61]

---

59 On this relation of truth to pain, see Hans Blumenberg, *The Legitimacy of the Modern Age* (trans. Robert M. Wallace; MIT Press, Cambridge, Mass., 1983), 404.

60 Rousseau, *Écrits politiques*, 93.   61 Ibid. 94.

In short, the speaker in the state of nature described here has a rather schizophrenic attitude to the world of exteriority. Living in what is effectively a timeless condition of the continuous present tense, the speaker is able to experience everything intensely and transparently: for this subject, speech *is* action and all speaking is conditioned as a proto-Austinian performative. The language in question would be extremely odd, for it would have to be one which was constructed almost entirely of neologisms: every new experience would require the invention of more vocabulary. This speaker is also unable to reflect on any experience that she or he undergoes, to know it *as* an experience, to codify it through an act of memoration which would be precisely a comparison allowing the *temporal distance* between two experiences to be eliminated. Memory—denied in this hypothesis—is an act which serves to homogenize that which is ostensibly heterogeneous, or to find uniformity amidst variety, as Hutcheson would have put it. If metaphor can be defined in the manner of Ricardou, as the shortest distance between two points, then, in the state of nature, and due to the fact that there can be here no memory, there is also no metaphor:

Toute idée générale est purement intellectuelle; pour peu que l'imagination s'en mêle, l'idée devient aussitôt particulière. Essayez de vous tracer l'image d'un arbre en général, jamais vous n'en viendrez à bout, malgré vous il faudra le voir petit ou grand, rare ou touffu, clair ou foncé, et s'il dépendait de vous de n'y voir que ce qui se trouve en tout arbre, cette image ne ressemblerait plus à un arbre. Les êtres purement abstraits se voient de même, ou ne se conçoivent que par le discours.[62]

In the state of nature, representation itself is impossible for the simple reason that insofar as something is natural at all, it is purely present and therefore purely singular; its condition is one to be described by Rosset much later as 'idiotic'. Baldly stated, Rosset's theory of *L'Objet singulier* states that an object is real insofar as it is unamenable to duplication: singularity (and therefore unconscionability) guarantees the reality of such-and-such an object *as*

---

[62] Rousseau, *Ecrits politiques*, 95. For the description of metaphor alluded to here, see Jean Ricardou, *Nouveaux problèmes du roman* (Seuil, Paris, 1978), 106; and cf. Ricardou, *Problèmes du nouveau roman* (Seuil, Paris, 1967), 134, where he had already described metaphor in terms of *exoticism*, the bringing together of an elsewhere with a here.

such.[63] In the terms of a thinker closer to the core of the present chapter, Benjamin states that 'language communicates itself'; for Benjamin, the singularity aimed at in this relation between language and entities depends upon an understanding of the proper name, which he describes as 'the point where human language participates most intimately in the divine infinity of the pure word, the point at which it cannot become finite word and knowledge':

The theory of proper names is the theory of the frontier between finite and infinite language. ... By giving names, parents dedicate their children to God; the names they give do not correspond—in a metaphysical rather than etymological sense—to any knowledge, for they name newborn children. In a strict sense, no name ought (in its etymological meaning) to correspond to any person, for the proper name is the word of God in human sounds. By it each man is guaranteed his creation by God, and in this sense he is himself creative, as is expressed by mythological wisdom in the idea (which doubtless not infrequently comes true) that a man's name is his fate. ... Through the word, man is bound to the language of things. The human word is the name of things. Hence, it is no longer conceivable, as the bourgeois view of language maintains, that the word has an accidental relation to its object, that it is a sign for things (or knowledge of them) agreed by some convention. Language never gives *mere* signs. However, the rejection of the bourgeois linguistic theory by mystical linguistic theory likewise rests on a misunderstanding. For according to mystical theory, the word is simply the essence of the thing. That is incorrect, because the thing in itself has no word, being created from God's word and known in its name by a human word.[64]

Benjamin, in this unpublished piece from 1916, trashes what was happening in Saussure's lectures in Geneva immediately prior to his writing, describing the kinds of position outlined in the *Cours de linguistique générale* (though not the hypogrammatic thought of Saussure's less celebrated or well-known—but much more interesting—work, presented by Starobinski as *Les Mots sous les mots*) as 'bourgeois' linguistics; but, perhaps more importantly for our present purposes, he also establishes a fundamental distinction between

---

[63] See Clément Rosset, *L'Objet singulier* (Minuit, Paris, 1979). It is worth comparing this with the Lacanian notions of the 'Real' as they are deployed in the work of Slavoj Žižek, especially in *The Sublime Object of Ideology* (Verso, 1989), and *Looking Awry* (MIT Press, Cambridge, Mass., 1991).

[64] Walter Benjamin, *Selected Writings*, vol. 1: 1913–1926, ed. Marcus Bullock and Michael W. Jennings (Belknap Press of Harvard University Press, Cambridge, Mass., 1996), 63, 69.

word and name which is germane to Rousseau's description of language in the state of nature. For it is becoming clear that for Rousseau, nature is somehow mute: its 'language' is akin to this 'naming'. As Benjamin puts it:

In name, the word of God has not remained creative; it has become in one part receptive, even if receptive to language. Thus fertilized, it aims to give birth to the language of things themselves, from which in turn, soundlessly, in the mute magic of nature, the word of God shines forth.[65]

Rousseau's 'truth' is precisely this emanation of the word of God in a 'mute magic'. For Rousseau, the state of nature would preclude the possibility of our ever comparing similars in order to establish types; and thus, in a state of nature, it is equally impossible for a subject to 'single out' one experience as the best or worst 'of its kind', for there simply are no 'kinds': singularity in the state of nature is non-evaluative.

The situation is altogether different in the sphere of the social, for sociality—talking together—depends precisely upon establishing the primacy of the Benjaminian 'word' over the 'name'. The social is that condition in which the human subject finds herself or himself 'located', first of all in a discursive situation, with regard to other subjects or with regard to alterity as such. Further, the subject is temporally dissociated from herself or himself: non-self-evidencing and dependent upon language and all its temporal conditions. That is to say that the social is that state of affairs in which all is not presence, but rather representation; and within representation, *paraître* supersedes and even controverts *être*.

Quite obviously, this fundamental discrepancy that exists between appearing and being for Rousseau rapidly becomes an issue not just of truth-telling but also of the justice associated with it (as we have already seen when Rousseau describes himself as being in danger of compromising Mme de Luxembourg in a court of law). In a famous reading of Rousseau, Starobinski takes an early example from the *Confessions* to demonstrate the link between theatricality and justice. In Book 1, Rousseau describes the false accusation leveled at him for breaking a comb belonging to Mlle Lambercier. He had been left alone in a room in which Mlle Lambercier had left her combs to dry; and when she returned, she saw that one of the combs had been

---

[65] Benjamin, *Selected Writings*, 69.

broken. As Rousseau himself readily concedes, no one else had been in the room other than him in the interim; and yet it was not broken by him. What we would call 'circumstantial evidence' (and what is taken here for self-evidencing)—and what Rousseau thought of as 'appearances' (*paraître*)—condemns him, and he is severely punished for the action which he swears he did not commit. He appears culpable, yet he is innocent: 'En même temps que se révèle confusément la déchirure ontologique de l'être et du paraître, voici que le mystère de l'injustice se fait intolérablement sentir à cet enfant.'[66] According to the analysis given by Starobinski, this is a formative episode for Rousseau: 'Qu'être et paraître se fassent deux, qu'un "voile" dissimule les vrais sentiments, tel est le scandale initial auquel Rousseau se heurte.'[67] Appearance (or aesthetics)—with which Rousseau associates representation, speech and theatricality—becomes a matter of critical judgement or justice (or politics); and the personal realm of factual subjective experience becomes thus the political realm of objective normativity, but crucially, the truth of the personal does not necessarily ground the political in truth. Aesthetic truth does not necessarily generate political truth or justice; and in fact, it may serve to do precisely the opposite and to generate injustice.

Given this initial injustice, we must ask how judgement itself is possible when, for Rousseau, a proper or adequate justice depends upon that which we do not have: the very transparency that would make justice and proper judgement—truth—self-evidencing (and therefore redundant). The loss of transparency goes along with this fissure between being and appearing; and Rousseau is suspicious of how the former—almost necessarily—deviates into the latter when we organize ourselves as speaking beings, as sociable. He knows that the social depends precisely upon that mode of language which, far from granting access to a self-evident truth, actually generates what Rousseau's great predecessor, Bouhours (long before Derrida) called 'undecidability'.[68]

[66] Starobinski, *Jean-Jacques Rousseau*, 19.   [67] Ibid. 15–16.

[68] On Bouhours and these problems of language, see Luc Ferry, *Homo Aestheticus*, 58. Bouhours, according to Ferry, praises equivocation ' "comme ces voiles transparents qui laissent voir ce qu'ils couvrent, ou comme des habits de masques sous lesquels on reconnaît la personne qui est déguisée" '—a formulation that begs to be recollected whenever we discuss Molière's *Le Bourgeois gentilhomme*, as in my discussion in Ch. 2. Ferry goes on: 'ce qui plaît dans l'équivocité, c'est justement qu'en elle il est un "reste" à jamais insaisissable par l'entendement', a formulation that suggests a link between equivocation and the sublime, rather than the beautiful.

As Ferry puts this, the emergence of the aesthetic sensibility in the eighteenth century leads to an interlinking set of problems. First, how do we judge of taste? If by reason, then we get the reduction of beauty to a purely epistemological category: the beautiful becomes simply a sensible representation of a truth potentially expressible in other ways; and the aesthetic loses its specificity. If we judge by sentiment, then we lose the principle of objectivity which would allow us to legitimize our judgements. There is thus a conflict, and:

les deux questions qu'il pose—celle de l'autonomie de l'esthétique comme discipline nouvelle, différente de la logique, et celle des critères de goût—renvoient au fond à un unique problème: celui de la communicabilité de l'éxperience esthétique en tant qu'expérience subjective, purement individuelle et cependant accessible à autrui sur le mode d'un 'sens commun', d'un *partage* que rien, semble-t-il, ne vient *a priori* garantir.[69]

Rousseau's preference, in this situation, is for a justice based upon the ethical priority of action (the ethics of which situates the action as one involving at least two subjects, and is therefore expressly a social priority), and specifically, of the actions of *pity*.

Judith Still, writing after Derrida, reveals what is at stake in Rousseau's pity as an ethical foundation of the social. Pity, she notes, is stimulated in Rousseau by spectacle (or what I call here theatricality); and she indicates the very noticeable prevalence of verbs concerned with vision in Rousseau's writings on the matter.[70] For present purposes, this simply demonstrates the centrality of theatricality to Rousseau's thinking—despite himself. Still explains the workings of pity and its usefulness in the social context: 'Pity works for the good of mankind not only by inspiring beneficence, but also by channeling energy away from amorous passion. Both pity and amorous passion are forms of self-love directed onto the

---

[69] Ferry, *Homo Aestheticus*, 52.
[70] See Judith Still, *Justice and Difference in the Works of Rousseau: Bienfaisance and Pudeur* (Cambridge University Press, Cambridge, 1993). Partly, this interest in the visual is to be expected (although Still does not comment on this) in a writing that takes its place alongside those meditations on the condition of consciousness that surround Rousseau at this time. The general debate is stimulated most directly by Diderot's *Lettre sur les aveugles* in 1749; and the argument takes the form of a debate over the whole concept of empirical sensibility. Interestingly, the debate has its more recent contributors, such as Derrida in his *Mémoires d'aveugle*.

other.'[71] Pity exists in a complex and competitive relation with love, then; but the situation is more complex than this at first suggests. Still, following Starobinski, sees Rousseau as a precursor of Freudian thinking in that he establishes a paradox in which the persistence of love is dependent upon obstacles to its progress:

Relations between the sexes are, for Rousseau, inaugurated with amorous passion and unthinkable without amorous passion. Only a shield (pudicity) can prevent the dire consequences of passion unleashed, amongst which perhaps the worst consequence is the death of passion and hence of sexual relations. Pudicity seeks to repeat, with regard to men and women, the original dispersion of humans: it keeps men and women apart. But it allows sociability among men (such as Emile and his tutor), and amongst women in their families.[72]

Clearly, there is a link here to the thinking of Hume, for whom woman seemed to act as some kind of threat to a masculine agency in history, requiring Hume to make his two interlinking moves: first, a deconstruction of the relations between men and women such that women are seen as the victims of a history which they threaten to enact, and men now become the agents; and second, an establishment of the priority of the nation-state (and the consequent establishment of England as a degree-zero of such nationality) as a determinant of action. For Rousseau, the social itself is a displaced sexuality or a displacement of ('pitiful') love; and hence is dependent upon a sexual difference that seems to trouble him. The fundamental conception of that sexual difference in Rousseau is one which depends upon an understanding—as in Hume—of gender and time, but in Rousseau with the added complication of the equalities or inequalities that would act as a spur or as an obstacle to democracy.[73]

I suggested above that there are at least two different kinds of

[71] Still, *Justice and Difference*, 82.
[72] Ibid. 10.
[73] On the centrality of gender to these questions of democracy, see esp. Alain Touraine, *Qu'est-ce que la démocratie?* (Fayard, Paris, 1994), 225-7. He writes there that 'La démocratie est impossible si un acteur s'identifie à la rationalité universelle et réduit les autres à la défense de leur identité particulière' (225); but this is precisely what has tended to happen in the establishment of the modern 'democracies' (now not at all democratic, or at least lacking in adequate legitimacy) when we operate according to a reason in which the male participant acts in the public sphere where he supposedly represents universal reason, while the female has to 'defend a particular identity'.

singularity operative in Rousseau's writings. The first, already discussed, is that singularity that exists in the continuous present tense—the schizophrenic intensity—of the state of nature. The second (the more important for our present argument) is that which exists within the social, and which is called into being by pity. Still indicates three stages of pity in Rousseau: (1) animal pity, which is the fundamentally acceptable instinct of self-preservation 'extended to other sentient beings'; (2) the 'devenir-humain de la pitié' (Derrida's words), which involves the capacity for reflection, for comparison, and for putting oneself in the place of the suffering other; (3) a fully social version of pity, in which pity itself is codified into morality, established through regulations which control the various performances of beneficence or what Shaftesbury and Hutcheson had thought of as benevolence.[74]

There is obviously a big difference between the most basic version of pity here (animal pity) and the two other more developed forms. The 'devenir-humain de la pitié' involves what I have already described as the 'tragic consciousness' in and through which the subject is able to see itself displaced into a representation in another subject, as in Cornelian tragedy. In Rousseau's terms, it involves a dissociation of the subject from itself, but a dissociation which is understood primarily in terms of a spatial displacement (seeing oneself represented in another person, a person whose mirroring representation of the self establishes a spatial distance between self and image). It is in the third stage of pity, the social stage, that we see the emergence of the real problem and issue for Rousseau, for it is in social pity that the subject is dissociated from itself in *temporal* terms, becoming a subject whose intrinsic nature is determined by abstract codes and regulations and not by any felt intensity of experience itself.

This third stage of pity can be explained partly by Rousseau's conception of love. Love, it turns out, is antipathetic to the conditions governing democracy, for love will be seen to be a major determinant cause of the inequalities that shape a society divorced from the state of nature. Love, as the capacity which enables the subject to discriminate among a community of similars in order to 'single out' one preferred object-choice, is the necessary precondition for the establishment of inequality within the social: in short,

---

[74] Still, *Justice and Difference*, 86–9.

it gives the wrong sort of singularity. Rousseau makes a distinction between physical love and moral love, the former of which is broadly compatible with 'animal pity', the latter of which is more akin to 'social pity':

Le physique est ce désir général qui porte un sexe à s'unir à l'autre, le moral est ce qui détermine ce désir et le fixe sur un seul objet exclusivement, ou qui du moins lui donne pour cet objet préféré un plus grand degré d'énergie. Or, il est facile de voir que le moral de l'amour est un sentiment factice; né de l'usage de la société, et célébré par les femmes avec beaucoup d'habilité et de soin pour établir leur empire, et rendre dominant le sexe qui devrait obéir.[75]

That moral love, in singularizing its object, is factitious, requires explanation; but the explanation has in a sense been already given in Rousseau's attitude to the origins of language and the singularity of being. The state of nature knows no comparisons, for, being based on a language which is entirely 'singular', or on a somatic relation to the world which is entirely rendered in a continuous present tense and in experience, it precludes the possibility of a subject ever representing to herself or himself any experience at all: in nature, one has experience, but cannot know it, cannot be dissociated from it. Transparency precludes love, we might say. It is only in the deviation from that state into the state of the social or of culture—we might now say into language itself—that representation (or theatricality) becomes at once necessary to—and yet simultaneously rejected by—Rousseau. Language—speech itself—becomes the obstacle between the subject and experience: it thereby renders the subject's desire for experience all the more intense, while constantly distancing the subject from precisely the experience of alterity that the subject so desires. Rousseau here not only prefigures the Eliot who says that 'I gotta use words when I talk to you' and who thinks of poetry as an 'intolerable wrestle with words and meanings', but also—and more pointedly—Beckett for whom 'I can't go on, I must go on, I'll go on' in a writing which uses language in order to search for a specific kind of silence or muteness.[76]

---

[75] Rousseau, *Écrits politiques*, 103.
[76] See T. S. Eliot, 'Four Quartets', in *Complete Poems and Plays* (Faber and Faber, 1969), 179; cf. Samuel Beckett, *Molloy, Malone Dies, The Unnamable* (John Calder, 1959; repr.1976), 418. On the paradoxical desperation of this condition, and for a work almost entirely founded in its pain, see Cioran *Œuvres* (Gallimard,

Once again, as in Hume, gender seems to be exerting a pressure on Rousseau's philosophy. In Hume, it led to a deconstruction and to the emergence of nationalism as a foundation for aesthetic sensibilities and their legitimization. In Rousseau, something slightly different happens, and woman—as a desired sexual object—becomes (at least tacitly) stigmatized as a kind of obstacle to republican equality. In the state of Rousseauvian nature, amorous passion is a matter of coupling and nothing more. In the social state of culture, however, where representation reigns over presence and where appearance controverts being, things are ordered differently. In the social, we live in and through a language that generates the necessity of that very abstract thinking the lack of which marks the state of nature and its mute magic. Thus, when Rousseau describes moral love as that kind of love which singles out a preferred object, he is describing a love that must of necessity be debased or factitious (and hence insincere) inasmuch as it is not founded in experience but in abstraction or reason. Instead of regarding different desired objects as simply A and B (as with oaks in the state of nature), the subject now regards A and B as two versions of the same, and can thus compare them with each other to establish a preference; but such a comparison has the necessary corollary that the subject who makes the comparison is temporally disjunctive with regard to itself: it is a subject-in-time, a subject not given to itself in a continuous presence but rather in a continual series of present moments or, in a word, given to itself in *representation* only. *Amour-de-soi*, that care *of* the self which Rousseau argues to be fundamental to self-preservation (and therefore entirely acceptable) deviates into *amour-propre*, that care *for* the self that hypothesizes an image of the self as it is seen by others.

Instead of a singularity in its preferred 'natural' condition, Rousseau sees in moral love the emergence of a new singularity, based upon a hierarchizing evaluation of *individuals* rather than

Paris, 1995). Cioran begins his published career with his book *Sur les cimes du désespoir*, which opens with a meditation, reminiscent of Pascal, on why we express ourselves: 'Pourquoi ne pouvons-nous demeurer enfermés en nous? Pourquoi poursuivons-nous l'expression et la forme, cherchant à nous vider de tout contenu, à organizer un processus chaotique et rebelle? Ne serait-il pas plus fécond de nous abandonner à notre fluidité intérieure...' (19). Interestingly, writing on Beckett, Cioran describes him in near nationalist terms, as one who always had the appearance 'd'être arrivé à Paris la veille, alors qu'il vivait en France depuis vingt-cinq ans' (1737).

singulars. With this new form of cultured singularity comes not only language and metaphor, but also the abstractions that allow for the possibility of preference, choice, selection: in short, what we see is the emergence of the codes governing beauty and aesthetics. Insofar as these are code-driven—insofar, that is, as moral love is born from abstraction rather than experience—beauty and aesthetics in the state of culture, paradoxically, cannot be based upon somatic experience or sensibility, for in this condition there is no experience since the subject is temporally dissociated from itself, seeing the world through the conventional and theatricalizing modes of reason, mores, even language itself. Oddly, then, moral love is non-sentimental, even non-sentient; and, by extension, the aesthetics of sensibility cannot be based upon any actual sensibility at all for the aesthetic is itself marked by the subject's powers of evaluation which themselves depend upon the subject's temporal dissociation from itself. Driven by the rational abstraction that allows us to compare two or more similars and to prefer one to the others, love and the aesthetic are also driven by pre-existing regulations that transcend the individual subject. In short, the rules of politeness cause a political problem for the simple reason that the rules of politeness require the temporal dissociation of the subject from itself (that is, they require that the subject be a subject-in-becoming, a *sujet-en-procès*); and, in requiring what is effectively the possibility of *memory*, they produce inequality.

Ethics thus can be said to found the possibility of the social; and yet, in its specific form of (moral) love, ethics also disrupts the very possibility of a proper social relation, a relation based upon the *experience*, somatic or otherwise, by one subject of another. Our temporal condition precludes the possibility of democracy, if democracy is understood to be based upon a presumed equality among the participants in a community, for temporality in which the subject is dissociated from itself leads to a theatricalisation of being in which the abstractions of consciousness required for the 'singling out' of preferred objects eventuates in a value-system based precisely upon inequality.

Rousseau maps this out in a broad-brush 'historical' sketch. Abstract reasoning, he says, is a form of technology. The technologized and technologizing subject can engage, through technology, in the process of house-building; in turn, such technology therefore produces the organisation of communities into familial units, based on 'les plus doux sentiments qui soient connus des hommes, l'amour conjugal, et l'amour paternel'.[77] Such an organization of the community produces time for leisure. Rousseau's analysis of this condition looks forward not only to Adorno but also to Gorz in their attacks on the 'culture-merchants' of the twentieth century; for, according to Rousseau, such leisure time as is produced is filled with commodities whose possession brings no joy (for they are not strictly necessary to our happiness), but whose loss brings pain.[78] In this spatio-temporal organisation, further, culture becomes possible.

Primarily, such culture arises in the form of the codes and conventions of politeness. Now, Rousseau had already proposed a link between culture and tribe in his first *Discours*, when he began his thoughts on the progress of the arts and sciences by stating that:

L'Europe était retombée dans la barbarie des premiers ages. Les peuples de cette partie du monde aujourd'hui si éclairée vivaient, il y a quelques siècles, dans un état pire que l'ignorance. ... Il fallait une révolution pour ramener les hommes au sens commun; elle vînt enfin du côté d'où on l'aurait le moins attendue. Ce fût le stupide Musulman, ce fût l'éternel fléau des lettres qui les fît renaître parmi nous ...[79]

In this same essay, Rousseau also attacks the supervention of politeness, claiming among its meretricious effects the reversal according to which 'Les haines nationales s'éteindront, mais ce sera avec l'amour de la patrie'.[80] This emergent national consciousness as a determinant of culture is one which permits of comparison between cultures. The ideas of merit and of beauty, available within the social sphere of moral love, has a much wider political series of ramifications, therefore, in which ideas of sameness (or tribal and cultural identification) vie with difference (or aliens, otherness, foreigners):

Tout commence à changer de face. Les hommes errants jusqu'ici dans les bois, ayant pris une assiette plus fixe, se rapprochent lentement, se réunissent en diverses troupes, et forment enfin dans chaque contrée une nation

77 Rousseau, *Écrits politiques*, 113.
78 On the culture-industry, see e.g. T. W. Adorno and Max Horkheimer, *Dialectic of Enlightenment* (1944; trans. John Cummings; Verso, 1979). See also André Gorz, *Farewell to the Working-Class* (1980; trans. Mike Sonenscher; Pluto Press, 1982).
79 Rousseau, *Écrits politiques*, 25.   80 Ibid. 28.

particulière, unie de mœurs et de caractères, non par des réglements et des lois, mais par le même genre de vie et d'aliments, et par l'influence commune du climat. Un voisinage permanent ne peut manquer d'engendrer enfin quelque liaison entre diverses familles. De jeunes gens de différents sexes habitent des cabanes voisines, le commerce passager que demande la nature en amène bientôt un autre non moins doux et plus permanent par la fréquentation mutuelle. On s'accoûtume à considérer différents objets et à faire des comparaisons; on acquiert insensiblement des idées de mérite et de beauté qui produisent des sentiments de préférence. A force de se voir, on ne peut plus se passer de se voir encore. Un sentiment tendre et doux s'insinue dans l'âme, et par la moindre opposition devient une fureur impétueuse: la jalousie s'éveille avec l'amour; la discorde triomphe et la plus douce des passions reçoit des sacrifices de sang humain.[81]

Love, thus, produces inequality because it is a prerequisite of love that it be able to distinguish, to discriminate, and thus to singularize and to evaluate identifiable objects within a community. In doing so, love establishes aesthetics (beauty) and morality (the evaluation of human subjects); but such ethical 'progress', in its production of moral (not natural) inequality, is at least questionable. Rousseau thus finds himself arguing for a first principle that turns out to be at the root of the very problematic situation he is ostensibly trying to resolve. The temporal dissociation of the subject from itself, so necessary for aesthetics at all, leads to the necessity of an inequality that is at odds with the 'democratic' impetus of Rousseau's writing.

Rousseau continues his brief history by arguing that with the establishment of the kinds of community described above, arts and culture begin to flourish:

... le chant et la danse ... devinrent l'amusement ou plutôt l'occupation des hommes et des femmes oisifs et attroupés. Chacun commença à regarder les autres et à vouloir être regardé soi-même, et l'estime publique eut un prix. Celui qui chantait ou dansait le mieux; le plus beau, le plus fort, le plus adroit ou le plus éloquent devint le plus considéré, et ce fût le premier pas vers l'inégalité, et vers le vice en même temps. ... Sitôt que les hommes eurent commencé à s'apprécier mutuellement et que l'idée de la considération fût formée dans leur esprit, chacun prétendit y avoir droit, et il ne fût plus possible d'en manquer impunément pour personne. De là sortirent les premiers devoirs de la civilité, même parmi les sauvages, et de là tout tort volontaire devint un outrage, parce qu'avec le mal qui résultait de l'injure,

---

[81]   Ibid. 114–5.

l'offensé y voyait le mépris de sa personne souvent plus insupportable que
le mal même.[82]

That inequality among nation-states leads to the demands for civil
rights within nation-states; and the consequence of this is not the
establishment of such civil rights but rather the scandal that is
'civility'.[83] There is therefore, for Rousseau as much as for
Benjamin, no document of civilization that is not also a document
of barbarity.

IV

What results from this collocation of Hume with Rousseau is a
problem regarding experience itself. For Hume, experience (and
this includes, centrally, *aesthetic* experience as a matter of subjective *fact*) is now itself conditioned or given by a predetermining
political state of affairs. It is as if 'England' makes art—or the critic's sensible experience of art—possible. For Rousseau, such experience is to be grounded in an ethical foundation, in which the subject's very being is conditioned by her or his relation to alterity as
to a single and specific other; but in this, singularity necessarily collapses into individuality, with the consequence that what should be
an ethical relation—in which, as in love, the very identity of the
subject would be endangered by the encounter with a singular
other—is thus always already a merely theatrical relation, and *hypocritical* or insincere. The problem, thus, is whether experience
itself can possibly constitute a basis for sociality; or, in other words,
can we mount a politics from an aesthetics? That is to say, can
sense be common? It is to this question—and to its ramifications
for the institutionalization of criticism—that I can now turn.

---

[82] Rousseau, *Écrits politiques*, 115.

[83] We know this today most immediately through those various discourses of
'political correctness' which masquerade as 'criticism', and in which the critic
claims, *à la Rousseau*, the status of victimhood: if you can't really be working-class,
at least you can be Irish—or, as this position is satirized in Alan Parker's film of
Roddy Doyle's novel, *The Commitments*: 'The Irish are the Blacks of Europe; the
Dubliners are the Blacks of Ireland; and the North-siders are the Blacks of Dublin.
So say it once and say it loud, "I'm black and I'm proud".' The discourse of vic-
timhood, so easily grasped by many *soi-disant* political critics, essentially trivializes
Benjamin's seventh thesis on the philosophy of history—and, of course, trivializes
Rousseau.

SECTION III

AESTHETIC EDUCATION

6

Pessimism, Community, and Utopia in Aesthetic Education

Hume famously woke Kant from his dogmatic slumbers in Konigsberg; but if the response to his work closer to home was somewhat delayed, the response there in Scotland was no less vigorous for its tardiness. Typical of those who placed themselves in the ranks of his (philosophical) enemies was James Beattie who, in 1770 in Aberdeen, published his *Essay on the Nature and Immutability of Truth*. Beattie had no time for the celebration of any mythic primal condition such as that explored by Rousseau; but he did share with Rousseau a passion for truth, even acknowledging in true Alceste-fashion, that he will probably have to be rude to those with whom he disagrees.[1] The target against which his essay ranges itself was the radical scepticism of Hume, which led inevitably, Beattie feared, to a form of extreme cultural relativism in which the absoluteness or 'immutability' of truth was threatened, and with it all standards of moral being (entailing the further loss, along with the standards of moral rectitude, of the guiding principles of Scottish education). The position is a familiar one, especially to the late twentieth century when a (sometimes explicitly) conservative reaction against a version of contemporary 'theoretical' and sceptical criticism (construed journalistically as nihilistic and contemptuous of values and of absolute standards of judgement) leads to a highly moralistic, ethnocentric appeal to a version of 'common sense'.[2] Sadly, those who participate in the

---

[1] James Beattie, *An Essay on the Nature and Immutability of Truth* (Kincaid & Bell, Edinburgh, 1777; facsimile repr., Garland Publishing, Inc., New York, 1983), 8.
[2] For the American version of this, see Stanley Fish, *There's No Such Thing as Free Speech* (Oxford University Press, Oxford, 1994), where Fish takes on his

contemporary debate (on both sides) are often ignorant of the very roots of Common Sense as itself a specific movement in eighteenth- and nineteenth-century philosophy in which anxieties about aesthetics, ethics, and politics were played out. In this first section of the present chapter, I shall outline some aspects of a Common Sense philosophy in its relation to truth, criticism, and the ethical dimensions of the social. This will open a problem of the relation of aesthetic sense to political truth, and will thus raise the issue of criticism in relation to those forms of education that are inherently Utopian, i.e. education that is 'disinterested', seeking the 'best that has been thought and said', seeking the 'better argument' without coercion—or, in two words, cultural education (*Bildung, formation*).

I

Against what he construes as Hume's radical scepticism, Beattie mounted one of the major and central statements in the philosophy of Common Sense, in which truth, fundamentally, was proposed as that which is self-evidencing and therefore beyond argument. The core of the argument relates truth to the problematic questions of time and of difference. Hume appears to have proposed a world of continuous mutability by calling into question the law or logic of causality. Not only do we now have history reduced to 'one damned thing after another' without any necessary or consequential linking of things or events to each other, we also have a state of affairs in which even the person herself or himself, construed as an entity that persists through time, is an illusion (however necessary it may be for us to maintain such an illusion for the normative functioning of society), for the person too is nothing more or less than a series of

conservative cultural-political enemies, notably Dinesh D'Souza. The issue is complicated by Fish's own subscription to what is itself an ethnocentric position (not adverted to as such), that version of pragmatism which, in its indebtedness to William James and John Dewey, is characterized as 'American' philosophy, especially by its contemporary foremost thinker and advocate, Richard Rorty. In England, the appeal to 'common sense' is usually accompanied by appeals to a mythical 'common reader' and, as in the books of John Carey, say, is basically grounded not in an anti-theoretical position, but rather, much more dangerously, in an anti-intellectualism. See e.g. John Carey, *The Intellectuals and the Masses* (Faber, 1993).

fleeting instances of perception or sensation. Beattie wants to argue against this, for he sees it as an opening to an absolute relativity of judgements and of values. According to his understanding of the Humean view, all judgements would now be reduced to the status of 'nonce'-judgements, that is to say, judgements made *in* the moment, *merely for* the moment and fully *of* the moment—but therefore with no value *beyond* the moment; and consequently, the judgement thus made has no *prescriptive* or predictive value or content. It therefore cannot propose norms for behaviour or practice, cannot generalize from its own particularity as a fact, and stands in a relation to time in which the morality or ethics of the future cannot be predicted or prescribed from the ethical content of the present instance of judgement. Therefore, any truth deemed to be constitutive of the present moment cannot have its substance guaranteed for any other moment, and truth has become vacuous because mutable. Beattie, not only as a moralist with a Christian formation, but also simply as a philosopher concerned with the pursuit of truth, is demonstrably unhappy with a position such as this which seems to call the entire project of philosophy—and especially that part of philosophy's project in which it assumes the task of moral judgement and edification, that is, *education*—into question. In arguing for the immutability of truth, he is setting out a position consistent with his theology, certainly, but also one that establishes some fundamental principles of a Common Sense philosophy whose ethical import is that it legitimizes that which is, he claims, commonly experienced, against that which is thought by one extremely singular individual. In short, his position is one which aims, in a certain way, to return philosophy to the people in their everyday practices of living.[3] It is worth looking at some of the steps of Beattie's argument in detail, for they develop the anxiety about the aesthetic-in-time that has become, as we have seen in previous chapters, a major concern for late eighteenth-century thought about the arts.

---

[3] It is worth noting, in passing, that this is precisely what is *not* being proposed in those contemporary conservative attacks on 'theory' made in the name of common sense. The conservatives and anti-intellectuals propose, in fact, the maintenance of various institutional exclusivist elites whose function has little or nothing to do with values or standards and instead everything to do with the maintenance of specific powers or cultural-political authority. The best analysis of this is still the work of Pierre Bourdieu, *Distinction* (trans. Richard Nice; Routledge & Kegan Paul, 1984); and for an analysis with specific reference to the academy, see Bourdieu, *Homo Academicus* (trans. Peter Collier; Polity Press, Cambridge, 1988).

'Truth, like virtue, to be loved, needs only to be seen', Beattie argued, claiming that truth is what happens when a proposition expresses something 'conformable to the nature of things'.[4] This leads to a basic, if implicit, premiss of Common Sense, that truth does not equate with any simple form of measurable or quantifiable 'adequate knowledge'. Indeed, it is almost as if Beattie is proposing an ontology of truth, in that, for him, truth appears to be rather a mode of being than a mode of knowing; or, better, truth is knowledge in the mode of being or what, in the terminology of the late eighteenth and early nineteenth centuries, we can call 'sensuous knowledge'.

Once again, this should be familiar, for the twentieth-century equivalent of this in criticism has been the emergence of a 'new pragmatism'. This is first developed in the trajectory of Fish's work, proceeding from its beginnings in a readerly-response lexicon, according to which the meaning of a text is what it *does* to a reader rather than what it might appear to *say* in any abstract or abstracted sense (so, as with Beattie, truth is something that happens, not something that exists only propositionally). As his thinking on this develops, Fish first makes the move to substantially concretize or realize this hypothetical reader as the real reader, Stanley Fish himself; and this then allows for the emergence of a position closely in alignment with Rorty's rehabilitated American pragmatism in which the event of reading is entirely circumscribed by the circumstances that made it possible in the first place: there is, as it were, no theory that will allow the critic to step outside of the position ascribed to her, and from which all is necessarily as it is or as it appears to be: truth is self-evidencing and necessarily conformable to what the critic takes to be the nature of things.[5]

Long pre-dating this, Beattie makes the claim (seemingly aware of the problems that Kant will try to address) for the possibility of some kind of adequation between the contents of consciousness and things-in-themselves:

4 Beattie, *Essay*, 19, 28.
5 For this trajectory, see the key steps in *Is There a Text in this Class?* (Harvard University Press, Cambridge, Mass., 1980), followed by the very explicit position described in *Professional Correctness* (Oxford University Press, Oxford, 1995), 48: 'one doesn't "choose" one's readings, one is *persuaded* to them, and one is persuaded to them not by calculating their political effects, but by coming up with answers to questions that are constitutive of the present practice of producing readings'.

there is in my mind something which induces me to think, that every thing existing in nature, is determined to exist, and to exist after a certain manner, in consequence of established laws; and that whatever is agreeable to these laws is agreeable to the nature of things, because by these laws the nature of all things is determined.[6]

He claims that one cannot *know* these laws, but they are nonetheless intimated to our feelings as credible and certain—they are as if 'given'; and it follows from this that:

I account That to be *truth* which the constitution of my nature determines me to believe, and that to be *falsehood* which the constitution of my nature determines me to disbelieve.[7]

There is thus a distinction to be made between the operations of Reason (which works by proof) and those of Common Sense (to which proof is superfluous, given the self-evidential nature of truth in this account). Once more, it is interesting to note that this formulation could have been written in our own day by Fish, who takes the view that I do as I do as a critic because of what I am (itself determined by my previous critical practices and predispositions). Common Sense is what we are left with when we decide to question—or to prove—no further; and Beattie's authority for this kind of manoeuvre is Aristotle who, it is claimed, demonstrates the necessity of taking some first principle for granted if we are to avoid a recursive pursuit of truth by proof and proof of proof *ad infinitum*. Common Sense, by taking some first principle—that of a belief based in 'the constitution of my nature'—puts a stop to the potentially endless temporality—the temporizing—of thinking, arguing, persuading. For Beattie, axiomatically, there must be some first principle that is not susceptible of proof, but which is rather self-evidencing; and he finds it in the constitution of consciousness itself: 'the constitution of my nature' which determines belief. The self-evidencing constitution of Common Sense has a precise relation to time: it is *immediate*, the validation of its propositions given all at once with the very philosophy which founds those propositions in the first place.[8]

---

[6] Beattie, *Essay*, 29.   [7] Ibid. 30.

[8] Insofar as this immediacy signals an unmediated relation between the subject and its objects of perception, it clearly constitutes a significant problem for subsequent philosophy. The unmediated relation would suppose the possibility of a total and precise identification of the subject with the object of perception; and it is against the scandal of this that Schopenhauer—and later Marx—will attend to the body of the subject as the site of mediation, and thus also of time and of history. See further, below.

Unlike Descartes who finds his first principle in the doubt that leads to the Cogito, Beattie takes the view that 'I am as I am and thus do I think'. Although he offers an early example of de Man's 'resistance to theory' argument, when he claims that many of his contemporaries are 'more concerned for their theory, than for the truth',[9] he nonetheless relentlessly justifies his own theory of the self-evidencing of truth in terms reminiscent of that Rousseauvian trope discussed in the previous chapter when he proclaims the easy availability of truth when we look into our own hearts: 'Physical and mathematical truths are often exceedingly abstruse; but facts and experiments relating to the human mind, when expressed in proper words, ought to be obvious to all'.[10]

In a central move, Beattie pushes Hume's arguments to what he proposes as the extreme of an impossibility:

If I were to believe, with Mr HUME, and some others, that my mind is perpetually changing, so as to become every different moment a different thing, the remembrance of past, or the anticipation of future good or evil, could give me neither pleasure nor pain; yea, tho' I were to believe, that a cruel death would certainly overtake me within an hour, I should be no more concerned, than if I were told, that a certain elephant three thousand years hence would be sacrificed on the top of Mount Atlas. To a man who doubts the individuality or identity of his own mind, virtue, truth, religion, good and evil, hope and fear, are absolutely nothing.[11]

This may appear to be a reasonable claim; yet it does not in fact follow from a Humean sceptical position regarding the persistence of the self. It is not a consequence of Hume's position that the concept of a past or of a future can have no present existence; and even causality, which appears to link two moments in time, can clearly be conceptualizable within any present moment (and indeed, it must be so for Hume to be able to attack it at all). Any individual moment could be marked by fear or hope (and thus directed towards a hypothesized future, a future now constitutive of the

---

    [9] Beattie, *Essay*, 6. Cf. Paul de Man, *The Resistance to Theory* (Manchester University Press, Manchester, 1986), especially the title essay where de Man writes, in a formulation typical of the essay as a whole, that 'the resistance to theory is in fact a resistance to reading' (p. 15). De Man wanted to hang on to the idea that texts disturb rather than confirm the prevailing theories with which one necessarily engages them; and it is precisely this that Beattie addresses here, with the purchase of the philosophy of Kant still pending.

    [10] Beattie, *Essay*, 17–18.   [11] Ibid. 75–6.

present), even though the temporality of the self is not transcendent: that is to say, the present moment of selfhood, if it has any substance at all, must be characterized by a specific content; and that content can just as easily be fear or hope directed towards a future hypothesized from the present as it could be pleasure or pain within the present. Indeed, the present self *must* be thus characterized if it is to be aware of itself *as* a present self. In one sense, the present is all that there is *in the present*, or, as Schopenhauer will later put it, 'time is merely the potential for conflicting states of the same matter, and space is merely the potential for the endurance of the same matter under all conflicting states'.[12]

Further, Beattie argues that when 'metaphysicians' (such as Hume) argue, for instance, that I cannot be the same at fifty years of age as I am at ten then they are in error; but, importantly, the difficulties operative in this question regarding the persistence of the self lack substance, being 'rather verbal than real'.[13] In allowing this, Beattie concedes the opposition being elaborated in Konigsberg by Kant between things-in-themselves (the real, in Beattie's terms) and the contents of consciousness (the verbal). For the argument against Hume to work in the terms elaborated above, Beattie would require the elision of this distinction between what we might call the factual and the conceptual; yet this is precisely the distinction that he has to maintain if he is to validate the immutability of truth in the face of historical difference. In terms of the 'change' between a man of ten and the 'same' at fifty, Beattie allows that I may change in substance, but I nonetheless remain 'animated' by 'the same vital and thinking principle'.[14]

This enables Beattie to make a very important observation about the possibility of difference within sameness, of conceiving of the same (the immutable) as indeed constituted by difference. Given that truth is what happens when a proposition expresses something 'conformable to the nature of things', it follows that, for Beattie, it must be possible to bring the verbal and the real into alignment, so that we are able to validate the real (the thing-in-itself) through the operations of a consciousness possessed of Common Sense (the verbal). Now, given also that the immutably true may be constituted

---

[12] Arthur Schopenhauer, *World as Will and Idea*, ed. David Berman (trans. Jill Berman; Everyman, 1995), 66.

[13] Beattie, *Essay*, 85.   [14] Ibid. 87.

by difference, it follows that there are different ways of 'telling the truth', of bringing the immutably real into alignment with the verbally mutable (or even ambiguous). Philosophy makes a mistake when it sacrifices the real, the thing-in-itself, for language or for the contents of consciousness. Indeed, this is another way of phrasing Beattie's early and prefigurative version of de Man's complaints about the 'resistance to theory': it is important that the philosopher does not simply provide a linguistic or autonomous system, answerable to itself and coherent with respect to its internal logic, for she or he must also maintain the possibility—or rather the necessity—of establishing a correspondence between verbal and real, between system and fact.

Given that the same can be different, it follows also that that which is constant—such as truth—may yet be characterized by a series of differences in appearance. So truth, though always the same, may appear different from time to time. This is an important concession, for while it is striving to maintain a correspondence-theory of truth-telling, it opens the door to a legitimation of appearance: appearance need not now be the mere contrary of reality or truth, but might rather be the very condition under which truth is manifest or self-evidencing.

Beattie needs this authentication of appearance for his greater argument against his version of Hume. It is a condition of knowledge and of experience itself, argues Beattie, that we are able to trust memory which is, of course, an appearing of things to consciousness that are not present in themselves. He writes that:

If we had no memory, knowledge and experience would be impossible; and if we had any tendency to distrust our memory, knowledge and experience would be of as little use in directing our conduct and sentiments, as our dreams now are.[15]

In order to be able to act at all, either in terms of responding to material historical conditions or in terms simply of thinking and reasoning in a consequential fashion, Beattie claims that we must axiomatically trust this memory; but he also claims that we cannot help but trust it:

The same Providence which endued us with memory, without any care of ours, endues us also with an instinctive propensity to believe in it, previously

---

[15]   Beattie, *Essay*, 90.

to all reasoning and experience. Nay, all reasoning supposeth the testimony of memory to be authentic: for, without trusting implicitly to this testimony, no train of reasoning could be prosecuted; we could never be convinced, that the conclusion is fair, if we did not *remember* the several steps of the argument, and if we were not certain that this remembrance is not fallacious.[16]

This allows Beattie to claim a persistence of self identified through memory (as a form of representation) and therefore to assert the truth of selfhood or identity (its self-evidencing self-sameness) across time based upon the authenticity of its several appearances (or representations). It is this that allows Beattie to assert the possibility of (and to predict the necessity of) rational behaviour in the future, based upon a notion of causality that has been demonstrated in the past:

In all our reasoning from the cause to the effect, we proceed on a supposition, and a belief, that the course of nature will continue to be in time to come what we experience it to be at present, and remember it to have been in time past. This presumption of continuance is the foundation of all our judgements concerning future events.[17]

Paradoxically, however, this does not run quite as smoothly as Beattie would want it to; for in this very formulation we see a demonstration of the presentness of the future or of the past: that is to say, we see that Beattie accepts that a present moment can be characterized by or conditioned by a content described as 'futurity' or 'pastness', but that these futures or pasts are never themselves really present to experience but are only present as elements of a present consciousness. In short, this is not an adequate answer against what Beattie takes from Hume's scepticism regarding the persistence of the self in time.

In a lengthy footnote, Beattie proposes a summation of his argument as a whole. All objects of human understanding, he claims, are reducible to two classes, 'abstract ideas' on one hand, and 'things really existing' on the other (two classes that will recall our previous opposition between theory or universals on one hand, history or particulars on the other). In respect of the former, all our knowledge is certain, for it is based on mathematical evidence (which includes intuitive evidence of a neo-Cartesian kind), and the evidence of strict demonstration, where the strictness of

[16] Ibid. 91.   [17] Ibid. 121.

the demonstration is measurable in terms of the demonstration's conformity with the rules of the systems of mathematics—with the autonomous laws of mathematics—themselves. This we might call, in terms more approximate to our own vocabulary, a knowledge based in the adequations of theory. With respect to 'things really existing' or the realm of material or historical facticity, we judge, claims Beattie, either from our own experience or from that of others. This gives us certain knowledge when we can support our claims by reference to the evidence of the senses, of memory, or of legitimate inference of causes from effects (deduction); and it gives us probable knowledge when we argue for the likely eventuality of any specific outcome or situation from an inference based on our past experience of similar facts. Crucially for my present argument, Beattie then addresses in this footnote the state of affairs in which we base our knowledge upon the experiences of others regarding things really existing. Here, he says, we have the evidence of the testimony of those others, and 'The mode of understanding produced by that evidence is properly called *Faith*; and this faith sometimes amounts to *probable opinion*, and sometimes rises to *absolute certainty*'.[18]

I do not wish here to make an argument regarding Beattie's final discovery of foundations for his philosophy in a theology; rather, I insist on hearing in the term 'faith' a specific notion of trust (friendship) or, better, a commonality of pursuit among a community. That is the argument with which the contemporary theorist will be more familiar in the lexicon of criticism from Leavis to Steiner.[19] We have to place a bond of trust in the others whose experiences we validate in and through our belief that they are appearances of the truth; and another name for this is, of course, 'society' or ethics—or, in one very specific form, *education*.

The fundamental principles of truth cannot be open to the process of reasoning, for if they were, we would have to be sure that we had heard all the possible or conceivable arguments for and

[18] Beattie, *Essay*, 52–3 n.

[19] I refer, of course, to F. R. Leavis, *The Common Pursuit* (Penguin, Harmondsworth, 1952; repr. 1976); and to George Steiner's 1985 essay on what he calls 'Real Presences', the succinct version of which appears in his *No Passion Spent* (Faber and Faber, 1996). Steiner's debt to the Pascalian 'wager', *le pari* of *Les Pensées* allows for a peculiar combination, in Steiner, of a peculiar theology with the totally different thinking of another notorious 'gambler', Baudrillard.

against any specific proposition before deciding on its truth; and we could never know that there would not be some future or other argument that could eventually serve to modify whatever position or judgement we arrive at. From this it follows not only that the self-evidencing nature of truth is fundamental or foundational; it also follows that we have a commonality of sense, or else 'every man would be a law unto himself'.[20] The very existence of the social—we might even say of a rational society—depends therefore upon the faith in the commonality of common sense. That very commonality, argues Beattie, is evidence enough that Common Sense cannot be taught, even if reason can; and this is so even if it is demonstrably the case that the degree of Common Sense might vary from person to person: 'Such diversities are ... to be referred ... to the original constitution of the mind, which it is not in the power of education to alter.'[21] Hence, we have the different appearances of Common Sense, all demonstrative of its fundamental truth.

Moreover, the commonality of sense is consistent with another basic truth for Beattie concerning human freedom and autonomy. The question concerning autonomy is to be asked in terms of the opposition between: (1) believing oneself to be free, and therefore acting in a morally responsible fashion, accepting innocence or guilt; and (2) believing oneself a 'necessary agent', and therefore amoral (or, eventually, immoral). Beattie's question is simple: if we subscribe to (2), then how is it possible for us to act at all; and, more pointedly for present purposes, how could society—friendship, as he puts it—subsist under such circumstances?[22] The commonality of sense thus produces freedom in society; and that is the mark of progress or civilization.

The society in question quickly becomes identifiable as a national one. A digression on Aristotle's justifications of slavery allows another attack on Hume's perceived racism;[23] and here Beattie prefigures Conrad's great opening of *Heart of Darkness*, when he writes:

---

[20] Beattie, *Essay*, 141.
[21] Ibid. 45; cf. ibid., 43–4.
[22] Ibid. 370. Cf. Alain Finkielkraut, *La Sagesse de l'amour* (Gallimard, Paris, 1984), 104, 112–13, and see also my commentary on this in Docherty, *Alterities* (Oxford University Press, Oxford, 1996), 206–7.
[23] Beattie, *Essay*, 479.

The inhabitants of Great Britain and France were as savage two thousand years ago, as those of Africa or America are at this day. Civilisation is the work of time. And one may as well say of an infant, that he can never become a man, as of a nation now barbarous, that it never can be civilised.[24]

Progress is possible, even if a certain form of education is not. Importantly, despite the fact that Beattie adopts a tone in which he equates his drive for truth-telling with rudeness, a tone that is explicitly reminiscent of Rousseau and of Molière's Alceste, we now have a state of affairs in which truth is identified not by the singularity of the truth-teller, but rather truth is marked by its commonality—or, in a word, by its *nationality*. The subject is in the truth when she or he is in conformity with a sense held in common, based on the optimistic view that people normally tell the truth (even liars do, most of the time, says Beattie). It is the person who confuses theory with practice, the abstract with the specific (like the metaphysical Hume) who is, *ipso facto*, out of the truth: idiosyncracy is no longer the mark of truth, but rather of error or of the barbarous need to progress towards a commonality of sense (as held by the commonality of Great Britain, or that of France, or even that of Peru[25]). Truth is not a matter of reason; and hence the reasoning individual is no more likely to be in truth than the unreflective. Beattie finds an answer to the problem of legitimation: the question 'how can my experience become normative for a community' is, for him, a non-question: axiomatically, the truth of one's experience is so self-evidencing that only the perverse (and therefore blameworthy, like Hume) will refuse to acquiesce in it. Truth is common *before* it is experienced by the individual or singular; that is to say, truth pre-exists the subject who would speak it. In these conditions, how can we say still that truth can be *immediately* given? The temporality of truth in its relation to a subject who is always, of necessity, *belated* in respect of the truth (and thus in need of *education* or edification) seems to be at odds with the Common-Sensical view that such an education (with its highly specific sense noted above) is impossible. It is this seeming contradiction that is Beattie's legacy for the nineteenth century.

---

[24] Beattie, *Essay*, 480.   [25] Ibid. 481.

II

It is clear that eighteenth-century aesthetics produces a significant problem regarding the relation between beauty and time or, more crucially still, between truth and time. Emerging from this, and consequent upon it in the turn into the nineteenth century, are two fundamental ways of addressing the issues of the relation of aesthetics to truth, of the relation of truth and the subject to democracy, and the question of all of these before history and the European nation-states.

On the one hand, time is seen as that which will offer the possibility of an aesthetic or sentimental education, as in Schiller or, later, Flaubert. In this, what we do not know now—that is, what we cannot yet aesthetically or sensibly experience—we may well know in a future moment; and hence, through an exercise in *Bildung* or *formation* we can ameliorate the conditions of the world or of history, bringing about the conditions in which we can live more fully. This, indeed, is how Eagleton once justified the necessity of Marxism, writing that 'The goal of Marxism is to restore to the body its plundered powers; but only with the supersession of private property will the senses be able fully to come into their own. If communism is necessary, it is because we are unable to feel, taste, smell and touch as fully as we might.'[26] For a thinker before Marx, such as Beattie, this aligned time with a version of progress: history is seen as a civilizing process, leading ever onwards to a present in which we are, finally, in the truth, living its intensities. This position is one which, as my preceding sentence already suggests, is founded upon a theology rather than an epistemology. In our day, Michel Serres has exposed the profound optimism (and Optimism) of this belief, for, according to those who subscribe to such a version of progress, the past is characterized by the condition of error and then, suddenly, 'Ouf! Nous sommes enfin entrés dans le vrai.'[27] We live the truth or are in the truth because—and only because— we are here, now. Truth has become nothing more or less than a function of a linguistic proposition whose truth is guaranteed by

[26] Terry Eagleton, *The Ideology of the Aesthetic* (Basil Blackwell, Oxford, 1990), 201.
[27] Michel Serres, *Éclaircissements: Entretiens avec Bruno Latour* (1992; Flammarion, Paris, 1994), 76.

the supposed self-presence, the 'here-now' that is the subject, 'I', as a grammatical element constitutive of truth's sentences or phrasing.

On the other hand, art becomes increasingly considered to be a privileged kind of object, one capable of taking the subject out of a particular objective time—the historical or secular time that is the condition of the artificial or constructed material object—entirely, as in Hegel and, in an extremely different fashion, Schopenhauer. In this account, art takes the subject out of time only so that the subject can then replace an individual relation to the world of particular objects or history with a communal—ethico-national—relation to such a world. That is to say, those subscribing to this view give up on the primary identification of subjects with objects as the ground for their truthful propositions, replacing that subject–object relation with a primary identification of subjects with other 'similar' subjects against 'different' objects (which may, in their turn, simply be other subjects who fail to resemble us). This latter we have learnt to call civilization; but it involves an at least tacit nationalism and, as the writers of an emergent imperialism knew, it also involves the stigmatization of others as 'under-developed', tardy, belated in respect of ourselves and caught up in the mire of nature itself.

It is by now conventional to see aesthetic modernity as a product precisely of this moment of a European post-Enlightenment. Kant is usually taken as the first leading figure, who raises questions and answers them in a way that was unacceptable to Hegel, who in his turn is controverted by Marx and Nietzsche, from whom all our critical problems derive, especially in the form in which the Nietzschean and Marxist legacies are given to us, after Heidegger, by Derrida, Foucault, Lyotard, Deleuze. This chain of names, all German up to Heidegger, all French after Derrida,[28] is itself significant. Though this has been noted before, by Habermas among others, the national identities of these philosophers have not been regarded as somehow *constitutive* of their positions. My contention in this book is that the conventional version of aesthetic modernity, as it is articulated in, for example, Andrew Bowie's *Aesthetics and Subjectivity*, does not give sufficient attention to the

---

[28] Derrida himself, of course, is in a slightly different position from the other named French philosophers, as an Algerian increasingly aware of his 'national' status and identity.

location of aesthetics and criticism within a contestation among emerging national powers and national consciousness.[29] Once we attend to the question of the nation-state within Europe, we can discern this more pan-European series of intellectual debates; and other thinkers assume a greater importance. One such is Schiller.

Schiller took, for his most celebrated theatrical productions, matter from the history of Scotland (in its relation to England) in *Mary Stuart*, or from Spain, in *Don Carlos*. He inherited from Kant the great modern problem of legitimation: how can we move from a factual subjective experience of the world to the establishment of a condition in which we find normative agreement about what constitutes the good, the true and the beautiful; and, further and more basically, how can we find the possibility of non-coercive intersubjective communication at all? Schiller, though, inherits this question with a profound awareness, writing alongside Goethe, of 'Germany' as a nation-state. He fits, thus, more centrally into the history of modern aesthetics than does Kant (although Kant's philosophy, more far-reaching and consequential in its ambit obviously, has had a much more significant purchase within contemporary philosophy).

Schiller's response to the Kantian problem of legitimation, within this new national condition, is instructive and influential. He takes it as read, partly from the presiding cultural conditions, that beauty is the key to freedom; but in discussing the ways in which we have to mediate between human consciousness and the world of nature (between *phenomena* and *noumena*), Schiller explicitly indicates that the governing medium is the State itself. It is the State that will go between what Schiller calls the 'physical' and the 'moral'; for the State is that which will allow the fullest possible play to both the physical realm of nature (which seems to be a constraint upon human possibility or to set the limitations of human being) and the moral realm of humanity (which threatens the realm of nature with mastery, domination, exploitation). The opposition between these ostensibly polar forces has to be reconciled, for Schiller, with maximum efficiency to produce a maximal energy. He writes:

[29] See Andrew Bowie, *Aesthetics and Subjectivity* (Manchester University Press, Manchester, 1990) for a brilliant, lucid exposition of the consequential chain of modern philosophical aesthetics. Cf. Luc Ferry, *Homo Aestheticus* (Grasset, Paris, 1990), for another view which, though more attentive to traditions other than the German, nonetheless rehearses the same trajectory from Kant to Hegel to Nietzsche.

it will always argue a still defective education if the moral character is able to assert itself only by sacrificing the natural. And a political constitution will still be very imperfect if it is able to achieve unity only by suppressing variety. The State should not only respect the objective and generic character in its individual subjects; it should also honour their subjective and specific character, and in extending the invisible realm of morals take care not to depopulate the sensible realm of experience.[30]

Broadly, Schiller's position is one which follows a 'dissociation of sensibility' thesis, the terms of which are outlined in his fifth and sixth letters. There, he laments the present condition of humanity as one in which either: (1) people follow a neo-Rousseauvian line on the state of nature, but pervert it into a legitimation of savagery or primitivism; or, (2) people adopt a variation of the proto-pragmatist quietism of a common-sensical view, and thereby allow themselves to fall into lethargy and the coming fashionable cultural mood of *ennui*:

Man portrays himself in his actions. And what a figure he casts in the drama of the present time! On the one hand, a return to the savage state; on the other, to complete lethargy: in other words, to the two extremes of human depravity, and both united in a single epoch![31]

This state of affairs is immediately politicized by Schiller. For him, it is the lower classes who, in their masses, unleash 'crude, lawless instincts' in a common pursuit of their 'animal satisfactions'; but the upper classes are deemed by Schiller to be even worse in their lethargy and depraved character. In a foreshadowing of Adorno, Schiller writes despairingly of Enlightenment:

That Enlightenment of the mind, which is the not altogether groundless boast of our refined classes, has had on the whole so little of an ennobling influence on feeling and character that it has tended rather to bolster up depravity by providing it with the support of precepts.[32]

As Eliot will do much later, Schiller compares his present day with an imagined earlier epoch. For Schiller, it is the ancient Greek

---

[30] Friedrich Schiller, *On the Aesthetic Education of Man* (bilingual edn.; ed. and trans. Elizabeth S. Wilkinson and L. A. Willoughby; Clarendon Press, Oxford, 1967; repr. 1982), 19.

[31] Ibid. 25. The *ennui* to which I allude here will be stylized by Baudelaire. Something of its flavour persists in the 'world-weariness' associated with Richard Rorty's pragmatism.

[32] Schiller, *Aesthetic Education*, 27; see also ibid. 25.

world and character that highlights the problems of his contemporary world: 'Why,' he asks, 'was the individual Greek qualified to be the representative of his age, and why can no single Modern venture as much?' Immediately, he offers what is to him the obvious reply, and one which establishes the terms of what will become a persistent conception of a dissociated sensibility: 'Because it was from all-unifying Nature that the former, and from all-dividing Intellect that the latter, received their respective forms.'[33] Intellection here serves the function of dissociating sensibility so that no single individual can speak on behalf of all and the consequence is that no one subject can have her or his experience legitimized as being representative of a whole or of a norm, and that representation has itself therefore become problematic and an issue for theoretical, cultural, and political interest.

Intellection is for Schiller what Reason was to Beattie: in its capacity for temporizing, it dissociates the subject from herself or himself in time. Whereas Beattie counters these temporizing effects of Reason with his Common Sense whose function—in its immediacy—is to heal the threatened temporal fracture that would constitute the dissociated subject, Schiller turns instead to the State.[34] Unable to propose any immediately satisfactory response to the problem of legitimation consequent upon the dissociation of sensibility, Schiller proposes that the State can take on the role of mediation and legitimation. This is an important difference between Beattie and Schiller: for Beattie, Reason is problematic because it is temporal and temporizing, and his counter to it is the *immediacy* of Common Sense; for Schiller, faced with the same problem, the response to the temporality of reasoning and its attendant dissociating of sensibilities is not, in this first instance, a response grounded in time but rather one grounded in *place* or space, in the State. One might explain this, of course, by the simple observation that Beattie has just recently lost his own nation-state while Schiller is

---

33 Ibid. 33.
34 That dissociated subject is described by Deleuze as the 'je fêlé'. In his *Différence et répétition* (PUF, Paris, 1985), 116–17, he describes a fundamental difference between Descartes and Kant. For Descartes, 'je pense' *proves* 'je suis', while for Kant the truth of each of these two propositions cannot be determined one from the other: 'la forme sous laquelle l'existence indéterminée est déterminée par le Je pense, c'est la forme du temps ... mon existence indéterminée ne peut être déterminée que *dans le temps* ... D'un bout à l'autre, le JE est comme traversé d'une fêlure; il est fêlé par la forme pure et vide du temps.'

writing at a moment of the new formulation of his own Germany out of Prussia. In the ideal State such as Schiller envisages it, all human possibilities can be explored, enhanced and accommodated, and in these conditions there will be no repression—and much less, oppression—of the subject's social capacities.

This, however, is not as simple or straightforward as it may seem, for the State itself is in need of reform; and the problems of the dissociated sensibility and of Schiller's contemporary political situation are interrelated. The terms of the problem will by now be familiar. While the human condition is characterized by a dissociated sensibility, the relation between the subject and the State is at best purely formal, void of content, vacuous in its unreality. In the condition of dissociation, the subject's relation to the State is, as we might now say after Althusser, *imaginary*,[35] in that it is not a lived or organic relation. Singular or individual experience has to be ignored, its specificity misconstrued, to make it conform to an abstract version of hypothetical norms given by the State. The subject is characterized in terms of how it *ought* to be rather than in terms of how it *is*:

little by little the concrete life of the Individual is destroyed in order that the abstract idea of the Whole may drag out its sorry existence. And the State remains for ever a stranger to its citizens since at no point does it ever make contact with their feeling.[36]

The consequences are disastrous, and could have been predicted from Hutcheson and others. In the terms given by Schiller in the passage just quoted, we have a return to Hutcheson's thesis of the proper relations between uniformity and variety. Rewritten with the explicit politics of Schiller in mind, this becomes a thesis regarding the oppression of the realm of subjective experience (in all its infinite variety) at the hands of a State concerned to impose uniformity, and thus needing to 'translate' various experiences into an abstract model of what the citizen ought to be, how she or he ought to experience the world. In short, the State is in danger of establishing *norms* for experience *before* it takes account of the *facts* of experience. The State thus gives the citizen her or his 'subjectivity', but without any reference to her or his 'feeling' or sensibility.

---

[35] See Louis Althusser, *Essays on Ideology* (Verso, 1984), for a definition of ideology in these terms; and cf. Eagleton, *Ideology* (Verso, 1991).

[36] Schiller, *Aesthetic Education*, 37.

Hutcheson's discovery of beauty in the relation of uniformity and variety is here rewritten in terms of Schiller's discovery of a *conflict* between State and subject; and consequently, it gives us the very opposite of beauty and, with it, the opposite of all that aesthetic beauty has implied: evil.

In such a condition, what is the individual to do, if not to distrust experience, to relegate experience itself to the status of the merely accidental in the interests of the pursuit of forms of legitimation based upon abstraction:

> In its striving after inalienable possessions in the realm of ideas, the spirit of speculation could do no other than become a stranger to the world of sense, and lose sight of matter for the sake of form.[37]

Despite such alienation, however, Schiller also sees that there is a virtuous circle into which we might break:

> the State as at present constituted has been the cause of evil, while the State as Reason conceives it, far from being able to lay the foundations for this better humanity, would itself have to be founded upon it ... The present age, far from exhibiting that form of humanity which we recognized as the necessary condition of any moral reform of the State, shows us rather the exact opposite. If, therefore, the principles I have laid down are correct, and if experience confirms my portrayal of the present age, we must continue to regard every attempt at political reform as untimely, and every hope based upon it as chimerical, as long as the split in man is not healed, and his nature so restored to wholeness that it can itself become the artificer of the State, and guarantee the reality of this political creation of Reason.[38]

We have a paradoxical situation in which intellectual education is to bring about moral education; while, simultaneously, this latter

---

[37] Ibid. 37–9. Interestingly, this formulation could be usefully compared with Walter Benjamin's argumentation in the celebrated 'Work of Art in the Age of Mechanical Reproduction' essay. There, Benjamin addresses the loss of the 'aura' of a work of art, the loss of its concrete specificity given to us as 'the unique phenomenon of a distance', in which we can be aware of its location in a specific place and in a specific time, carrying within it its own history. In the age of mechanical reproduction, when art is made *for* reproduction, we can lose such an 'aura'—which Schiller writes of here in terms of 'matter'—while yet being fully aware of the form in which the work is given to us. In terms of art history, we lose sight of the struggles inscribed within a specific painting, say, and see instead just a pretty or beautiful image; in terms of politics, we lose subjective experience and become literally 'conformist', legitimized by forms or decorum or theatricality.

[38] Schiller, *Aesthetic Education*, 45.

(moral education) is the very condition of the possibility of the former (intellectual improvement). Likewise, on a grander, more political, scale, the relations between political improvement and the ennobling of character: political improvement will permit for the ennobling of character; but without an ennobling of character in the first place, the very political improvement requisite for such ennobling will not be possible. Beattie, we will recall, faced a similar problem; and his response was to deny the possibility of the education of sense, but allow for the educability of reason. Schiller's proposed solution to this problem, his way of breaking into the virtuous circle, lies in something that is not provided by the State: fine art, as that which 'whatever the political corruption, would remain clear and pure'. Schiller argues that:

Art, like Science, is absolved from all positive constraint and from all conventions introduced by man; both rejoice in absolute immunity from human arbitrariness. The political legislator may put their territory out of bounds; he cannot rule within it. He can proscribe the lover of truth; Truth itself will prevail. He can humiliate the artist; but Art he cannot falsify.[39]

In this, Schiller is proposing that Art can, as it were, 'exceed' the artist: there is no simple identification of the subject of the artist with the object, the artifice, that she or he makes. That discrepancy is also instrumental in allowing Schiller to deal with the kind of anxiety about personal identity that had been expressed by Beattie in a very different way from that proposed by Common Sense. As a fundamental basis or precept for his thought on aesthetic education, Schiller argues that abstraction, at its highest levels, 'distinguishes in man something that endures and something that constantly changes. That which endures it calls his Person, that which changes, his Condition'.[40] The variety of conditions operates within the uniformity of person; and this therefore reformulates Hutcheson's aesthetics, but this time applied directly to the human subject and across time. In Schiller, there is an explicit political dimension to this, for the relation of Person to Condition is fundamentally the relation between freedom and time. Foreshadowing

---

[39] Schiller, *Aesthetic Education*, 55. It is important to note here that Schiller concedes that many artists will strive only to gratify the degraded tastes of humanity, working within rules; yet, despite such artists (or scientists), art itself will 'struggle triumphantly to the surface', beyond the control of specific individuals.

[40] Schiller, *Aesthetic Education*, 73.

Schopenhauer on the relations between subjects and objects, Schiller argues that in terms of the relation between Person and Condition, neither can singularly be deemed to be foundational, the ground upon which the other subsists:

Not because we think, will, or feel, do we exist; and not because we exist, do we think, will, or feel. We are because we are; we feel, think, and will, because outside of ourselves something other than ourselves exists too

from which it follows that:

The Person therefore must be its own ground; for what persists cannot proceed from what changes. And so we would, in the first place, have the idea of Absolute Being grounded upon itself, that is to say, Freedom. The Condition, on the other hand, must have a ground other than itself; it must, since it does not owe its existence to the Person, i.e., is not absolute, proceed from something. And so we would, in the second place, have the condition of all contingent being or becoming, that is to say, Time.[41]

The human condition is now proposed by Schiller as an interplay between consciousness and history, between what he thinks as the Freedom that is consciousness and the constraints imposed by the time that is history. He understands this interplay in terms of forces or drives, bringing the 'sensuous drive' into contact and potential conflict with the 'formal drive'. The business of the 'sensuous drive' is to set the subject 'within the limits of time, and to turn him into matter', matter here being understood as change itself or, as Schiller calls it, 'reality which occupies time':

Consequently, this drive demands that there should be change, that time shall have a content. This state, which is nothing but time occupied by content, is called sensation, and it is through this alone that physical existence makes itself known.[42]

The key element for us here is the idea of 'time occupied by content', for this speaks directly to the fundamental philosophical problem inherited, as I noted previously, from Augustine, regarding experience or time itself. In this state, governed by the sensuous drive, the human subject is only 'an occupied moment of time', which is to say that, as Person, she or he *is* not at all, for, as Schiller has it, her or his personality is 'suspended as long as he is ruled by sensation, and swept along by the flux of time'. This sensuous

---

[41] Ibid.   [42] Ibid. 79.

drive, therefore, seems to make experience possible in that it gives a content to time in an intense present; and yet, paradoxically, it is precisely in binding subjectivity to this sensuous drive that we limit and circumscribe the possibility of experience or of empirical fulfilment. If the subject is exclusively governed by the sensuous drive (by the desire to give the present a content), then the subject is bound to a world of *mere* sensation:

With indestructible chains it [the sensuous drive] binds the ever-soaring spirit to the world of sense, and summons abstraction from its most unfettered excursions into the Infinite back to the limitations of the Present. Thought may indeed escape it for the moment, and a firm will triumphantly resist its demands; but suppressed nature soon resumes her rights, and presses for reality of existence, for some content to our knowing and some purpose to our doing.[43]

That is to say, if we give a content to time, then, paradoxically, we are limiting the freedom of the subject. In this, the subject loses autonomy and becomes itself merely a counter in a play of forces that we will call 'experience': it is as if the subject can no longer distinguish itself from other physical entities in the world and is, instead, condemned to be at the mercy of the relations among objects, and among their forces, that keeps the world moving. That is to say, in this state of affairs, the world—and within it, the art-object—moves the subject, and the subject becomes merely the victim of such movement. In Schiller's terms, the subject is all Condition, and does not arrive at Personhood.

Against the sensuous drive, the formal drive is that which allows the subject to bring harmony to her or his manifold experiences, or to produce that uniformity from the variety or diversity of experiences that constitutes her or his history. The formal drive allows the subject 'to affirm his Person among all the changes of Condition'. Consequently, this drive has as one of its explicit functions the annulment of time, the annulment of change. In this, the formal drive annuls time in the interests of a 'real' which is deemed to be necessary and eternal. Put another way, the formal drive annuls time in the interests of a specific version of truth, one in which truth is considered to be (as it is for Beattie) immutable.

Truth exists, therefore, out-of-time, according to the logic of this

---

43 Schiller, *Aesthetic Education*, 81.

tension between the two drives. The concept of truth thus overlaps here with that of Rousseau as well as that of Beattie. The logic is one that suggests that truth, in its alignment with the formal, has no content: that is to say, truth can be given, but cannot be 'experienced' by a subject as a lived condition of her or his present: it cannot be felt. Feeling, for Schiller, is explicitly 'occasional', while thought is 'eternal'. The subject can thus 'know' the truth, but cannot, in these terms, 'believe' it. In such a state of affairs, what has happened to the possibility of education?

While the sensuous drive provides 'cases' whose effect is to involve the subject, the formal drive provides 'laws', with the truth of which the subject is constrained to conform, regardless of her or his beliefs in specific cases. Schiller's response to this predicament, caused by truth's problematic relation to time, is to argue that it is the business of culture and of education to *regulate* the play between the two drives, not through the prioritization of one over the other, but rather through establishing the conditions for their fullest mutual realization.[44] Education, therefore, intensifies our passivity to the utmost, so that we will be receptive to the fullest possible sense-experience (of an art-work, say); and it simultaneously intensifies our activity to the utmost, so that we will be able to reason to the highest degree without such reasoning being determined by exterior forces (such as that of the art-work itself).

What counts as aesthetic education for Schiller is precisely what I. A. Richards, later, will describe as the condition of tragedy. Here is Schiller:

Where both these aptitudes are conjoined, man will combine the greatest fullness of existence with the highest autonomy and freedom, and instead of losing himself to the world, will rather draw the latter into himself in all its infinitude of phenomena, and subject it to the unity of his reason[45]

---

[44] It is instructive to compare this with Coleridge, who argues for much the same thing in the *Biographia Literaria*, ed. George Watson (Dent, 1975), 174 (and also the whole of chapters 12 to 14); and with I. A. Richards, who finds in tragedy an art that brings into the fullest play two opposed forces, and allows them their fullest articulation without suppression. See I. A. Richards, *Principles of Literary Criticism* (1924; rev. and repr. Routledge & Kegan Paul, 1976) 193. It should be noted here that Richards has effectively eradicated the question of the nation-state in a formal criticism located in an abstract human subject, that provided by psychoanalytical models of the subject.

[45] Schiller, *Aesthetic Education*, 87–9.

and here is Richards:

What clearer instance of the 'balance and reconciliation of opposite or discordant qualities' can be found than Tragedy. Pity, the impulse to approach, and Terror, the impulse to retreat, are brought in Tragedy to a reconciliation which they find nowhere else, and with them who knows what other allied groups of equally discordant impulses. Their union in an ordered single response is the *catharsis* by which Tragedy is recognized, whether Aristotle meant anything of this kind or not. This is the explanation of that sense of release, of repose in the midst of stress, of balance and composure, given by Tragedy, for there is no other way in which such impulses, once awakened, can be set at rest without suppression.[46]

The combining thus of the sensuous with the formal is a combining of the temporal with the true, giving history (the temporal) in the form of necessity (the true) to Schiller. Schiller describes this as that which eventuates in a third drive, which he calls the 'play drive'. In Schiller's German, 'play' is *Spielen*, a verb which brings together notions of ludic activity, gaming, with, crucially, *theatricality*. Theatre is that which will reconcile history with necessity, the vagaries of our temporal condition with our immutable eternal truth. As Schiller has it:

The sense-drive demands that there shall be change and that time shall have a content; the form-drive demands that time shall be annulled and that there shall be no change. That drive, therefore, in which both the others work in concert (permit me ... to call it the play-drive) ... therefore, would be directed towards annulling time within time, reconciling becoming with absolute being and change with identity.[47]

Although this playing gives us a theory which has become essentially a theory of *tragedy*, it is important to note that it is not in any sense pessimistic. On the contrary, the reconciliation of history with necessity is tied fundamentally to an Optimism. History and necessity are, for Schiller, what variety and uniformity were for Hutcheson; but in the later writer, the terms are marked primarily by an ostensible incommensurability in their different attitudes to *time*, in which secularity and non-secularity have to be thought together and all at once. In aesthetics, the content of the work of art has to be reconciled with its own capacity for exceeding itself, for reaching beyond itself to encompass values unknown to the art

---

[46]   Richards, *Principles of Literary Criticism* 193.
[47]   Schiller, *Aesthetic Education*, 97.

or to the artist. In education, the experience of the Person at a moment of her or his Conditioning has to allow that moment to reach beyond its own content to a form that exceeds it. These things, for Schiller, happen in *Spielen*, in the game that is theatre: and this becomes a primary site for education, therefore. Yet, as the foregoing argument in this book has made clear, theatre has also been precisely the site of a *national* education. It is the history and the necessity of the nation and its national character that are thus being reconciled, and the nation-state finds its justification in theatrical practice and in aesthetic theory.

In Schiller's case, this tacit nationalism is mediated in an extremely neutral form, for he is concerned not so much with the nation as with an explicit concept of the State. It is for the State to regulate this aesthetic education, this reconciliation of history with necessity, of time with truth. In this, therefore, the State has a role to play in the question of theatre (and this, perhaps, is why Rousseau, under other circumstances, might have agreed with d'Alembert on the desirability of a theatre in Geneva); additionally, such theatre has to find a role for what we now identify as *tragic* production, in which the spectator is brought to her or his fullest possible condition of being and becoming, both at once;[48] and thirdly, the education consequent upon this is to be one in which the realm of the object and of the objective is to be brought within the purview of the subject, such that the subject can gain freedom and autonomy rather than being enslaved to the world of necessary force and objects.

Schiller warns against what can happen if the relations between the sensual and the formal drives are not properly regulated. He repeatedly stresses the importance of having these drives as fully realized, brought into 'play' as fully as possible, so that they operate without any repression. Given their necessary interplay, it would be all too easy to establish a state of affairs which is precisely the contrary of that which Schiller desires. What he desires is a mode of organic form or what he terms 'living form', in which the State becomes more than some abstract entity, and is rather legitimized by being a vigorous and vibrant part of the being of the subject or citizen. The State would make what Gramsci will later call 'organic intellectuals' of us all. It is too easy, argues Schiller, to

---

[48] That is to say, the theatre in question should be governed by what we now recognize as a Coleridgean notion of *organic form*.

miss our destiny as such organic intellectuals. We can fail in two ways: either we can 'let the sensuous drive encroach upon the formal' the consequence of which would be to give too much determining force to sensuality or feeling (art controls or determines the subject); or we can let the formal encroach upon the sensuous, thereby substituting thought for feeling (the subject is not 'touched' by art, knowing what to think and allowing such thought to predetermine the feeling—and thereby to deny the experience of feeling in relation to any single specific art-work).

In the first case, he [the subject] will never be himself; in the second he will never be anything else; and for that very reason, therefore, he will in both cases be neither the one nor the other, consequently—a non-entity.[49]

It is therefore important for Schiller that a principle of undecidability regarding the relative priority of the sensual and the formal drives does not fall simply into a mixture or confusion of the two drives. They must be distinguished one from the other; but they can still have their relation *regulated*, and such regulation happens through the experience of 'living form', or the State characterized by organic intellect.

In short, criticism now, as part of the pedagogical function of the State, is institutionalized. Especially in its task to reconcile history and necessity, it is thus clearly related to Utopianism: criticism, as an aesthetic education, will produce an ameliorated human condition, and the ethics of the social will be dependent upon our capacities for freedom, capacities themselves dependent upon the State's ability to regulate *theatricality* or to generate 'play'.

III

So much for art 'in time'; what of that other strain in early nineteenth-century aesthetics to which I adverted above: the tendency of art to remove the subject from time, as evidenced in Hegel and, yet more importantly, in the great pessimist Schopenhauer? It is to this that I now attend briefly, before focusing on the main topic here: how an institutionalized form of aesthetic education conspires to suppress Pessimism.

---

49   Schiller, *Aesthetic Education*, 89.

Schiller died in 1805, just as Hegel was preparing his first major work, the *Phenomenology of Spirit*, with its magisterial opening section devoted to a meditation on the present, the 'here-now' of the 'I'. There, Hegel tries to address the question of 'sense-certainty', or modes of knowledge dependent upon consciousness. He rapidly discovers that what is fundamentally at stake is a relation between something that can call itself 'I' in the face of something that it takes as its specific object, a single item. Perception is thus of the nature of an event, a confrontation between two forces. What results is the realization that 'in sense-certainty, pure being at once splits up into what we have called the two "Thises", one "This" as "I", and the other "This" as object', and, further, that the sense-certainty is not given simply *immediately* in this aesthetic or perceptual experience, but is also *mediated* therein, in that the 'I' is mediated to itself by the object, and the object is itself in a situation of sense-certainty courtesy of the 'I' distinguishing it or singling it out.[50]

In thinking of this 'event' as something happening 'here', 'now', Hegel also proceeds to evacuate the here and the now—the present or presence—of all specific meaning, by rendering the terms fully deictic. This allows Hegel to establish a purely formal constitution of the subject, the 'I', along with a sense of 'here' and of 'now' as at once site-specific terms and also utterly general terms, allowing a philosophy based upon a distinction between 'essence and instance' as he calls it,[51] or between being and time as Heidegger will later term it. It was not until the 1820s, when he was installed in Berlin, that Hegel began systematically to apply this philosophy of the 'essence and instance' to aesthetics; and while he was lecturing to packed halls in his tortuous prose, Schopenhauer, who had arrogantly set his own lectures at the same time as Hegel, lectured to silence—to empty halls—next door. The confrontation in these two— between, on the one hand, a Hegelian philosophy of 'essence and instance' whose fundamental model is Optimistic in its Christianity (in which Christ is the perfect 'instance' of God as 'essence') and, on the other, a Schopenhauerian philosophy indebted to Indian religions, but atheist in itself—is the nineteenth-century's founding version of that nationalism in aesthetics that

[50]   Hegel, *Phenomenology of Spirit* (trans. A. V. Miller; Oxford University Press, Oxford 1977), 59.   [51]   Ibid. 59.

shapes the eighteenth century. In its great confrontation of 'West' with 'East', it also opens the question of national aesthetics to imperialism.

Hegel starts out by setting an opposition between necessity and beauty. The realm of nature (in which Hutcheson, of course, had found a primary version of beauty, 'original' beauty) is dismissed by Hegel as a realm of indifferent necessity; and beauty is identified with the free operation of the mind, no matter how banal the inventiveness of any specific mind may be:

if we look at it *formally*—i.e. only considering in what way it exists, not what there is in it—even a silly fancy such as may pass through a man's head is *higher* than any product of nature; for such a fancy must at least be characterized by intellectual being and by freedom. In respect of its content ... the sun, for instance, appears to us to be an absolutely necessary factor in the universe, while a blundering notion passes away as accidental and transient; but yet, in its own being, a natural existence such as the sun is indifferent, is not free or self-conscious, while if we consider it in its necessary connection with other things we are not regarding it by itself or for its own sake, and, therefore, not as beautiful.[52]

Hegel is at pains right from the start to assert the relation of aesthetic beauty to freedom, as was Schiller; but where Schiller saw this freedom as a material and political freedom—the autonomy of the subject—Hegel rather sees it as a matter purely for consciousness, or at least for the mind. Insofar as art depends upon the mind's capacity for inventiveness or construction, it demonstrates the freedom of the mind; and, further, it is in the mind and not in the realm of nature that we are to seek truth. Truth is a matter of mind, in relation to which the beauty that we may see in nature is but a *reflection* of this higher intellectual beauty.

This equation of beauty with freedom allows Hegel to argue that art is marked precisely by its *unpredictability*, by its escape from rules and regulation: 'artistic production is not formal activity in accordance with given determinations', as he puts it.[53] It follows from this 'irregularity' of art that there is, at best, an uneasy relation between art and science; for while art, as a presentation to sense, necessarily attends to particularity, science, 'everyone

---

[52] Hegel, *Introductory Lectures on Aesthetics* (trans. Bernard Bosanquet; introd. Michael Inwood; Penguin, Harmondsworth, 1993), 4.
[53] Ibid. 30–1.

admits, is compelled by its form to busy itself with thought which abstracts from the mass of particulars'.[54] Hegel here has taken but one aspect of what Hutcheson had seen as constitutive of beauty—general abstraction, or what I called 'theory'—and called it science. He thus manages to break totally, for the first time in modern aesthetics, with what had been the prevailing disposition in which beauty had always been seen, in various ways, as an effective reconciliation of the demands of particularity with the demands of generality.

Hegel also breaks with Schiller on the question of aesthetic education. He concedes the ready availability of the Schillerian thesis: 'reflection soon suggests the notion that art has the capacity and the function of mitigating the fierceness of the desires', by 'educating' the impulses, desires, and passions of the subject 'so that they don't occupy the whole man'.[55] In his consideration of this, Hegel sees that the 'savageness' of passion consists in the fact that the subject of the passion becomes effectively subject to the passion, for she or he is so fully identified with and in the passion that the subject is left with no will outside of the particular passion, leaving her or him entirely circumscribed by the limitations of desire. The thesis regarding art's capacity for education rests on the claim that art can externalize such emotion, or can effectively *alienate* it for a subject, allowing the subject to gain self-consciousness; and, in turn, this leads to the idea that art should have a specific moral content. Hegel finds this interesting, but inadequate. Its inadequacy lies in the fact that it will lead to a constant opposition not between essence and instance, but between universal and particular; and he wants fundamentally to get beyond such oppositions, with their inherent drive towards the 'reconciliation of opposing forces', to a more serious kind of progressive opposition: dialectics. To do this, we must acknowledge the limitations inherent in seeing art as a utilitarian or instrumental exercise. We should avoid, argues Hegel, the confusion of the question 'what is the *aim* of art' with the question of 'what is the *use* of art':

The perverseness of this [confusion] lies in the point that the work of art would then be regarded as aspiring to something else which is set before consciousness as the essential and as what ought to be; so that then the work of art would only have value as an instrument in the realization of

54 Ibid. 7.   55 Ibid. 53.

an end having substantive importance *outside* the sphere of art. Against this it is necessary to maintain that art has the vocation of revealing *the truth* in the form of sensuous artistic shape ... and, therefore, has its purpose in itself.[56]

Other matters, such as instruction, edification, education, and so on, thus have nothing whatever to do with the work of art for Hegel, and certainly cannot play a determining role in its conception.

Having made these two turns, away from the Hutchesonian legacy and away from Schillerian principles regarding aesthetic education, Hegel then makes a third fundamental shift. The argument against aesthetic education rests on the pillar that art, insofar as it is art at all, is marked by non-functionality. That is not to deny that art can be used or can be made to have a utilitarian purpose: it is simply to assert that when it does so, it stops being art. Interestingly, this third turn involves, once more, space, place and nation. Art, he argues, is not real art unless and until it is free, such freedom being constituted as a matter of the freedom of the mind. It only comes fully into itself when it assumes the same kind of status as religion or philosophy, becoming thus 'simply a mode of revealing to consciousness and bringing to utterance the Divine Nature, the deepest interests of humanity, and the most comprehensive truths of the mind'.[57] This rather grand claim for art, in which it appears to be entirely divorced from material considerations, assuming some kind of transcendental existence (putting it outside of time) , is *immediately* relativized by Hegel. His next sentence suggests that these truths may not be quite so comprehensive, for they are spatially *located*:

It is in works of art that nations have deposited the profoundest intuitions and ideas of their hearts; and fine art is frequently the key—in many nations there is no other—to the understanding of their wisdom and of their religion.[58]

Art, thus, is tied to the *nation* which gives it its specificity; and one gets access not to a universal truth but rather to a national truth through it. Art reveals national character and is founded upon it. This sudden intrusion of the concept of the nation is itself quickly made more general by Hegel; for rather than addressing directly

---

[56] Hegel, *Introductory Lectures on Aesthetics*, 61.   [57] Ibid. 9.
[58] Ibid.

specific nation-states, he returns to the negativity of his preferred deictics; and art becomes that which engages a *here* and a *beyond*. It is a *here* and *beyond*, not a *now* and *then*, importantly: primarily spatial rather than temporal, or, better, temporal only insofar as it is realized in space. In this, we also see the development of a dialectical thinking, in the confrontation of the demands of the here (the instance) with the beyond (another instance) whose collision opens the way to truth (the essence). Art is given to the senses and is thus *here*, certainly; but it also is based in a capacity for what the romantics had called 'imagination', a capacity for thinking *as if* from 'there'. Here is Hegel:

This is an attribute which art shares with religion and philosophy, only in this peculiar mode, that it represents even the highest ideas *in sensuous forms*, thereby bringing them nearer to the character of natural phenomena, to the senses, and to feeling. The world, into whose depths *thought* penetrates, is a supra-sensuous world, which is thus, to begin with, erected as a *beyond* over against immediate consciousness and present sensation; the power which thus rescues itself from the *here*, that consists in the actuality and the finiteness of sense, is the freedom of thought in cognition. But the mind is able to heal this schism which its advance creates; it generates out of itself the works of fine art as the first middle term of reconciliation between pure thought and what is external, sensuous, and transitory, between nature with its finite actuality and the infinite freedom of the reason that comprehends.[59]

Art is the product of the confrontation of the here with the beyond (of a specific nation with its others, say). It does not *reconcile* the particular with the general; rather, it is the product of a clash between the demands of immediacy (the here, the sensuous, the 'instance') and those of the ideal (the beyond in all its generality and alterity, thought, the 'essence'). Art, in short, is what happens when a specific nation (here) starts to think itself in relation to the world and to history (beyond), and is forced to give a content to presence, to the here-now or the 'I' that is the subjectivity, the character, of the nation as it emerges. Thus can an absolute knowing reveal itself in and through a particular identity, as in Hegel's model, Christ. What this amounts to, in sum, is a transcending of the here and the beyond in the interests of a universalism, whose effect is to eradicate the fundamental differences between the here

[59] Ibid. 9–10.

and the beyond (a beyond which, of course, from a certain point of view, is only an other 'here').

Badiou, writing recently of Saint Paul, is instructive here. For Paul, Christ is an 'event', the effect of which is to establish a new relation of the subject to what it takes as its object: 'le discours chrétien est dans un rapport absolument nouveau à son objet.'[60] The ostensibly single subject is, in fact, the binding together of two subjectivities, named by Paul as that of the spirit and that of the flesh, and 'Il est de l'essence du sujet chrétien d'être, par sa fidélité à l'événement-Christ, divisé en deux voies qui affectent en pensée tout sujet.'[61] Further, the real, according to this divided subjectivity, is now thinkable in two ways, that of the flesh and that of the spirit. Badiou translates *Romans* 8: 6 to mean (in terms that would have been entirely consistent with Hegel's thinking described above) that 'La pensée de la chair est mort, la pensée de l'esprit est vie.'[62] Given, under these circumstances, that the object of thought is the totality of the world as given for subjectivity or, in Hegel's terms: 'Truth could not be, did it not appear and reveal itself, were it not truth *for* someone or something, *for* itself as also *for* Mind,'[63] we can now say, with Badiou, that:

Le réel cause le désir (philosophique) d'occuper adéquatement la place qui vous est distribuée, et dont la pensée peut ressaisir le principe. Ce que la pensée identifie comme proprement réel est une place, un séjour, auquel le sage sait qu'il faut consentir.[64]

For Paul, however—as now also for Hegel—Christ-the-event 'indique précisément la vanité des places'; and instead, the real can be attested to wherever the subject becomes conscious of its own limitations, which is to say, *universally*. Where this allows Paul to declare the identity of the Jew with the Greek, it allows Hegel and Hegelian logic to be profoundly aware of place (Germany) while yet negating its national specificity, its relativity. To think Hegelian is not to think German, but to think world (and world-as-German). Once more, the difficulties for aesthetic philosophy consequential upon the relativisms occasioned by the awareness of national consciousness, national institutions, national theatres and cultures, are

[60] Alain Badiou, *Saint Paul* (PUF, Paris, 1997), 59.
[61] Ibid. 60.   [62] Ibid. 59.
[63] Hegel, *Introductory Lectures*, 10.
[64] Badiou, *Saint Paul*, 60.

Optimistically eradicated: difference is identity, in this case, Christian identity.

Things are somewhat different for Schopenhauer. Like Schiller, Schopenhauer sees the world as an arrangement of subjects with objects; but one in which neither subjectivity nor objectivity are given as such: 'this whole world—is only object in relation to the subject', such that the instantiation of the subject is itself as much an effect of a specific arrangement of forces as is the instantiation of the object. Nothing is therefore 'essentially' subject or object.[65] The world is a series of Humean events, a concatenation or series of conjunctures in which subjects and objects are constituted as such through the interrelation of forces: 'where the subject ends, the object begins', as Schopenhauer has it.[66] It follows from this that Schopenhauer must begin from a conception of time in which the present—the site that would normally be that of sensuous experience—is radically empty; and he indeed argues that each moment in time exists only insofar as it has effaced the preceding one and only to be effaced in its turn: 'The past and the future ... are empty as a dream, and between them runs the present as a mere boundary-line without extension and without duration.'[67]

Schopenhauer defines the subject as 'that which knows all things, and is known by none'.[68] Given this, how can we reconcile the pure 'eventness', the pure transience of the instanced with this essence of the subject? Schopenhauer's answer to this, famously, lies in his giving a full philosophical significance to the body. A specific series—indeed a *sequence*—of subject–object relations are realized in and through my body; and thus my body—specifically my body as Schopenhauerian *will*—becomes a mediation between subjective and objective realms (it is of both), and thereby constitutes me as an individual:

the knowledge which I have of my will, though it is immediate, cannot be separated from the knowledge that I have of my body. I know my will not as a whole, not as a unity, not completely according to its nature, but I know it only in its individual acts, thus in time, which is the form of the phenomenal aspect of my body as it is of every object.[69]

If the experience of art—as of aesthetic objects not identifiable solely with my body, objects offering a form of resistance to my body—is

[65] Arthur Schopenhauer, *World as Will and Idea*, 4.
[66] Ibid. 5.   [67] Ibid. 7.   [68] Ibid. 5.
[69] Ibid. 34.

through my body, the clear consequence is that I will engage in a purely egoistical way with the world: 'It is precisely by way of this special relationship to one body that the knowing subject is an individual'.[70] That is to say, the instance of art will confirm the essence of the subject; and all art, therefore, would be *merely* a reflection of the subject, having thus only a phantasmal existence. This, clearly, is not the case; indeed, Schopenhauer describes it as madness to subscribe to this egoistical view.[71]

Against such egoism, Schopenhauer proposes an aesthetic that he derives from Platonic notions of the Forms. Before outlining that, however, it is vital to attend to how Schopenhauer sees Plato, as fundamentally the inheritor of an *Indian* philosophy, in which truths, directly accessible only to a few, are realized for the many in the figures of myths. Addressing the specific myth of the transmigration of souls, through which an economy of justice is understood, he writes:

Never has a myth more closely allied itself ... to the philosophical truth which is accessible to so few, than this ancient doctrine of the noblest and oldest of peoples. Degenerate as this [Indian] race may now be in many respects, this doctrine still holds sway as the universal belief of the people, and has a decided influence on life to-day as it had four thousand years ago. Hence, Pythagoras and Plato admiringly took up that *ne plus ultra* of mythical representation, adopted it from India or Egypt, respected it, applied it, and (we know not in how far) even believed it themselves. We, on the contrary, now send to the Brahmans English clergymen and pietistical Moravian linen-weavers in order, out of compassion to set them right and to tell them that they are created out of nothing, and that they ought gratefully to rejoice in that. But what will happen to us is the same as what happens to the man who fires a bullet at a rock-face. In India our religions will *never* take root. The primeval wisdom of the human race will not be displaced by what happened in Galilee. On the contrary, Indian philosophy flows back to Europe, and will produce a fundamental change in our scholarship and in our thinking.[72]

Farewell Hegel; welcome Modernism, one might say. In this, Schopenhauer the atheist rails against missionary imperialism, clearly; but he also is making the point that his own Neoplatonic philosophy is itself indebted to the East; that for him as Western philosopher, the East is not simply an aspect of the world that is

---

[70] Schopenhauer, *World as Will and Idea*, 36.   [71] Ibid. 37.
[72] Ibid. 222.

there to bolster and consolidate his Western ego and its self-present truths.

It is art, fundamentally, that will produce the escape from aesthetic egoism. Art is not the instantiation of 'ideas'; rather, art is that which can reveal the Idea in its full Platonic sense. Such Ideas 'can become objects of knowledge only on condition that the individuality of the knowing subject is suspended'; and 'the subject, insofar as it knows an Idea, is no longer an individual'.[73] The logic of this is that in art, the body is to be, in a strict sense, suspended, for the body as concretized will presupposes a temporal existence only. Time, argues Schopenhauer 'is only the fragmented and piecemeal view which the individual being has of the Ideas, which are outside time and consequently *eternal*'.[74] Hence, the individual (i.e. the subject as embodied) may have the intimation that an Idea is to be known; but she or he can only know it insofar as they give up on the body or the will.

It is this austerity, characteristic of some Indian philosophies, which opens Schopenhauer to his fundamental Pessimism. He concedes that it is the knowledge of particularity that is usually accepted as our normal meaning of knowledge. To get from this—which is necessarily temporal and thus also necessarily egoistical—to the Idea, the subject must forget the interrelatedness of the object of perception (in Kantian terms, its time, space, causality), and look instead at the *what* that it is, such that the whole subject loses herself or himself, *as if* the object were there *without a subject of perception*. At that point, what is known is not the idea (which is of necessity an aspect of subjectivity), but rather the Idea:

> what is known is no longer the individual thing as such, but the Idea, the eternal form ... The person rapt in this perception is thereby no longer individual ... but he is a pure, willess, painless, timeless *subject of knowledge*.[75]

The individual may know particular things; but the pure subject of knowing has only Ideas; or, the individual is limited to her or his historical instance, while the subject of knowledge enters the realm of eternity. Art, thus, takes the subject out of time, leaves her or him *disinterested*. For Schopenhauer, the nation will not supplement this loss of individuality, for it is precisely the interestedness

[73] Ibid. 98, 100.   [74] Ibid. 100.   [75] Ibid. 102.

of the subject as an instance, such as the instantiation of a national character, that has been the issue. In returning the East to our aesthetics, Schopenhauer also offers a counter to aesthetic imperialism.

Such disinterestedness, necessary for our acceding to the truth, gives us a version of truth that can be known but not historically or materially lived. The freedom that Hegel finds in art is, for Schopenhauer, simply a negative concept, the 'denial of necessity'.[76] The striving after happiness, which is for Hegel and for Schiller before him, part of the point of this freedom is, for Schopenhauer, vain, for, in the end, all such 'freedoms' gained, all such autonomy won, leads to the inevitability of death, before which 'all life is suffering'.[77] Sounding increasingly like a direct precursor of Cioran, he finds the opposite of suffering in boredom; and it follows from all of this that optimism 'appears not merely as an absurd, but also as a really *wicked* way of thinking, and as a bitter mockery of the unspeakable suffering of humanity'.[78]

What, after this, has happened to the Utopia promised through aesthetic education?

IV

Utopia, paradoxically, is an evasion of the historical. In this concluding section of the present chapter, I shall argue that, within any text that thinks of itself as modern, as part of a project of modernity or of modernization, there is an avoidance of history or of the time that I have shown to be central to the construction of the aesthetic. Paradoxically, the modern text avoids the very history that we would need to allow us to proceed from where we are now to a better tomorrow. The collocation I make here—of the modern with the Utopian—will show that a text is Utopian precisely to the degree that it denies us access to a condition of pleasure, by denying us the possibility of the real historical advancement that would be required for us to attain to Utopia. In short, the Utopian text offers a vision of pleasure precisely by denying us access to such pleasure: all Utopian discourse is dystopian, conditioned by a pessimism which the Utopian text exists ostensibly to deny. Further, I

---

[76] Schopenhauer, *World as Will and Idea*, 187.   [77] Ibid. 197.
[78] Ibid. 206.

want to suggest that the condition I describe here with respect to the literary text is also a condition of modern literary conscious-ness: the dystopian Utopia is our modern way of thinking, and is the ground on which criticism, as the institutionalized form of aes-thetics, is based.[79] Dystopia is at the core of the academy, despite the fact that the space in which we might 'play' as Schillerian teach-ers ostensibly exists for the amelioration of the social.

Utopia is always an island, always concerned with the distinc-tion of a place from its environs. Cioran is able to relate this to the nation:

Just as a nation, in order to set itself apart from the others, in order to humiliate and overwhelm them, or simply in order to acquire a unique physiognomy, needs an extravagant idea to guide it, to propose goals incommensurable with its real capacities, so a society evolves and asserts itself only if ideals are suggested to it, or inculcated in it, out of all pro-portion to what it is. Utopia fulfills, in the life of collectivities, the function assigned to the notion of 'mission' in the life of peoples. Hence ideologies are the by-product and, in a sense, the vulgar expression of messianic or Utopian visions.[80]

Further, this Utopian thinking is related to the human desire to be historical:

Wisdom—fascinated by nothing—recommends an existing, a *given* happi-ness, which man rejects, and by this very rejection becomes a historical ani-mal, that is, a devotee of *imagined* happiness.[81]

The island, especially the explicitly Utopian island (or city, or state) has to present itself as being self-sufficient: it requires nothing more than its own constitution. Indeed, any excess, anything external (as in the form of imported disease, say) threatens its very being.[82] Part of the very nature of Utopia is its exclusivity, its capacity for erect-ing boundaries; and what it must exclude is, by definition, the harmful, the excessive insofar as it—excess—is harmful. Utopias

---

[79] E. M. Cioran, *History and Utopia* (trans. Richard Howard; Quartet Books, 1996), 91, makes this a yet more general claim: 'So deeply have Utopias marked us, that it is from outside, from the course of events or from the progress of collectivi-ties that we await our deliverance. Thus was devised the Meaning of history, whose vogue would supplant that of Progress, without adding anything new to it.'

[80] Ibid. 93.   [81] Ibid. 81.

[82] On the relation of Utopia to imperialism, especially with respect to the ques-tion of disease, see Alfred Crosbie, *Ecological Imperialism* (Cambridge University Press, Cambridge, 1986).

are built upon a kind of perfect economy, in which all internal forces are held in a final balance or harmony, even if there is, within the Utopia itself massive energy. Utopia is the site *par excellence* of *regulation*. Cioran again: 'Hostile to anomaly, to deformity, to irregularity, it [Utopia] tends to the affirmation of the homogeneous, of the typical, of repetition and orthodoxy.'[83] As such a perfect, and hence necessarily exclusive economy, Utopia is necessarily an island, even if it is a city as in Plato's *Republic*, or a dystopian nation, as in *1984*. It must be isolated, even desolate, like a character in tragedy who is facing her or his bare or basic human condition. Tragedy, we might say, is what happens when someone has been stripped so bare of interhuman or social relation that all she or he has left is a kind of being-towards-death, a self-presence so extreme that no possibility of any further change is possible. Such a character, in her or his full self-presence, has her or his present moment as a moment full of content, not dependent on a hereafter or a foregoing; and consequently, such a character has no history. She or he becomes pure space: a pure presence, a Cleopatra held up to view, a Hamlet borne aloft, a Cordelia held up by Lear, as in those Shakespearean tableaux. Death, in tragedy, is an isolation occasioned by the giving of content to the present moment to such an extent that the present loses all form, and with it all relation to a formative past or a future determinable from it. This present, the present marked by a fullness of content, has been written of before, in another Utopian text, Augustine's *City of God*, in which the passage of time is compared to the passage through a liminal present moment characterized as a moment 'in death'. Augustine tries to identify and to characterize the moment of a person's death, and discovers that:

there are three situations: 'before death', 'in death', and 'after death', and three corresponding adjectives: 'living', 'dying', and 'dead'. This makes it very hard to define when he is dying, that is 'in death'; a state in which he is neither living (which is the state *before* death) or dead (which is *after* death), but dying, or 'in death'. It is evident that as long as the soul is in the body, especially if sensibility remains, a man is alive, his constituent parts being soul and body. Consequently he must be described as being still

---

[83] Cioran, *History and Utopia*, 86. Cioran goes on: 'But life is rupture, derogation from the norms of matter. And man, in relation to life, is heresy to the second degree, victory of the individual, of whim, aberrant apparition.'

'before death', not 'in death'. But when the soul has departed and has withdrawn all bodily sensation, a man is said to be 'after death', and dead.

Thus between these two situations the period in which a man is dying or 'in death' disappears. For if he is still alive, he is 'before death'; if he has stopped living, he is by now 'after death'. Therefore he is never detected in the situation of dying, or 'in death'. The same thing happens in the passage of time; we try to find the present moment, but without success, because the future changes into the past without interval.[84]

Jameson, too, has argued the intimacy of Utopia to death, claiming that 'there is no discrepancy between Utopia and death, the former being what you do to distract yourself from the organic boredom of the latter'.[85] Death, for Jameson, is essentially a matter of spatial perspective, and he describes it as 'the aftereffect and sign that the perspective of Utopia has been reached, which consists in a great and progressive distance from all individual and existential experience, from individual people, from *characters*', from which it follows that 'the emergence of death is then ... the signal that it has been possible to take the point of view of the species upon human existence'.[86] It is important to note here the Augustinian collocation of a Utopian moment with the loss of experience, and specifically of precisely that sensuous experience—that sensibility—on which the emergence of aesthetic modernity had been ostensibly based. Jameson allows the establishment of an opposition between history and death (an opposition that is surely counter-intuitive, given the necessity of death for personal history or biography): history is marked by time and by difference, whereas Utopian death (with its achieved perfect economy, its exclusivity, its isolation) is now marked as a *space* that has eradicated the need for any further change or for history itself.

The fact that Utopia is an island (that 'no-*place* is an island', so to speak) means that Utopian texts must present a place that is strictly speaking impossible: a place that can admit of nothing exterior to itself (and which therefore cannot even admit of anything

[84] Augustine, *City of God* (trans. Henry Bettenson; Penguin, Harmondsworth, 1972), 519–20. I quote this at length partly to indicate the possibility that the great philosophical precursor of Beckett is not, as is so often thought, Descartes, but rather Augustine, whose style, with its concern for such precision, is extremely premonitory of Beckett, and also of Beckett's friend, Cioran.

[85] Fredric Jameson, *The Seeds of Time* (Columbia University Press, New York, 1994), 111.

[86] Ibid. 122–3.

interior to itself): Utopia is, of necessity, *fiction*, and fiction is its condition. From this, it follows of necessity that, in the Utopian text or condition, all narrative has to tend towards the condition of *description*. Even if there is a narrative story to be told ('this, and then this, followed by that, in consequence of which this', etc.), such a narrative must be proposed as something that exists out-of-time. It will be either something that *has* happened (as with the French preterite tense), in the discovery, foundation or formation of the Utopia; or, much more likely, it will be presented as something that is *constantly happening* as in the continuous present tense of Keats's Grecian Urn, whose 'happy melodist, unwearied' is 'For ever piping songs for ever new'.

Another way of putting this would be to say that, in the Utopian text or condition or mentality, all time veers towards the condition of space, to the establishment of a point of view and of a position for its subject. Time here—the time that would be required if a reader were ever to try to modernize by reaching a condition akin to the Utopia ostensibly desired—exists only in order to establish a locatedness for the reading subject and for the subject of and in the Utopia. It would be a simple conclusion now to suggest that the modern nation-state exists as precisely such a Utopia for aesthetic modernity; but I want to offer a yet more precise identification of the real Utopian condition than this.

In Louis Marin's terms, 'le discours utopique occupe la place vide—historiquement vide—de la résolution historique d'une contradiction',[87] by which he means that Utopia is always neither one thing nor the other. In the case of Thomas More, for example, it is neither England nor America, neither ancient nor modern; rather, Utopia is proposed as a fictional manner of dealing with the seeming necessity of choice between such undecidable possibilities. Utopia is thus a kind of zero-degree of the dialectical synthesis of contraries or, in Marin's terms, it is the discursive expression of the neutral. Utopian discourse allows the imagining of a fictional solution of real contradictions or antinomies, and is thus 'le simulacre de la synthèse'.[88] We should recognize in this neutral, this neither-one-thing-nor-the-other, not only Augustine's moment 'in death' but also Beckett's Unnamable:

---

[87]   Louis Marin, *Utopiques: jeux d'espaces* (Minuit, Paris, 1973), 9.
[88]   Ibid. 26.

perhaps that's what I feel, an outside and an inside and me in the middle, perhaps that's what I am, the thing that divides the world in two, on the one side the outside, on the other the inside, that can be as thin as foil, I'm neither one side nor the other, I'm in the middle, I'm the partition, I've two surfaces and no thickness, perhaps that's what I feel, myself vibrating, I'm the tympanum, on the one hand the mind, on the other the world, I don't belong to either, it's not to me they're talking, it's not of me they're talking, no, that's not it, I feel nothing of all that, try something else, herd of shites ...[89]

This neutral is something that engenders a space, a perspective or a way of seeing things: a mentality. Importantly, the neutral does not require the reader to make a decision, but rather to stay in the realm of the neutral (the realm, now, of the dead). One way of saying this is to state that the Utopian text requires the reader to effect a shift in her or his thinking and to move from a realm of sense-experienced and empirically verifiable facts to a realm of abstract norms—but yet to be 'of' neither realm fully ('on the one hand the mind, on the other the world, I don't belong to either').

Utopia is, therefore, this moment of 'in-between-ness'. Were I a deconstructor, I might call it 'undecidability'; were I a New Critic, I would call it variously 'irony' (Booth), 'ambiguity' (Empson), 'paradox' (Brooks), 'tension' (Tate); but were I Augustine, I would recognize it as a moment 'in death'. Utopian discourse thus projects a fictional space which is a median point between two conditions. In 'nationalist aesthetics', it might be the fictional nation that is, for example, Hume's 'zero-degree England'. More generally, as such an ineffable median point, Utopia is the discourse *par excellence* of modernization, not only suggesting that we can get from a dreadful condition to a better one by way of literature, but also suggesting that we are, in a sense, already there is our undecidedness, our prevarication, our lack of commitment.

In the projection of a Utopian condition, one hypothesizes a state of affairs in which there can be a specified moment when there is no discrepancy between the subject's factual condition and her norms. That, actually, will also serve as a definition of metaphor; and as I indicated in the previous chapter, following Ricardou, metaphor is 'the shortest distance between two

[89] Samuel Beckett, *Molloy, Malone Dies, The Unnamable* (1959; repr. John Calder, 1976), 386.

points'.[90] Utopian discourse is metaphor in this sense that it collapses together two moments, a present one in which change is desirable and a future one when that change will have been so successfully accomplished as to have annihilated all possible futures *and pasts*, including the one from which the change is projected in the first place. What links those two moments is death, the moment of undecidability, the neutral that is metaphor. Yet in saying that this is metaphor, I can now also say that the modernization that is at once inscribed in and prevented by Utopian discourse is also the academy and its pedagogy, including especially its aesthetic education: for what is teaching if not—*inter alia*—the bringing us from an undesirable position of ignorance to one of knowledge, and of establishing, as the link between the ignorant condition and the knowledgeable condition the acculturated subject herself or himself?

Our university—that of modernity—prides itself upon a liberal disinterestedness, the Socratic method: neutrality. Not only is this Utopian, it is also prematurely Utopian and hence also dystopian: it is a recipe for the isolation of the academic from the community, a death-warrant. It is the university that has now assumed the mantle of Utopia, replacing the nation-state as the zero-degree from which all sensibility can be measured; and yet, as my final chapter will show, the university or the academy, especially in its role as aesthetic educator or in its production of *criticism* as we now know it, remains firmly tied to the ideology of the now impossibly self-contradictory nation-state: the place that is 'no-place'.

[90] Jean Ricardou, *Nouveaux problèmes du roman* (Seuil, Paris, 1976), 106.

7

Education, English, and Criticism in the University

I

In or about December 1810, humanistic education changed. The turn of that century was a period in which there was much lively debate over what constituted the nature of the university; and, importantly, it was in this period that the question assumed the corollary task of identifying a national culture and a national character through education, most often through an education grounded in a conception of a foundational philosophy which served to unify the variety of the disciplines. The modern university is thus in a very precise sense, an aesthetic institution, indebted to the principles of regularity and harmony in which ostensible difference or variety can be found (in the manner of Hutcheson and subsequent aesthetics) to occlude an essential unity and identity. The classic formulation here, of course, is that of Humboldt, who, in 1810, wrote his report on the founding of the University of Berlin. As is well known, and as has been noted most pointedly recently by Bill Readings, Humboldt's conception of the university, his 'idea of the university', was fundamentally aligned with the formulation of the German nation-state: university education in Berlin was to be a 'university of culture'. In the terms of Readings's argument, such an institution

draws its legitimacy from culture, which names the synthesis of teaching and research, process and product, history and reason, philology and criticism, historical scholarship and aesthetic experience, the institution and the individual. Thus the revelation of the idea of culture and the development of the individual are one. Object and process unite organically, and the place they unite is the University, which thus gives the people an idea of the nation-state to live up to and the nation-state a people capable of living up to that idea.[1]

In this, that paradoxical and Utopian idea addressed by MacIntyre via Augustine, according to which the education gained through reading is precisely the education required to have allowed one to read in the first place, is ostensibly addressed. As MacIntyre puts this:

> The reader was assigned the task of interpreting the text, but also had to discover, in and through his or her reading of those texts, that they in turn interpret the reader. What the reader, as thus interpreted by the texts, has to learn about him or herself is that it is only the self as transformed through and by the reading of the texts which will be capable of reading the texts aright. So the reader ... encounters apparent paradox at the outset ... it seems that only by learning what the texts have to teach can he or she come to read those texts aright, but also that only by reading them aright can he or she learn what the texts have to teach.[2]

In Humboldt, the university exists in a dialectical relation with the people and the nation-state. Its function, thus, is to address and even to constitute a national culture, not in any abstract sense, but rather in terms of making such a culture, making the nation, *available* to its people, who can now live the nation-state empirically, can embody it in actual and specific practices. Those practices now constitute what we call culture—in this case, specifically that culture that emerges, at this historical moment early in the nineteenth century, as the culture of 'Germany'.

This state of affairs is a long way removed from what had been apparent to Vico, at the turn of the previous century, when he delivered his inaugural orations in the University of Naples. It is in the second of these orations, delivered on October 18, 1700, that Vico addresses the relation of wisdom to virtue, and in which he distinguishes the wise from the foolish. Vico argues that 'while other created things must follow their nature, man instead must follow his wisdom as his guide'.[3] In doing this, Vico takes it for

---

[1] Bill Readings, *The University in Ruins* (Harvard University Press, Cambridge, Mass., 1996; repr. 1997), 65.

[2] Alasdair MacIntytre, *Three Rival Versions of Moral Enquiry* (Duckworth, 1990), 82.

[3] Giambattista Vico, *On Humanistic Education (Six Inaugural Orations, 1699–1707)* (trans. Giorgio A. Pinton and Arthur W. Shippee; Cornell University Press, Ithaca, 1993), 57.

granted that there is a clear separation of the sensible from the rational; and, following Cicero *On Laws*, he prescribes that we be directed by the priorities of the rational:

let the mind know the true from the false and not be dominated by the senses; let reason be the interpreter of life and its guide and overseer; let desire submit to reason. Let mind judge of things not on the basis of opinion, but according to profound reason, and the spirit's quest for the good be according to reason and not passion; let man earn for himself a lasting renown by the good arts of the spirit...[4]

The century which follows this oration in Europe, as we have seen in the course of this book, complicates what is for Vico the ready availability of such a clear opposition between sense and reason. In Vico's oration, the fool, who acts in contravention of these prescriptions, is 'guilty of treason', a precursor of those intellectuals who will be attacked some two centuries later by Julien Benda in his study of *La Trahison des clercs*, intellectuals who sacrifice their proper intellectual pursuits in the interest of bureacratically serving the nation-state. Vico's fool is condemned to wage a dreadful war against himself. 'The weapon of the fool is his own unrestrained passion';[5] and such passion is grounded in a love which paradoxically always undoes itself. Vico writes:

there are two powers like a pair of horses in that part of the spirit which is distinct from reason. One is easily provoked to anger, the other easily inclined to lustful desires. The first is male and thus rebellious, spirited, and impetuous; the other female and thus pliable, languid, and idle. The inclination in the former leads toward harsh and difficult tasks while the other embraces light and pleasant things. How many enemies that were hidden come out from those two horses as if each had been a Trojan horse! In fact, when an overwhelming longing for that which has the appearance of good invades the spirit of the fool, love, which is the origin and source of all passions, is born. If this good is remote, then desire for it is born. If it can be obtained, then hope is built. If it is present, then great joy is aroused. If that good is considered so great and complete that only one man can obtain it, then jealousy and rivalry take over. If one has much of it and we none, then we are consumed by envy. But once we are in possession of what we at first thought as good, its mask now removed, we see

---

[4] Ibid. 58.
[5] Ibid. 61. On the more recent 'treason' to which I refer here, see Julien Benda, *La Trahison des clercs* (1927; repr. Bernard Grasset, Paris, 1975), especially Benda's Preface to the 1946 edn., repr. here 41–104.

its true nature standing forth. What previously had the appearance of good has now disclosed the evil hidden within itself. Then hate, the opposite of love, immediately takes over.[6]

What begins as love ends in an endlessly repeating and deepening cycle of hatred and despair, in which the fool is the victim of himself. Vico, suspicious thus of 'love', is suspicious of precisely that which will condition the emergence of the aesthetic in the century following his orations. Love, in its forms of pity or benevolence, invades (as we have seen in my previous chapters) the domain of reason and of politics within Europe, and when that invasion extends also to the realms of education, it gives us what we will eventually recognize as 'culture', the *Bildung* that unites historical scholarship with aesthetic experience, individual with institution, history with reason, as described in Readings's delineation of Humboldt's idea of the university of (national) culture.

At precisely the same moment that Humboldt was adjudicating between the rival proposals of Fichte and Schleiermacher for the principles governing the University of Berlin, there was another significant debate going on about the idea of the university, in Britain. Between July 1809 and April 1810, the *Edinburgh Review* ran a series of pieces systematically questioning 'English' education, by which the reviewers meant specifically Oxford University.[7] The grounds of the attack were fundamentally that the recently 'reformed' Oxford programme was excessively narrow, mechanical, useless, parochial, and incompetent. The charge of incompetence came first, in Richard Payne Knight's review of the Oxford edition of Strabo's geography, which he succinctly described as a 'pile of rubbish'.[8] He justifies this severe criticism of the edition by enumerating a huge number of errors in the edition, most of which are due to an extremely impoverished understanding of Latin: 'If this be the kind of Latin now taught and written in the University

---

[6] Vico, *On Humanistic Education*, 62. On this gendering of virtue and wisdom in relation to the priorities of sense and passion, cf. Rousseau, *Émile* (1762; repr. Garnier-Flammarion, Paris, 1966), 490–1.

[7] At the time, of course, there was only one other university in England; and, as has been pointed out by A. L. Walker, this compares very unfavourably with Scotland, especially when one compares demographic statistics of the two countries. See Walker, *The Revival of the Democratic Intellect* (Polygon, Edinburgh, 1994), chs. 2 and 3.

[8] *Edinburgh Review*, 14 (July 1809), 441.

of Oxford, we have only to observe, that it is an original indige-
nous speech of their own.'[9] As is clear from this, Knight intends not
simply to attack the edition, but also to launch an attack on its
provenance and on the values of the University of Oxford.

Oxford and the Clarendon Press, argues Knight, have been a
constant disappointment, apparently unable to provide any decent
home-grown English scholarship:

> though this learned Body have occasionally availed themselves of the
> sagacity and erudition of Rhunken, Wyttenbach, Heyne, and other *foreign*
> professors, they have, of late added nothing of their own except what they
> have derived from the superior skill of British manufacturers, and the supe-
> rior wealth of their establishment; namely, whiter paper, blacker ink, and
> neater types.[10]

In this, the attack on Strabo becomes rather incidental to what is
essentially a greater cause, the argument about national cultures,
an argument about politics and culture. Knight has argued that
Oxford's endowment stands as the greatest in Europe, and that in
Oxford, the veneration paid to the Greek and Latin languages is
without comparison. Competence in the ancient languages is nearly the only intellectual requirement to enable an individual to enjoy
all of Oxford's privileges; but more than this:

> a critically accurate knowledge of them is justly esteemed the most safe and
> effectual means of forming the taste, moulding the judgment, and direct-
> ing the imaginations of those, whose stations or talents befit them for more
> active scenes of life, and open to their dawning ambition the more brilliant
> prospects of political advancement.[11]

A classical education is thus also the key to government and power.
The implication is clear: to demonstrate incompetence in the classics among the English is to demonstrate incompetence in English
government and politics in the still uneasy 'union' that brings
Scotland and England together, especially if one accepts Knight's
assertion that 'In every free state, eloquence is the principal medium of government, and the most direct and honourable road to
rank, power and reputation.'[12] The catalogue of errors that Knight
then educes constitutes an attack not just on scholarship, but also
on the national culture of England. It is an attack, essentially, on an

---

[9] Ibid. 433.   [10] Ibid. 431.   [11] Ibid. 429–30.
[12] Ibid. 430.

ideology that is inscribed in the pedagogical practice of an England which can boast but two universities whose main claims to excellence internationally—or at least within Europe—lies in the size of their *financial* and not their legitimate *intellectual* endowments. Knight dresses up his attack as an 'admonishment', saying that:

> The very serious concern which we feel at seeing the literary reputation of the country tarnished and degraded in the estimation of Europe, by such expressions as the above [solecism in the Strabo edition], issuing, in barbarous abundance, from the fountain head of learning, taste and science among us, must be our apology for entering into so minute a grammatical discussion.[13]

He claims to be writing 'so as to make them [Oxford scholars] shake off the benumbing influence of port and prejudice,—do themselves and their country honour, and the republic of letters essential service';[14] but the real point is to raise the spectre of a different education, that proposed in Edinburgh and the other Scottish universities, as being more relevant to the contemporary world, more useful to contemporary humanity, attuned to an entirely different pedagogy from that of the English.

   The next number of the *Review* carried Sydney Smith's criticism of *Essays on Professional Education*, by R. L. Edgeworth (the father of Maria). Once more, the topic is the classics; and Smith's piece is concerned to establish a proper place for the classics in education. Edgeworth claimed that the 'principal defect' in the great schools is that they devote far too much time to the teaching of Latin and Greek, a pedagogy imitated by Trinity College Dublin. Smith shares this view, but mounts from it another attack on English education. While he stresses the importance of a classical education, arguing for example that 'we should consider every system of education from which classical education was excluded, as radically erroneous, and completely absurd', Smith nonetheless rails against a system—the English, Oxford system—which focuses on the classics *exclusively* in the studies that a student makes up to the age of about twenty-three.[15] The consequence of such an education, ignorant of advances in science, moral philosophy, European literatures or anything else that

---

[13] *Edinburgh Review*, 434.   [14] Ibid. 441.
[15] Sydney Smith, review of *Essays on Professional Education*, by R. L. Edgeworth, *Edinburgh Review*, 15 (Oct. 1809), 45–6.

Smith describes as 'useful', results in what he describes as 'a style of elegant imbecility' in the English graduate:

the matter of fact is, that a classical scholar of twenty-three or twenty-four years of age, is a man principally conversant with works of imagination. His feelings are quick, his fancy lively, and his taste good. Talents for speculation and original inquiry he has none; nor has he formed the invaluable habit of pushing things up to their first principles, or of collecting dry and unamusing facts as the materials of reasoning. All the solid and masculine parts of his understanding are left wholly without cultivation; he hates the pain of thinking, and suspects every man whose boldness and originality call upon him to defend his opinions and prove his assertions.[16]

Smith argues, in what we now know as the argument for the 'democratic intellect', for a mode of education that will embrace the diversity of forms of knowledge, that will combine the aesthetic with the practical or, in his preferred term, the useful. The distaste of the Oxford scholar for the necessity of proving his assertions stems from what will be eventually analysed by Bourdieu as the self-legitimizing stance of an 'aristocracy of culture', a self-satisfying 'aristocracy' of scholars who are in the right (or who satisfy themselves that they are in the right) because of who they are (Oxford scholars) rather than because of what they do (make supposedly fine translations, say—but translations marred by fundamental errors in Latin). As Smith puts this, the point of the Oxford education which is being attacked is the production of a self-satisfying group or class. Having acknowledged that those who have spent all their youth studying only Greek and Latin will not be too pleased to hear that this is all misplaced energy, Smith writes that:

A certain sort of vanity, also, very naturally grows among men occupied in a common pursuit. Classical quotations are the watchwords of scholars, by which they distinguish each other from the ignorant and illiterate; and Greek and Latin are insensibly become almost the only test of a cultivated mind.[17]

I will return to the Leavisite tag (that 'common pursuit' productive of vanity) later; but suffice to note here that, for Smith, the common pursuit in question is entirely vacuous, in that the scholars described have come to appreciate not the *content* of what they are reading in Greek or Latin, but rather simply the *fact* that they are reading it:

[16]   Ibid. 49.   [17]   Ibid. 43.

Another misfortune of classical learning, as taught in England, is, that scholars have come, in process of time, and from the effects of association, to love the instrument better than the end;—not the luxury which the difficulty encloses, but the difficulty;—not the filbert, but the shell;—not what may be read in Greek, but Greek itself.[18]

or, as we might now say, following Adorno, 'not Italy, but the fact that it exists'. Here lies the source of this 'elegant imbecility' which Smith discerns in the vacuities of the Oxford system, resulting in a class-system in which the very possibility of human maturity (*Bildung*) or autonomy is lost:

The bias given to men's minds is so strong, that it is no uncommon thing to meet with Englishmen, whom, but for the grey hairs and wrinkles, we might easily mistake for schoolboys ... His object is not to reason, to imagine, or to invent; but to conjugate, decline and derive.[19]

Against 'elegant imbecility', Smith posits a system based on 'the only proper criterion of every branch of education—its utility in future life';[20] but such 'utility' is not merely technological, for it embraces the usefulness of education for improving the lot of human happiness within a society; and any such society will, if it serves the good, be multifarious and diverse. Its education system, thus, will embrace many disciplines, so that while Smith agrees that 'A great classical scholar is an ornament, and an important acquisition to his country', he also insists that 'in a place of education, we would give to all knowledge an equal chance for distinction; and would trust to the varieties of human disposition, that every science worth cultivation would be cultivated'.[21]

In short, what we have is an opposition between uniformity and variety, but one now in which these two terms have been 'nationalized', such that 'English' education is seen to be all uniformity,

---

[18]   *Edinburgh Review*, 47. At this point, the correspondence between Molière's celebrated 'doctors', whose respect for the 'forms' of medicine and for decorum ensures that they neglect the practical matters of life and death, and this characterization of the Oxford scholar, is clear. The same kind of argument persists, from Molière to Smith, from France to Scotland.

[19]   Smith, Review of Edgeworth, 46. The system, of course, persists; and in precisely the form described by Smith. Those who doubt it might attend some English 'society' events such as, for example, Henley during 'regatta-week', where they will see any number of relevant examples of men who, even in their forties, fifties, sixties and beyond are still wearing their schoolboy uniform.

[20]   Ibid. 44.   [21]   Ibid. 51.

with its attendant narrowness, ignorance, parochialism and inability to encounter difference or intellectual non-conformity; and against this is hypothesized a 'Scottish' education that is multiple, diverse, open, democratic, useful, relevant to the modern world and society. We have what Snow will later diagnose (in different circumstances and with a different content) as a clash between 'two cultures', but at this historical moment, the two cultures are also two nation-states 'united' politically, but clearly in a state of extreme cultural tension.[22]

When Edward Copleston, Fellow of Oriel College, became aware of these attacks on Oxford, he rose to the defence of the institution and its values. Indeed, he took what was for him the rare step of publication, writing *A Reply to the Calumnies of the Edinburgh Review against Oxford*; and this, in turn, was reviewed in the *Edinburgh Review* of April 1810, by Richard Payne Knight and John Playfair. Once again, the attack was continued, and its basis in national differences made explicit. Copleston points out (in precisely the kind of formulation that would antagonize a thinker such as Benda in a later century and in another nation) that it had been difficult in Oxford to abandon the principles of, for example, Aristotelian Physics when such an abandonment might have clashed with the terms of the university statutes. Needless to say, Knight and Playfair pounce on this as 'disgraceful', going on, in a passage that would excite one of Copleston's allies and friends, Cardinal Newman, in these terms:

This is the constitution of both the English universities ... It is the case of all universities that, originating in the Catholic times, and constructed on the principles of a church that claimed infallibility, either retain their original constitution, or have been but slightly reformed. The Scottish universities happily have not retained this pernicious structure; and, perhaps from the greater extent to which the Reformation was carried in the northern part of the island, or, still more, from the poverty of establishments that had no means of distinction but those derived from exertion, they are without any of those artificial impediments which, in the south, have so effectually resisted the progress of improvement. Hence it is that our universities have been so rapid in following, and so instrumental in

---

[22] See C. P. Snow, *Two Cultures*, ed. Stefan Collini (Canto edn.; Cambridge University Press, Cambridge, 1993); and note here that the version of Scottish culture advanced by the Edinburgh reviewers is one that embraces both science and literature.

forwarding the improvements of knowledge. The university of Edinburgh was the first in Britain, perhaps in Europe, into which the Newtonian philosophy was introduced; and that of Glasgow the first in which the subject of moral philosophy was raised to the place which it is entitled to occupy ...[23]

This makes clear the opposition between, on one hand, an English system of education, characterized (or caricatured) as monolithic, narrow, homogeneous and lacking in the capacity to give autonomy to its participants—or, in a word, lacking culture; and, on the other hand, a Scottish system mooted as pluralist, democratic, 'cultivated', cosmopolitan, heterogeneous, and guaranteed to produce that diversity among its participants that is required for the elaboration of a democratic culture.

What is being celebrated, at least tacitly, in these pages of the *Edinburgh Review*, is a philosophy of education in which there is an intimate link between the intellectual life and the practical life. This, in Scotland, is more or less equivalent to the 'university of culture' advocated by Humboldt in Berlin. It gives a model of the university—and within that, of the aesthetic sense characterized by the capacity for wedding uniformity to variety—as liberally and disinterestedly serving the pursuit of truth; but serving that pursuit in the belief that its discovery will lead to the amelioration of the conditions of life for all members of a community, broadly identifiable now as a *national* community. In what follows, I shall explore how this conception of the university has come under pressure.

II

Is not the university the site where precisely the kinds of conflict described above between the Scots and the English can be rationally debated and eventually reconciled? Such might have been the belief of Vico, with his essentially Utopian wish for a great citizenry of scholars, from which one can only be excluded through one's own folly. That, clearly, would be the case only with an ideal or 'virtual' university; but in the eighteenth century, the work of the universities

[23] Knight and Playfair, review of *A Reply to the Calumnies of the Edinburgh Review against Oxford*, in *Edinburgh Review*, 16 (Apr. 1810), 168.

was actual, engaged in the formation of national cultures with all the attendant political realities. The reconciling of such differences, then, given that they can be fundamentally political and national, carries with it its own set of problems. MacIntyre has drawn attention recently to 'the capacity of the contemporary university not only to dissolve antagonism, to emasculate hostility, but also in so doing to render itself culturally irrelevant'.[24] It was not always thus.

Such a situation was not the case when, for example, Newman was invited, in April 1851, to help found a Catholic University of Ireland, a university which in time developed into the National University of Ireland. In his Discourses, he explicitly alludes to the *Edinburgh Review* controversy some forty years since, and he is keen to counter what he sees as the Scottish guiding principle of *utility*, at least as that principle—fundamentally driven by a concern that the aesthetic should have a practical as well as an intellectual and theoretical component—was expressed by the reviewers. While conceding that utility is quite obviously a requirement of the contents of a university education, he makes a significant shift in this, for he claims that 'intellectual culture', which he has described as the proper business of a university, 'is its own end; ... [and] what has its *end* in itself, has its *use* in itself also'.[25] Newman's text introduces a specific version of liberal education in which types of knowledge can be evaluated. Like Vico, he makes a sharp distinction between sensation and knowledge, putting this, admittedly, in an extreme form: 'I say, it seems to me improper to call that passive sensation, or perception of things, which brutes seem to possess, by the name of Knowledge.'[26] In this questioning of the centrality of what elsewhere might have been called aesthetics, Newman establishes the grounds for distinction among different kinds and forms of knowledge. In the first place, he separates 'Useful Knowledge' from 'Liberal Knowledge', the end of the former in education being 'mechanical' and of the latter, 'philosophical'. In his idea of the university, he favours the latter:

Let me not be thought to deny the necessity, or to decry the benefit, of such attention to what is particular and practical, as belongs to the useful or

---

[24] MacIntyre, *Three Rival Versions of Moral Enquiry*, 218–19.
[25] John Henry Newman, *The Idea of a University*, ed. I. T. Ker (Clarendon Press, Oxford, 1976), 142.
[26] Ibid. 104.

mechanical arts; life could not go on without them; we owe our daily welfare to them; their exercise is the duty of the many, and we owe to the many a debt of gratitude for fulfilling that duty. I only say that Knowledge, in proportion as it tends more and more to be particular, ceases to be Knowledge.[27]

The knowledge proper to a university, then, is a knowledge that is general, 'theoretical' in the sense I have earlier given this word, grounded in the capacity for seeing a general law as the ground on which a particular case may be said to exist.

In his rationalization of this, Newman argues in a fashion that has allowed him to be seen, by Readings for example, as an imitator of the Oxford system;[28] but Newman himself is concerned to distinguish what he does in Ireland from his own English formation, arguing that a servile imitation of England's universities 'will result in nothing better or higher than the production of that antiquated variety of human nature and remnant of feudalism ... called a "gentleman" ';[29] and while he is sympathetic to the production of gentlemen, Newman nonetheless sees Rome rather than Oxford as that which gives the institutional structure within which we can produce *gentility*. The similarities, nonetheless, are there, in that Newman argues that grammar should be the foundation of a university education:

I hold very strongly that the first step in intellectual training is to impress upon a boy's mind the idea of science, method, order, principle, and system; of rule and exception, of richness and harmony. This is commonly and excellently done by making him begin with Grammar ...[30]

Newman here is also reiterating Vico, who in his sixth oration (delivered in 1707), puts eloquence at the foundation of knowledge, arguing there that 'even before true and effective principles concerning language, it is necessary that we first have speech that is grammatically correct. What then follows is knowledge of the

---

[27] Newman, *Idea*, 104.

[28] Readings, *University in Ruins*, 74: 'Significantly, Oxford is the model for Newman's *Idea of a University*.'

[29] Newman, *Idea*, 5–6; cf. pp. 10–11, 120, 124–5, 127.

[30] Ibid. 12. In hinting that Newman is interested in *gentility* rather than the *gentleman*, I am, of course, hinting also at the notion that Newman is interested in the *gentile*, with its connotations both of the concept of 'the people' and of the non-Jewish. This might be seen as one foundation of the conceptual opposition of Hebraism and Hellenism as operated by Arnold, say.

divine'.[31] Like Vico, Newman finds in the adequacy of the *logos* a fundamentally theological foundation for knowledge and for the university. Inasmuch as grammar is, broadly, 'theory', it is grammar that allows the student to see the relation between particular and general, or between his present instant and the eternal, between the secular and the sacred.

In his Sixth Discourse, Newman builds on this in order to allow him to demonstrate what he sees as three stages and three kinds of knowledge. In the first place, there is what he calls 'mere' knowledge. Such knowledge is that which is associated with the acquiring of *matter* or materials, as, for example, in acquiring certain facts and being able to store them in memory or in some other mental archival fashion. This stage is a primary stage in human and intellectual development, one in which the mind is impressed by the constantly brave new world which it discerns and of which it is made aware; 'and when he [the student] is leaving for the University, he is mainly the creature of foreign influences and circumstances, and made up of accidents, homogeneous or not'.[32] We might think of this, accordingly, as 'accidental' knowing, a knowing in which the subject is at the mercy of the influence of the objective world around her or him. This, however, cannot be the whole story, argues Newman.

He goes on in this Discourse, in pages which (he says) reprint almost word-for-word his fourteenth Oxford University Sermon, to hypothesize the case of a person who leaves 'the more calm and unpretending scenery of these islands, whether here or in England' to go to places 'where physical nature puts on her wilder and more awful forms, whether at home or abroad'.[33] This person, suggests Newman, is literally disoriented, 'decentred'; but also intellectually enlarged thereby, possessing now 'a range of thoughts to which he was before a stranger'. The logic of this argument is that to venture into a new area is akin to venturing into a new discipline or into one with which we have hitherto been unfamiliar. Such enlargements happen also within single disciplines, whenever we try to process new materials; and so, Newman argues for a degree of autonomy as intrinsic to knowledge:

---

[31] Vico, *On Humanistic Education*, 132; cf. 125–30 on the relation of language to nation-formation.
[32] Newman, *Idea*, 116.   [33] Ibid. 118.

The enlargement consists, not merely in the passive reception into the mind of a number of ideas hitherto unknown to it, but in the mind's energetic and simultaneous action upon and towards and among those new ideas, which are rushing in upon it. It is the action of a formative power, reducing to order and meaning the matter of our acquirements; it is a making the objects of our knowledge subjectively our own.[34]

Without the ability to *inform* the matter of our intellects or experience, we cannot attain to anything worthy of the name of philosophy, argues Newman, in terms extremely close to those which will form our notions of the 'democratic intellect'. We may meet persons who have any amounts of detailed memories of events,

but who generalize nothing, and have no observation, in the true sense of the word. They abound in information in detail, curious and entertaining, about men and things; and, having lived under the influence of no very clear or settled principles, religious or political, they speak of every one and every thing, only as so many phenomena, which are complete in themselves, and lead to nothing, not discussing them, or teaching any truth, or instructing the hearer, but simply talking.[35]

It follows from this, argues Newman, that knowledge is only genuine when it is 'Universal' (by which he must also imply 'Catholic', of course); that is, only when the particular case can be seen and understood as playing its part in a more general—universal—state of affairs.[36] Hence, knowledge is aware that there are many compartments or disciplines into which it is separated—and within each of these one will have 'expertise' or professional knowledge (as in Fish's most recent work, say); but these disciplines and their ostensible separation one from the other attain to the condition of true knowledge only when they are referred to the overarching system or general state of affairs from which they derive their being (an impossible project for a thinker such as Fish, who prefers to limit us to our 'professional' correctness). It follows from this Optimistic and Utopian view that 'the true and adequate end of intellectual training and of a University is not Learning or Acquirement, but rather, is Thought or Reason exercised upon

---

34 Newman, *Idea*, 120.

35 Ibid. 121–2. Cf. Molière's Jourdain, 'drowning in experience'.

36 On this issue of universalism and its relation to a Catholic theology, see the recent work of Badiou and of Vattimo: Alain Badiou, *Saint Paul* (Presses Universitaires de France, Paris, 1997), and Gianni Vattimo, *Credere di credere* (Garzanti, Milan, 1996).

Knowledge, or what may be called Philosophy'.[37] We see here a project akin to Humboldt's, in which the university organizes knowledge into its several disciplines; but also hypothesizes a position from which the diversity of knowledges can be eventually regulated or reconciled into a single or absolute knowing. Philosophy becomes, in the university of culture at least, the metadiscipline.

Newman's Seventh and Eighth Discourses then flesh out the terms and condition of professional knowledge and philosophical knowledge; and this latter devolves explicitly into theology or into an acknowledgement of the proper relations between knowledge and religious duty, such that theology—and specifically the moral prerogatives of Catholicism—becomes the fundamental ground on which even the meta-discipline of philosophy is based.

Newman certainly sees the university, then, as a place with a variety of disciplines, but that variety is underpinned not simply, as was the case in Berlin, by a general system of knowing called philosophy, in and through which individuals will find their proper and adequate citizenry in a nation-state; but rather a general system called theology, in and through which the difference between England and Ireland will disappear through their fundamental underpinning in Rome:

The past never returns; the course of events, old in its texture, is ever new in its colouring and fashion. England and Ireland are not what they once were, but Rome is where it was, and St. Peter is the same: his zeal, his charity, his mission, his gifts are all the same. He of old made the two islands one by giving them joint work of teaching; and now surely he is giving us a like mission, and we shall become one again, while we zealously and lovingly fulfil it.[38]

While the English Oxford model might have produced scholars who knew only the intricacies of Greek (however well or badly),

---

[37] Newman, *Idea*, 124–5.
[38] Ibid. 31–2. It is instructive to compare this with Erich Auerbach's closing meditations in *Mimesis* (1946; trans. Willard Trask; Princeton, 1968), 552, where he wishes away the racism of Nazism by an appeal to a common humanity. Writing of Woolf's interest in the random, he claims that 'In this unprejudiced and exploratory type of representation we cannot but see to what an extent—below the surface conflicts—the differences between men's ways of life and forms of thought have already lessened. ... There are no longer even exotic peoples'—and this, of course, written in Turkey where Auerbach wrote, in exile from Nazi persecution. See my comments on this in Docherty, *After Theory* (rev. and expanded 2nd edn.; Edinburgh University Press, Edinburgh, 1996), 144–6.

Newman's University, even while it acknowledges the huge diversity of disciplines demanded by the Scottish reviewers, nonetheless can relate everything back to a knowledge which is fundamentally and essentially homogeneous: religious knowledge. The concept of the 'University', qualified by the adjective 'Catholic', produces what is for Newman essentially a tautology.

Acknowledging the diversity of the disciplines, in among which the arts come rather low down in Newman's priorities on the grounds that they are not intimate with truth, Newman argues that the university is a site for the *regulation* of these various discourses:

An assemblage of learned men, zealous for their own sciences, and rivals of each other, are brought, by familiar intercourse and for the sake of intellectual peace, to adjust together the claims and relations of their respective subjects of investigation.[39]

Through this, the student benefits from the 'pure and clear atmosphere of thought', gaining the privileges of a liberal education whose characteristics are 'freedom, equitableness, moderation, and wisdom'.[40]

By the middle of the nineteenth century, then, we have two models for the university, with two corresponding positions for the place of art and aesthetics within knowledge and now also within the social. In Berlin, we have the classic formulation of the university of culture, in which the university establishes the conditions for the possibility of autonomous citizenship within the nation-state. In this model, aesthetics plays a fundamental role in *Bildung*, in representing to the potential citizen her or his models for adequate moral and social being within the collectivity that is the nation. Here, we have the realization of Schiller's argument that the State assumes— specifically in the form of its pedagogical apparatuses—the function of healing the 'dissociation of sensibility'. The result is the production not only of knowledge, but also of a specific position within such knowledge for the intellectual— and most specifically, for the intellectual engaged in aesthetic practices—as a key figure in the identity and autonomy of the nation. It is the aesthetic intellectual, aspiring to a philosophical and critical consciousness, who is able and required to give to the nation

---

[39] Newman, *Idea*, 95.   [40] Ibid. 96.

its consciousness and self-consciousness. Hence, the intellectual in the university of culture provides not only for the conditions governing the possibility of a national identity, but also for the conditions governing the possibility of a critique of such identity from within the nation itself. The key discipline is the metadiscipline of philosophy; and the structural indebtedness of this thinking to that medieval division of knowledge into the trivium (grammar, rhetoric, knowledge) and the quadrivium (arithmetic, geometry, astronomy, music) is fairly clear: philosophy unifies the disparities and varieties of disciplines. Such an indebtedness reveals, of course, the continuing fundamental similarity of this structure to the theological conception of knowledge that it is supposed to secularize in the first place.

In Dublin, we have a slightly different model. Newman shares with Humboldt the optimistic belief in the Utopian possibility that all heterogeneous knowledges can finally be homogenized, through the production of a philosophical cast of mind that can finally be identified as Catholic. In this, the nation-state is thought entirely differently: the specificity of Ireland is ignored in a move which tries to unite England and Ireland under the presiding power of Rome and of the Catholic Church. It is here that we see the 'aestheticization of the university', in a specific sense: the 'beauty' of Newman's project lies in its capacity for establishing a fundamental identity between dissimilars, of finding transcendent (or religious) uniformity in the midst of national variety. Here, it is important to note the precise relations among education, morality, and nation that drive Newman's thinking. In a somewhat shocking passage, Newman adjudicates between two kinds of university. The first is that which is more or less explicitly *professional*, which has 'dispensed with residence and tutorial superintendence', giving degrees to candidates who pass examinations 'in a wide range of subjects'; and the second—rather amateur—is that 'which has no professors or examinations at all, but merely brought a number of young men together for three or four years, and then sent them away'.[41] If asked to decide which of these 'was the more successful in training, moulding, enlarging the mind', Newman says, 'I have no hesitation in giving the preference to that University which did nothing, over that which exacted of its members an acquaintance with every science

---

[41]   Ibid. 129.

under the sun'.[42] This would be shocking but for the important caveat that Newman is clear in stating that in such a decision, he is ruling out of present consideration the question of morality; so what he is arguing is that an *amoral* education can be achieved—and would indeed be excellent in the production of citizens well-equipped for public and secular society—without professors or examinations. This, of course, is precisely the description of the unreformed Oxford University, which is alleged to have reneged on its duties to teach and to examine, preferring instead the casualness of an extremely unstructured and undemanding community of people who, basically, simply talk to each other in a gentlemanly fashion (called the tutorial). An ethical university, argues Newman, would organize things differently. Institutions which 'did little more than bring together first boys and then youths in large numbers, these institutions, with miserable deformities on the side of morals, with a hollow profession of Christianity, and a heathen code of ethics'[43] may indeed lack an ethical foundation; but they 'have made England what it is,—able to subdue the earth, able to domineer over Catholics'.[44] Clearly, Newman fundamentally is not sympathetic to the model of the university that best prepares the citizen for public and secular life, given that it produces a nation which is inimical to Catholicism. It follows that Newman's model of the university must be one that can embrace the pedagogical possibilities of community while also instilling an ethics that ostensibly transcends national locatedness. Unlike Humboldt, Newman favours a university that is ostensibly tied not to place but rather to the Utopia that is 'no-place', to a Catholic theology that disregards its specific national location. As Satan has it in Milton, 'The mind is its own place.' It is, of course, somewhat paradoxical, then, that in this model of the university, the arts are deemed to have a rather lowly place on the grounds that literature, say, is not grounded in empirical truth but concerns itself rather with imaginary spaces.

While Newman was making his discourses, and taking into account the pressures from the Scottish universities, things in Edinburgh differed somewhat. In 1760, Hugh Blair had been chosen to occupy the Chair of Rhetoric and Belles-Lettres,[45] and,

---

[42] Newman, *Idea*, 129.   [43] Ibid.   [44] Ibid. 130.
[45] The Chair was royally endowed only in 1762; and Blair became the first Regius Professor of Rhetoric and Belles-Lettres in that year.

for the next twenty-four years, he had given a course of lectures on his subject. The lectures were published and republished in various editions right the way through into the middle of the nineteenth century, and their influence had an international reach, with some arguing that their rules of rhetoric had a pronounced impact on the drafting of the American constitution.[46]

In the lectures, Blair follows what was for him the still pertinent Vichian logic of beginning a formal university education with the study of language. He considers the relation of speech to society, and indicates the undecidability of the relative priorities to be given to either of these, pointing out that speech appears certainly to be a prerequisite of society, while society is simultaneously a condition of speech:

Think of the circumstances of mankind when languages began to be formed. ... One would think that, in order to any language fixing and extending itself, men must have been previously gathered together in considerable numbers; society must have been already far advanced; and yet, on the other hand, there seems to have been an absolute necessity for speech, previous to the formation of society. For, by what bond could any multitude of men be kept together, or be made to join in the prosecution of any common interest, until once, by the intervention of speech, they could communicate their wants and intentions to one another? So that, either how society could form itself previously to language, or how words could rise into a language previously to society formed, seem to be points attended with equal difficulty.[47]

Blair follows the Rousseavian line that language originates in cries of passion, which eventually lead, via onomatopoiea, to a mimetic articulation of objects, and then on into increasing abstraction and arbitrariness. He argues, from this, for an origin of language which transcends place, for, long before Derrida, he is able to claim that figures are foundational for speech and not ornamental additions to some basic tongue. The claim is based in the empirical evidence:

The style of all the most early languages, among nations who are in the first and rude periods of society, is found, without exception, to be full of

[46] See Walker, *Revival of the Democratic Intellect*, 308. On Blair's preference for the oral delivery, and on the conditions governing the necessity of seeing these lectures printed and published, see Penny Fielding, *Writing and Orality* (Clarendon Press, Oxford, 1996), 12.

[47] Hugh Blair, 'Rise and Progress of Language', in *Lectures on Rhetoric and Belles-Lettres*, ed. Rev. Lionel Thomas Berguer (T. and J. Allman, 1827), 56-7.

figures; hyperbolical and picturesque in a high degree. We have a striking instance of this in the American languages, which are known, by the most authentic accounts, to be figurative to excess. The Iroquois and Illinois carry on their treaties and public transactions with bolder metaphors, and greater pomp of style, than we do in our poetical productions.[48]

This style, of which Blair gives a splendid example in a footnote citation from Cadwallader Colden's *History of the Five Indian Nations*, is not limited to America. He immediately points out that the style of the Old Testament is extremely similar to this, for there we find abstract concepts represented by concrete particulars: 'Iniquity, or guilt, is expressed by "a spotted garment"; misery, by "drinking the cup of astonishment"', and so on. Such a style, which would be characteristically referred to as 'Oriental' is clearly not specific to the Orient, given its similarity to the figural origins of Occidental speech. Hence, figure can be seen 'to be common to all nations in certain periods of society and language'.[49]

However, things appear differently once we consider the origins of writing, according to Blair. The non-locatedness of speech, whose characteristic is its concrete particularity and force, or motivation by the *sensible*, gives way to an explicit geo-politics once we encounter the facts of the origins of writing. In the seventh lecture, on the 'Rise and Progress of Writing', Blair follows the same logic of communication as a representation of objects to which the elements of communication refer. Accordingly, he notes the pictorial nature of hieroglyphics, which were 'employed at first from necessity', and which count as a mode of communication in desperate need of refinement. Interestingly, he considers, again in a Rousseauvian fashion, the consequences of that form of nominalism in which every discrete particular in the world must be given its own separate name. This state of affairs which, in Rousseau, leads to the inability to comprehend two oak trees, say, as being fundamentally related or being two examples of the one kind leads, as Blair points out, to the condition of the Chinese languages. This, argues Blair, is a state of affairs which slows down human and social progress, for it takes a lifetime of learning simply to deal with the language or medium in which the learning is supposedly being done. What we need is, clearly, that form of abstraction which allows for permutation of signs called the alphabet. While

[48] Blair, 'Rise and Progress of Writing', 64.   [49] Ibid. 65.

the origins of speech cannot be located, the origins of the alphabet can be tracked down, according to Blair; and he discovers that 'the most probable and natural account of the origin of alphabetical characters is, that they took rise in Egypt, the first civilized kingdom of which we have any authentic accounts, and the great source of arts and polity among the ancients'.[50] Egypt, and specifically Egypt as a nation conditioned by the demands of arts and polity, provides the source of that form of abstraction that we call writing.

Although Blair claims that writing 'is clearly an improvement on speech',[51] he nonetheless makes a distinction between the two that seems to favour speech as a sensible, immediate, living kind of communication. Speech is that which gives the present moment a material content, whereas writing, in its capacity for—and indeed, demand for—abstraction, is that which gives the present moment a *form*: writing refers its own present moment to both that which precedes and that which follows it, and its present is dependent not upon the intensity of an intention informing the word but rather upon the relations of that present word to the words around it. Writing thus locates the present in an abstract relation to the progress of time—becoming—itself, whereas speech gives the present an intensity of being. If we now recall Augustine, writing occupies that moment 'in death', a moment which is *evaded* by constantly referring it to its precedents ('before death') or its consequents ('after death'). Speech, by contrast, is the being-towards-death itself. He closes his lecture with a comparison between speech and writing or, in an uncanny prefiguration of the Lyotard of *Discours, figure*, what he calls 'words uttered in our hearing, with words represented to the eye'.[52] The comparison allows him to stress what he calls the great superiority that speech has over writing in point of force, energy, vigour: in speech situations, there is an *immediacy* of communication, a near-unmediatedness of communication, effected by the fact that the present instant of communication is characterized by a force playing directly upon concrete sensibility:

The voice of the living speaker makes an impression on the mind, much stronger than can be made by the perusal of any writing. The tones of the voice, the looks and gestures which accompany discourse ... render discourse

50 Ibid. 75.
51 Ibid. 70.   52 Ibid. 76.

... infinitely more clear, and more expressive, than the most accurate writing. For tones, looks, and gestures, are natural interpreters of the sentiments of the mind. They remove ambiguities; they enforce impressions; they operate on us by means of sympathy.[53]

Writing, on the other hand, establishes not the force of a sensibly experienced present moment, but rather the abstract and reasoned relation of that moment to other moments. Writing, we are told,

prolongs this voice to the most distant ages; it gives us the means of recording our sentiments to futurity, and of perpetuating the instructive memory of past transactions.[54]

This perhaps sits slightly uneasily with what Blair has said about the origins of speech and of writing. The origin of speech, in its poetic figurality, is non-site-specific; whereas the origin of writing is very precisely located, in Egypt. Now, discussing the advanced condition of humanity, these characteristics seem to be reversed: speech is very site-specific, whereas writing has abstracted all content from the present, constructing a present which is entirely dependent upon its reference to precedent and consequent moments for its substance. Progress, thus, for Blair, is characterized by the triumph of reason and understanding over the vigour and liveliness of sense-perception:

Language is become, in modern times, more correct, indeed, and accurate; but, however, less striking and animated: in its ancient state, more favourable to poetry and oratory; in its present, to reason and philosophy.[55]

In his obvious and often-stated preference for speech over writing, Blair clearly feels unhappy with such 'progress'. For Blair, writing gives effectively what is but the shell, the form, of experience without any kernel or content; it is speech alone which gives the possibility of a present moment characterized by a fullness of content. What he laments, thus, is what we can call the demise of experience or what Agamben more recently has described as the 'destruction of experience', a destruction consequent upon the primacy of reason over sensibility, according to Blair's logic.[56] The opposition of speech to writing allows for a corollary opposition between the

---

[53] Blair, 'Rise and Progress of Writing', 77.   [54] Ibid. 76.
[55] Ibid. 70.
[56] See Giorgio Agamben, *Infancy and History* (1978; trans. Liz Heron; Verso, 1993).

fullness of the present (which is to say, the full experience of the moment 'in death') and the vacuity of such a moment (which is to say, the articulation of the *form* of the present, and thereby the openness to something called 'life'). This devolves, in our time, to an opposition between sensibility and the 'felt life' on the one hand, and philosophy on the other; and the name for this, in criticism, is, of course, Leavis. But the position of Leavis—which is above all conditioned by the nation that is 'England', not Britain, nor indeed the anglophone states, certainly not the Scotland of Blair—has to be more fully situated still; and, prior to discussing the specifically English condition of criticism, it is to the more general situating of the twentieth-century problematic of the institutionalization of criticism and of the intellectual that I now turn.

III

Alain (Emile Chartier) in France was as suspicious of intellectualism as was Blair in eighteenth-century Scotland. However, in his *Propos sur l'éducation*, he advocated a mode of education that would be difficult—that might indeed even celebrate difficulty and hard work—and would certainly not be driven by the pleasures of experience. Crucially, as the opening gambit for this section of this study, he wrote that 'l'homme pense l'humanité, ou bien il ne pense rien'.[57] This, written in 1928, comes in a proposition whose thrust prefigures that of Auerbach during the Second War in that it is directed against the 'facts' of national identity in favour of a universal humanity. It goes hand-in-glove with a piece written in 1931 in which he argued, typically and in what will come to be insistently, for the necessity of the student's engagement with abstract thinking, the necessity of getting beyond the particular data that is given to the subject by the objective world. This, he argues, is precisely the condition of autonomy, the moment when 'le petit d'homme nait une seconde fois; il se sait esprit; il a saisi cet instrument admirable dont Descartes parlait'.[58] Precisely at the time when Alain was publishing such propositions, Julien Benda took

---

[57] Alain, *Propos sur l'éducation; suivi de Pédagogie enfantine* (1932, 1963; repr. Quadrige, PUF, Paris, 1986; repr. 1995), 176.
[58] Ibid. 72.

his more famous stance on *La Trahison des clercs*, in an argument claiming that the intellectuals had betrayed their abstract and transcendent calling in order the better to become bureaucrats acting as instruments of the nation-state. The logic of Benda's position in 1927 is that the intellectual should be fundamentally noninstrumental, that her or his task was to be 'non-site-specific' in her or his thinking. This articulates forcefully the notion of the intellectual as 'disinterested', simply pursuing the best that has been thought and said on any subject, or looking always for the better argument in a way that considers the intrinsic logic of arguments without attending to their instrumental consequences: very 'unScottish', therefore.

Were such intellectuals to form the basis of a university education, especially one in which the arts or the aesthetic played any part or in which it was thought that there could be an ethical amelioration of the human lot, then we would have a serious challenge to the 'university of culture'; for, as Readings has argued, such a university must be tied to a project that is site-specific, national (though that, of course, does not imply nationalist). After the Second War, this becomes a crucial issue, perhaps especially in Germany and in England.

Jaspers is the philosopher who takes it upon himself to rehabilitate the Humboldtian idea of the university in Germany after 1945. In his 1946 *Idea of the University*, he makes an appeal to the fundamental principle of academic freedom as that which should govern the university and guarantee its autonomy. Like the Church for Newman, academic freedom is a transcendent principle for Jaspers; and like Newman, Jaspers considers that the ostensible disparity of various disciplines is underpinned by an implied unity of all knowledge, though for Jaspers this does not imply a 'catholicity' but rather a totality of knowing. Whereas for Newman, theology becomes the underpinning 'catholic' metadiscipline, from Jaspers we have an argument according to which disciplinarity *implies* a wholeness that cannot in and of itself be known to any one subject. There is, as it were, a relation in the university between the particularity of beings and the totality of Being. He writes:

We are mistaken ... when we attempt to regard knowledge as an absolute. Knowledge is possible only where the laws of logic are respected. Consequently, what is known is not Being *per se* but those aspects of reality which present themselves in terms of the conditions imposed by our own thinking processes.[59]

Unlike Newman, Jaspers sees an intimate link between teaching and research, and places research at the centre of the university's activities. Such research is involved in the discovering of truth, which is at the ethical and cultural axis of the institution. Jaspers, however, takes his research in what may seem an unexpected direction. The consequence of placing such research at the centre of university activity is itself the production of a specific kind of committed ethical or moral individual:

Because truth is accessible to systematic search, research is the foremost concern of the university. Because the scope of truth is far greater than that of science, the scientist must dedicate himself to truth as a human being, not just as a specialist. Hence, the pursuit of truth at the university demands the serious commitment of the whole man. The university's second concern is teaching, because truth must also be transmitted.[60]

This is highly significant. It accords in some ways with Newman's observation that in the university, professional knowledge (here 'specialist' expertise) related to a single discipline is not yet adequate to the full requirements of the idea of the university. For Jaspers, it is not enough to know the technical truths of philosophy, say, it is also required that one *lives* those truths, that one's life as a human being is determined by their axiomatic ethical demands. This is what we might call a recipe for a kind of *pensiero forte*, a strong culture; anathema to the Fishian notion of professionalism. Yet more important than the obvious derivation of this from existentialist philosophy is the fact that, for Jaspers, the disinterested pursuit of truth in this manner leads inexorably to the requirements of a form of social cohesion or consensus. Science and scholarship, he argues, discover 'a kind of knowledge which is intellectual, cogent, and *universally valid*'; and this proposition means that the cogency of a particular finding can be in principle verified by anyone, with the consequence that 'Consensus is the mark of universal validity'.[61] In sum, not only does the intellectual extend her or his professional expertise into the domain of the entire ethical life; but

[59] Karl Jaspers, *The Idea of the University*, ed. Karl Deutsch (1946; trans. H. A. T. Reiche and H. F. Vanderschmidt; Peter Owen, 1960), 34.
[60] Ibid. 21.   [61] Ibid. 24, 25.

further, the intellectual's life is in turn validated by the community's legitimation of her or his knowledge, a legitimation guaranteed by the community's own moral being, lived experience, or *culture*. The shift that Jaspers makes from Humboldt's position—a shift that could be thought to be required after the atrocities of the Second War, but which it would be an oversimplification to consider in this way—is a slight but significant one, in that Humboldt's nation-state as final arbiter of the validity of the idea of the university is here replaced by a more abstract and general consensus. The principle, however, remains the same: universal legitimation derives from the ethical pursuit of truth, itself dependent upon intellectuals who see their work as demanding the commitment of the whole self, the total subject. In this state of affairs, knowledge becomes once again a matter of experience or the felt life. As Jaspers has it, 'Only experience can test the truth of scientific assumptions.'[62]

Such experience must consist in the totality of the subject's living. Jaspers argues that 'individual disciplines are meaningless apart from their relation to the whole of knowledge';[63] and that it is only the unity of knowledge that can give meaning to the search for truth demanded of the intellectual. Such unity is, of course, elusive, not given as such to any one subject. We thus need a leap of sorts, that existentialist *acte gratuit* which is akin to MacIntyre's description of the Augustinian culture of the book, to commit ourselves—in the dark—to knowledge before we will get such knowledge: 'Only after we have committed ourselves to the quest for knowledge can we learn the source and meaning of knowledge.'[64] Necessarily, after making such a commitment, we ask ourselves why we do so; and for Jaspers, the answer to this is strangely reminiscent at once of both Schopenhauer and Newman (and behind these, Hegel). He writes:

If I ask myself where all this knowledge is headed for, I can only answer in metaphorical terms. It is as though the world wanted itself to be known; as though it were part of our glorification of God in this world to get to know the world with all our God-given faculties, to rethink as it were the thoughts of God, even if we ourselves can never grasp them except as they are reflected in the universe as we know it.[65]

---

[62] Jaspers, *The Idea of the University*, 26.   [63] Ibid. 59.
[64] Ibid. 39.   [65] Ibid.

As Sartre would put this, 'man is the being whose project is to be God',[66] or to inhabit the position of the totality of knowing.

The *acte gratuit* made, culture then becomes possible; for Jaspers thinks of culture as the coming into material effectivity of our ideas, or, as the terms of this book would have it, the establishment of a determining link between aesthetics and politics, art and the social. This culture need not now be national, though it often can be:

> At times an entire nation has adopted the cultural ideal of a particular class, thus making it general. In this way, the set and uniform characteristics of the English gentleman or the Frenchman became possible, while in Germany no one class had developed a cultural ideal of sufficient suggestive power. Because of this the German lacks a uniform national culture; as a mere member of his nation he remains barbarian. For the German, culture is always a purely personal matter.[67]

In the light of this, Jaspers prizes the liberal arts precisely because they give access to a tradition or to the awareness of human possibilities for the establishment of a culture. Yet one can also see here something familiar from the British context in the eighteenth century. Jaspers presents the culture of Germany as precisely the lack of a single unified homogeneous culture. Such a move recalls very clearly Hume's establishment of England as a zero-degree of national identity in the eighteenth century, in which England's national character is precisely that it has no national character. Despite himself, Jaspers is still caught up in precisely the logic of nationality that his idea of the university seeks to contest. The philosophical basis he wishes to establish for the idea of the university is, seemingly inevitably, caught up in a logic given by the demands of an identification between culture and the nation-state.

Further, behind that, there lies a conception of the university and its functions as basically a theodicy. In my earlier elaboration of the difference between the models proposed by Humboldt and Newman, Berlin and Dublin, I showed that the difference is not as great as it might appear. In both models, there is a subscription to the belief that it is at least hypothetically possible to reconcile the different knowledges gained from the different disciplines under

---

[66] Jean-Paul Sartre, *Being and Nothingness* (trans. Hazel E. Barnes; Philosophical Library, New York, 1956), 566.

[67] Jaspers, *Idea of the University*, 47.

one metadiscipline, be it philosophy or theology. Both, further, are marked by the identification of that philosophy/theology with a national identity. In these, what is fundamentally at stake is the view that it is possible and desirable to reconcile the realm of experience with that of knowledge or, as philosophy and aesthetics have put this, to reconcile the demands of sense with those of reason. In these, as with Jaspers, we have what I am calling (in contradistinction to a *pensiero debole*) a form of *pensiero forte*, in which the intellectual must be 'committed': her or his life, the experienced, examined or felt life must be consistent with the demands of her or his consciousness. Universities, in this way of thinking, are fundamentally institutions geared to the production of individuals whose behaviour or sociality (experience, in sum) is regulated: the primary, though not always stated, task of the university is to produce an acceptable human agent, and not purely a subject of knowledge or of consciousness. In this state of affairs, although the intellectuals produced are necessarily 'committed', they are all necessarily marked by the particular treachery of which Benda accused them, for they are all guilty of introducing the will into the operations of reason; and their judgements, thus, are necessarily instrumentally-determined or, in a word, *prejudicial* to the proper operations of reason as such.[68]

Meanwhile, in England, there is being developed another idea of the university, and one which certainly does not place philosophy at the centre of the totality of knowing, but prefers instead to replace philosophy with 'Eng. Lit.', in the interests of refining judgement, certainly, but still with a question of the moral being of the individual who engages with knowledge as a key issue. It is to this that I now turn.

IV

Leavis would certainly not have thought of the human subject as a project to 'be God'; rather, he was constantly engaged in the strug-

---

[68] On the problem of the introduction of the will into reason, and for a demonstration of how this separates the thinking of Lyotard from that of Habermas, see Jean-François Lyotard, 'Svelte Appendix to the Postmodern Question' (trans. Thomas Docherty) in Richard Kearney (ed.), *Across the Frontiers* (Wolfhound Press, Dublin, 1988), esp. 285.

gle to 'be English'. The vehicle for this project was to be the university study of English Literature, a discipline which, though it had its origins in the eighteenth-century appointment of Hugh Blair to the Regius Chair in Edinburgh, came more fully into its proper self-identification in the 1850s, coincidentally the decade in which we also see the triumph of the particularist 'English' educational philosophy over the generalist 'Scottish' approach. It was in this decade that Scottish students began spectacularly to fail in the examinations being set for enrolment in the imperial offices of the British Civil Service. The examinations, set in England, predictably suited the specialist education of that system, and, to compete at all, the Scottish universities had to begin to prepare their students in a more specialist fashion than heretofore. Coincident with the moment of the emergence of the discipline of English, then, there arises a set of available oppositions for the construction and constitution of the pedagogy surrounding it: on the one hand, close and direct engagement with the specificities of a particular text, while on the other, an engagement with questions governing the text's possibilities, necessarily more distanced from the particularity of the specific text in question; on the one hand, a mode geared towards an essentially undemocratic colonial attitude, while on the other a desire for participatory democracy; on the one hand, immersion of the reading-subject in a text with a view to its mental *appropriation*, while on the other, a critical concern for information or *formation*. This is the background against which Leavis set himself the task of identifying and characterizing the project of university humanistic studies.

One insistent aim in Leavis's meditations on the nature of literary study is that it requires the operation of reason and sense together. Literary criticism, specifically under the rubric of 'English',

trains ... intelligence and sensibility together, cultivating a sensitiveness and precision of response and a delicate integrity of intelligence. ... [T]here must be a training of intelligence that is at the same time a training of sensibility ...[69]

This attempt to see, in English (and defiantly not in philosophy), the discipline that will deal with the problem of Enlightenment, the

---

[69] F. R. Leavis, 'Education and the University: A Sketch for an English School', in *Education and the University* (Chatto and Windus, 1943), 34, 38.

discipline that will reconcile the competing demands of reason and of sense, is already an oversimplification of the stakes of the discipline. In seeing English as a discipline that ostensibly regulates *both* reason and sense, Leavis actually avoids precisely the problem with which he is pretending to deal. As I have argued throughout this study, the contest between the demands of reason and of sense is one which has significant entailments: how is it possible *legitimately* to move from the *fact* of subjective liking of some aesthetic object (a 'sensible' response to it) to the establishment of a *norm* that sees the subjective response as inherently universalizable and given by the nature of the aesthetic object itself, and then on to an ethical demand that, insofar as another human subject is governed by reason, she or he too is compelled to evaluate the artifact positively—that is, to like it? Instead of dealing with the philosophical complexity of this (fundamentally a problem concerning the *legitimation* of aesthetic judgements and their consequent ethical entailments), Leavis simplifies the question, pretending to be able to deal with the potential *conflict* between the demands of reason and of sense by claiming what he will eventually refer to as the peculiar 'third realm' in which poetry operates, a realm in which this conflict has already been resolved such that the task becomes one simply of entertaining fully both reason and sense, rather than of regulating them in ways which can produce a *legitimizable* consensus of response or, in short, a *community*, national or otherwise, whose self-identification and whose identity or *mores* or codes, conventions and political actions can be *legitimized*. That is to say, Leavis's manner of thinking is already inherently anti-democratic.

To remark on Leavis's preference for elites is, of course, not entirely new: he did, after all, explicitly pronounce on this himself on numerous occasions. Yet in the foregoing, I want to suggest that within this anti-democratic impetus, there lurks an imperialist consciousness, and one which is governed by a specific version of 'Englishness'. That requires further argumentation. Leavis argues that the consequence of exercising simultaneously our reason and our sense is that we achieve a particular kind of 'inwardness'. The discipline of literary criticism can, 'in its peculiar preoccupation with the concrete, provide an inescapably inward and subtle initiation into the nature and significance of tradition'.[70] He argues that

---

[70]   Leavis, 'Education and the University', 35.

'the essential condition of a real education' is 'that inwardness with a developed discipline which can come only by working and living into it'.⁷¹ It is for these reasons that 'an approach is personal or it is nothing'.⁷² This inwardness, then, is a manner of appropriation of the otherness of a text and all its strangeness into the *living* of the reading subject or critic. This is precisely that kind of extension of 'professional knowledge' of which Newman wrote and which, in the hands of Jaspers, became a condition governing *commitment* of the university subject or academic to the totality of her or his life-choices in such a way that the academic work or profession was entirely consistent with the lived experience and ethico-political practices of the individual. In Leavis, we have, as it were, Jaspers without the social action (or Jaspers without content). Instead, we have the odd concept of 'commitment' to a principle or concept— 'life'—which is mythic, notoriously indefinite and undefined. To ask Leavis for such a definition of this thing to which we are to be committed is simply to demonstrate one's exclusion from the elite who have acquired an innate sense of what it might be, and with that to demonstrate not only one's lack of capacity for the requisite commitment but also, with that, the 'grade' of one's intellect and *person*.⁷³ Leavisite criticism is—perhaps despite Leavis's preferred politics—Bourdieu's 'aristocracy of culture' rewritten for the bourgeois class. Culture for Leavis is as much a personal matter as it is for Jaspers's 'German'; but Leavis, unlike Jaspers's German, does have a strong sense of the nation served by this personally lived culture.

In his proposals for a reformed Cambridge course, Leavis argues that the reformed Part II of the course 'would be essentially designed for an elite ... To be content with modest numbers, but to provide a standard, a centre and a source of stimulus and suggestion—that

---

⁷¹ Ibid. 37.

⁷² 'Literary Studies', ibid. 68.

⁷³ The actual consequences of that kind of position in the university are extremely disturbing. In one English department in which I have examined (in an institution which some have described as 'the last bastion of British imperialism'), I came under attack from a colleague on the grounds that I was marking and assessing examination performances. Instead, I was informed, 'What we are assessing here is *personality*', and I was asked to make a judgement of the *person* whose examination I was marking and grading. This still strikes me as improper and shocking; but it is, I think, a logical (though not a necessary) corollary of a specific kind of Leavisism.

would be the aim'.[74] At the core of this study should be a 'key passage in the history of civilization', such as the seventeenth century, chosen explicitly for its possibilities for the inculcation within the elite of the tradition of England: 'The Seventeenth Century is precisely that; and ... it lends itself admirably to study—integrating study—in terms of England.'[75] The purpose of English, thus, becomes clearer: it is to occupy the integrating function within the university that would otherwise have been the preoccupation of philosophy; it is to produce an elite who are to be valued for their *persons*, their capacity to have that fulness of life consequent upon the happy merger of reason and sense; and it is to provide thereby standards for the being of Englishness, for those others of us who wish fully to share in 'being English'. It is vital to recall here what being English means, for the texts in which these arguments are made constitute 'Leavis's War', written as they were during the period of the Second World War. It would be a falsification to describe these as informed by a wartime patriotism or even as a defence of some quintessentially 'English' values set against the nastiness of the national character of other nations; rather, Leavis's war (at least in the Second War) was an essentially parochial affair, a war *within* England and specifically within one institution in one town about the possibility of being genuinely (though fundamentally *mythically*) English.

If what is at stake is the production of the 'English person', how might we characterize that person? Interestingly, Leavis's prescriptions suggest an identification of this person as precisely the 'English gentleman' so desired by Shaftesbury, in at least one fundamental respect. What is to go on in the discipline of English Literature is, essentially, conversation. Leavis rules out of court the possibility of attempting, by such conversation, the proving of the validity of value-judgements. In 'Mutually Necessary', he resists the drive from philosophy to justify one's judgements on the grounds that 'you can't *prove* a value-judgment', even if he admits that 'you can always ... get beyond the mere assertion of personal conviction'.[76] The way to get beyond such personal conviction is

---

[74] Leavis, 'Sketch', in *Education and the University*, 42.
[75] Ibid. 48.
[76] Leavis, 'Mutually Necessary', in *The Critic as Anti-Philosopher* , ed. G. A. Singh (Chatto and Windus, 1982), 190.

through a very specific kind of conversation which has the merit of looking very Habermasian in the fact that it will arrive at conclusions based upon such conversation, but has the demerits of looking extremely un-Habermasian in that it is fundamentally coercive and not driven by the mere pursuit of the better argument (and thus is geared towards the production of a society—an 'Englishness'—that is basically irrational). The conversation is 'programmed', driven by the demands of being English; and consequently, it takes the form of a statement which seeks assent, the famous 'This is so, isn't it', dissent from which is certainly possible (even desirable) insofar as it can make for the minor modification of the statement. Dissent from the statement on the grounds that its philosophical basis is illegitimate, or even that there is another philosophical basis upon which another, equally relevant, statement might be made whose effect would be to contradict the very possibility of the first statement, is not what is sought; for that would be 'generalist' or foundational—'Scottish', in a word—and not based upon the necessary *appropriation* of the text.[77] Further, assent (even after the 'Yes, but' response) 'must be real, or it … brings no satisfaction to the critic'.[78] The similarity between this imagined confrontation of teacher and student on the one hand, and O'Brien and Winston at the end of Orwell's *1984* on the other, is striking.

Critical pronouncements or statements within 'English' need no justification on 'theoretical' or philosophical grounds; they contain within themselves their own self-legitimation, a self-legitimation whose ground, tacitly if fundamentally, is the achieved 'Englishness' of the speaker making the statement. That Englishness is historically tied up with the imperialist project of the nineteenth-century civil service, which demanded in its exams the

---

[77] Once again, this recalls the distinction made by Alasdair MacIntyre, in *Whose Justice? Which Rationality?* (Duckworth, 1988), 226–30, between Scottish and English law as conceived by Viscount Stair in Scotland and William Blackstone in England. See, esp., 230: 'Blackstone … absolutizes the rights of property. What obligations individuals have depends almost, if not entirely, upon their place within established property relationships. Stair by contrast makes the treatment and status of obligations prior to the treatment and the status of property'; by analogy, Leavis, and the centrality of that inward appropriation of a text to his work, conforms to the bourgeois laws of England, prejudiced by the ownership of the property of the text and thus incapable of precisely the moral judgement that is ostensibly the object of critique.

[78] Leavis, *English in our Time and in the University* (Cambridge University Press, Cambridge, 1969), 47.

attentiveness to particularity and the dismissing of that 'democratizing philosophy' which constituted a Scottish pedagogical practice—more importantly, a 'democratic' practice aiming at producing autonomy and culture within specific political conditions.

Should we require further evidence of the persistence of the imperialist strain and its anti-democratic values in Leavis, we need look no further than his essay on 'Research in English'. There, we find that he is dismissive of the concept of research in English; and more importantly, that the research student in English should not really require any supervision, 'having proved himself as a First Class Tripos man' (this in response to a letter in the *TLS* from Philip Hobsbaum, a former student, at that time lecturing in Queen's University Belfast). Leavis is writing this in the face of adversity (real or imagined, *à la* Rousseau), as usual. It follows his jeremiad about the alleged philistinism of Robbins whose report on education advocated mass expansion, thus denting Leavis's project for the production of an elite who would read the books and a mass who would respect the elite. He writes:

The university has a new duty, we are told: there is a besieging host, ever-increasing, of Indians, Africans, Commonwealth people in general, Levantines, who aspire to become university teachers of Eng. Lit., and must therefore have a Ph.D.—preferably a Cambridge one (though it is admitted that a large proportion of them couldn't hope to take the English Tripos with much credit—even if they could pass).[79]

Of course they could not pass, at least in the terms that would constitute a pass for Leavis: they are not 'English' persons.

What—it will immediately be asked—of the fact that Leavis writes in *The Great Tradition* about three novelists, two of them being foreign? How English are Henry James and Joseph Conrad? Leavis is aware of this, and has to deal with it. In the case of both writers, he finds that their being in the English tradition of which he writes necessitated them responding to a peculiar essence within themselves that demanded their internal colonization. In the case of James, for example, Leavis says that 'In seeing him in an English tradition I am not slighting the fact of his American origin'.[80] Indeed, he goes on to identify him firmly as a New Yorker; yet,

[79] Leavis, *English in our Time and in the University*, 194–5.
[80] F. R. Leavis, *The Great Tradition* (1948; repr. Penguin, Harmondsworth, 1974), 20.

within that New York milieu, he could not find an objective realm answerable to his internal or subjective demands, argues Leavis; so 'History ... was already leaving him *déraciné* in his own country'. This said, Leavis defends James against those who decry his 'pulling up his roots' on the grounds that 'the congenial soil and climate were in Europe rather than in the country of his birth'; and, within Europe, Leavis then finds reasons for James to see the limitations of the great rival tradition, that of the French. What makes James 'English' is a matter of personality, not a matter of birth:

James's wit is real and always natural, his poetry intelligent as well as truly rich, and there is nothing bogus, cheap, or vulgar about his idealizations: certain human potentialities are nobly celebrated.[81]

Being English is, as it were, a moral condition or state of mind. Thus, when we come to Conrad, the case is slightly more difficult; and Leavis, in fact, stresses his foreignness—'that he was a Pole, whose first other language was French'—but only momentarily. Immediately, Leavis recalls a conversation with André Chevillon on Conrad's decision to write in English, in which the Frenchman (himself bilingual)

went on to explain in terms of the characteristics of the two languages why it had to be English. Conrad's themes and interests demanded the concreteness and action—the dramatic energy—of English. We might go further and say that Conrad chose to write his novels in English for the reasons that led him to become a British Master Mariner.[82]

Conrad, a master of the English language 'chose it for its distinctive qualities and because of the moral tradition associated with it'.[83] It is that tradition which is unavailable for the 'besieging host' of colonized people whose research Leavis would be reluctant to supervise. The study of English is now the study of 'being English', nationally and even racially exclusive, and certainly inconsistent with anything approaching democracy or even the formation of the autonomous human subject, governed by rational principles.

The influence of Leavis on subsequent institutionalized criticism has been massive, especially—paradoxically or not—within those nations that once constituted a British Empire. Has there been any adequate response to it? Has it been possible to reconfigure aesthetic

---

[81] Ibid. 21–2.   [82] Ibid. 28.
[83] Ibid.

enquiry in such a way as to rehabilitate a democratic impulse? For answers to this kind of question we have, in this concluding section of this study, to investigate the terms and conditions of literary criticism as it occurs within the university; and that will also require a brief meditation on the form and function of the contemporary university.

V

Especially in Europe, but also elsewhere, the contemporary university has found itself in a predicament. On the one hand, its most recent 'liberal' or cultural traditions have required of it and its intellectuals an activity consistent with the formulation of consensually agreed standards for the regulation and evaluation of all forms of intellectual enquiry. The consequence of that has been the establishment of local—national—cultures, and the foundations of those modes of autonomy that constitute legitimate citizenship for the individual subjects within the states or nations in question. That is to say, the responsibility of the university has most recently been, fundamentally, to regulate and reconcile the demands of experience and those of reason, taking into account that separate states might have divergent views of what legitimately constitutes rational enquiry within their respective domains.

The very existence of such a university of culture is now in some question. Most governments—and many publics—consider the university not as being related to culture, but rather as having its primary identity given to it by business and economics. (In Britain, for instance, the governmental portfolio for education is merged not with that for culture, but rather with that for employment, underlining the consensual subscription to a rather crudely instrumentalist view of education and, within that, of the arts.) If culture remains in the frame at all, it does so only in the form of the culture industry, whose material contribution to national economies can be quantified in business terms. When Readings analysed this state of affairs, he saw the university of culture being replaced by a 'university of excellence', in which excellence had a purely formal existence and was actually and in substantive terms, vacuous, utterly devoid of meaningful content. In the particular case of the British university, the means for thus emasculating the university is none other than 'quality control', which concerns itself not with the content of what is taught and researched, but rather with the ways in which such content—regardless of its substance—is rendered transparent, self-evidencing, and thus supposedly 'accountable'. 'Excellence' is at best an administrative category, but mediated as a substantive intellectual matter by 'assessors' who have no particular knowledge of the content of what they are supposedly assessing; and the major contribution that 'excellence' and 'quality control' have made to university education is to drive down quality while preserving a mythic, empty, 'standard'.

The fundamental problem facing the academy (and within that, especially the study of aesthetic matters), as MacIntyre points out, is one of legitimation. When asked to justify its existence and privileges, the university should respond that 'universities are places where conceptions of and standards of rational justification are elaborated, put to work in the detailed practices of enquiry, and themselves rationally evaluated, so that only from the university can the wider society learn how to conduct its own debates, practical or theoretical, in a rationally defensible way'.[84] Yet such a claim is itself only valid if it is the case that the universities are themselves sites in which debates precisely *about* what constitutes rational justification can be entertained. However, disciplinarity, professionalization, technological specialization have all conspired to preclude this possibility. MacIntyre goes on: 'It is precisely because universities have not been such places and have in fact organized enquiry through institutions and genres well designed to prevent them and to protect them from being such places that the official responses of both the appointed leaders and the working members of universities to their recent external critics have been so lamentable.'[85] MacIntyre's history of the university traces the demise within the institution of the validity or centrality of moral and theological enquiry.

Broadly, the totalizing (or universalizing) view of the university as an institution in which the variety of disciplinary knowledges can be eventually reconciled into a unity, real or hypothetical, has come into conflict (especially since the nineteenth century) with the

[84] Alasdair MacIntyre, *Three Rival Versions of Moral Enquiry* (Duckworth, 1990), 222.
[85] Ibid. 222.

Nietzschean, genealogical, fragmenting view of what constitutes 'truth'. The incommensurability of these two positions—the one prioritizing the availability of uniformity, the other celebrating a variety whose very diversity defies universalizability—does not itself presently constitute (and in fact precludes) a legitimate confrontation between them within the institution that produces them. To put this crudely and with respect to the now central discipline of English, there is no debate available between the 'English' Leavisites and the (more 'Continental', more 'Scottish', certainly 'foreign') post-structuralists or post-colonialists; or, the conflicts between Dryden and Corneille, between the English and the Scots, between Hume and Rousseau are still with us.

The proposal made by MacIntyre in the face of this problem is that we should make such discords part of the very substance of what we teach, making the university 'a place of constrained disagreement, of imposed participation in conflict, in which a central responsibility of higher education would be to initiate students into conflict',[86] the model for which might be Paris in 1272; but the point would be, for example, to thematize the conflicting claims for legitimacy of Paris 1272 and Vincennes 1968, as MacIntyre graphically puts it. Those who charge such a proposal as Utopian, argues MacIntyre, simply demonstrate their incapacity for acknowledging that there might exist ways of thinking about the world that are different from their own; and he accordingly embraces the allegedly Utopian aspect of his proposals.

It is perhaps Habermas whose work offers a philosophical analogue of this. First of all, I can draw attention, in the work of Habermas and of MacIntyre, to the continuing centrality and relevance of Shaftesbury for contemporary theory. Shaftesbury's Whiggism, as a determinant of his philosophy of benevolent sociability, has its late twentieth-century version in a peculiar combination of Marxist cultural ideologies. In Europe, specifically in Germany, Habermas's version of the rational society founded not upon ideology but upon a theory of communicative agency in whose ideal speech-situations human subjects can find autonomy, is clearly akin to the Shaftesburian prioritization of the regulation of discourses as a founding condition of the social sphere. As in Habermas, that social sphere was for Shaftesbury an ideal space:

---

[86] MacIntyre, *Three Rival Versions of Moral Enquiry*, 230–1.

for Shaftesbury, the realization of such a space was probably an environment such as Will's famous coffee-house, though an ideal society could of course be found anywhere where gentlemen engaged in regulated polite conversation; for Habermas, the ideal space is to be realized more and more insistently in a whole variety of 'spheres of action' or associations of 'culturally mobilized publics',[87] of which the political is only one example in any complex social formation. Where Habermas differs from Shaftesbury is in stressing that civic identity is not single or singly determined by one's ethical or other commitments; rather, the civic subject for Habermas is one that participates in multiple spheres of action which are not necessarily hierarchized nor centred even in a political or an ethical sphere. It is, however, precisely such fora whose absence from our contemporary culture MacIntyre laments; and it is, in a way, a consequence of his proposals for the university that their revival would become possible.

However, as this study has shown, there is more at stake in this question of the rehabilitation of the university and the re-legitimization of the aesthetic intellectual. Fundamentally, we have a straightforward opposition, between what we used to consider as the 'committed' intellectual for whom aesthetics and politics were involved radically with each other and, on the other hand, the 'professional' critic for whom intellectual work is part of a coded set of conventions with its own internally given modes of legitimation and with no particular purchase, direct or otherwise, on political matters. Both Habermas and MacIntyre are, in a sense, looking for the possibility of a renewed notion of commitment; and against them, thinkers such as Fish or Rorty adopt the position that Rorty once described as that of the 'postmodern bourgeois intellectual' who has no particular social or political responsibilities.

I propose that we recast the terms of this opposition, in the light of the foregoing arguments of this book. It is by now evident that what I have called a *pensiero forte*—a commitment in which aesthetics is aligned intimately with politics such that the intellectual who makes aesthetic judgements thereby proposes concomitantly a mode of life or set of philosophical prescriptions for her or his

---

[87] Habermas, 'Three Normative Models of Democracy', in Seyla Benhabib (ed.), *Democracy and Difference* (Princeton University Press, Princeton, 1996), 30, 29.

experience—leads inexorably and necessarily to an aesthetics that is marked by *locatedness*. In brief, but not crude, terms, commitment implies national allegiance. The critic who looks for such an intimacy between the operations of reason and those of sense, between judgement and experience, is inevitably producing a subject the legitimacy of whose autonomy is given by her or his located affiliations; and these, almost equally inevitably, have been nationalist. It is a national community, a consensus given by the nation-state, that underpins the assumed legitimacy of propositions made by this kind of critic. Further, such a consensus is inherently non-democratic (and, in its more extreme forms, is irrational), for it replaces the ethical regard for others within the community with an ethnic regard for self-identification.[88]

Against this position in which the critic is identified and affiliated to place, as I have demonstrated, there is a recurring pressure upon the aesthetic of the problem of the temporality and historicity of judgement and of the subject. It does not follow from this that the opposite of commitment is 'postmodern bourgeois liberalism', nor even 'professionalism'; rather, it is the case that we should rethink that opposition in terms that attend to the philosophical issues that have governed modern aesthetics, at least as they have been formed within Europe. In this book, I have tried to show that these issues are best considered in terms of that way in which the critic thinks the problem of alterity, and, in the first instance, that means the otherness of the aesthetic entity itself: what if the aesthetic object is there precisely to resist appropriation by the subject's consciousness (especially the subject's 'English' consciousness)? To engage such an object, the critic would certainly need some theory: that is, she or he would need the capacity for identifying the object as a specific kind of object or, in the terms of this book, she or he would need to be able to see the particular object in more general terms as a varietal example of a more universal or

---

[88] It is, perhaps, matter for another book to trace the persistence of this attitude even through those ostensibly 'theoretical' criticisms produced in England over the last thirty years. My contention, however, is certainly that that eruption of 'theory' into the British version of 'English' studies (and its consequent production of disciplines such as 'cultural studies') has been entirely consistent with this tacitly nationalist impetus. It is not that theory as such has been inimical to democracy—far from it—but rather that the actual theoretical production of Britain in the last three decades has been so.

uniform set. More than this, however, the critic would have to maintain a vigilant regard for how this single and specific item shapes, forms, disrupts and interrupts the general uniformity that has made its perception possible at all. To put this crudely and with specific regard to the institutional and pedagogical issues at stake, we should not apply theory to texts, with all the tedious predictability that that entails; rather, we should apply texts to the production of theory (as did Barthes on Racine, Kristeva on Lautréamont, Cixous on Joyce, Derrida on Mallarmé, and so on).

In this latter condition, we have a criticism among whose tasks is the prioritization of the singularity of the *aesthetic event*: that is, not the singularity of the aesthetic object, but rather the singularity of the historical, temporal, *experiential* or empirical confrontation of a subject of consciousness with what it is taking as its object. This mode of criticism rehabilitates experience, not as a ground for legitimation of judgements, but as a condition of the possibility of aesthetics in the first place. As Agacinski would have it, anything else amounts to an egocentrism which precludes the possibility of the experience of the other—in this particular case, precluding the possibility of the experience of the work of art which forms the ostensible object of our intellectual and somatic engagements. She begins her *Critique de l'égocentrisme* by demanding that we ask again 'la question de l'autre':

Il faut la reposer, non pas à partir de la subjectivité, individuelle ou collective, qui croit savoir ce qui lui est propre, mais à partir de cette *épreuve de l'autre* qu'est immédiatement l'existence, une existence que l'autre vient toujours partager.[89]

Anything else denies time, denies the possibility that criticism can be open to a future. Here, then, is the possibility that criticism can be firmly linked to modernity, to an experience of art that gives the present a content while also respecting the alterity, the foreignness of the past and the unpredictability of a future. That this is a risk is what makes the practice of criticism not only worthwhile, but possible.

---

[89] Sylviane Agacinski, *Critique de l'égocentrisme* (Galilée, Paris, 1996), 11.

Index

DATE DUE

NOV 0 7 1999		
MAR 0 1 2000		